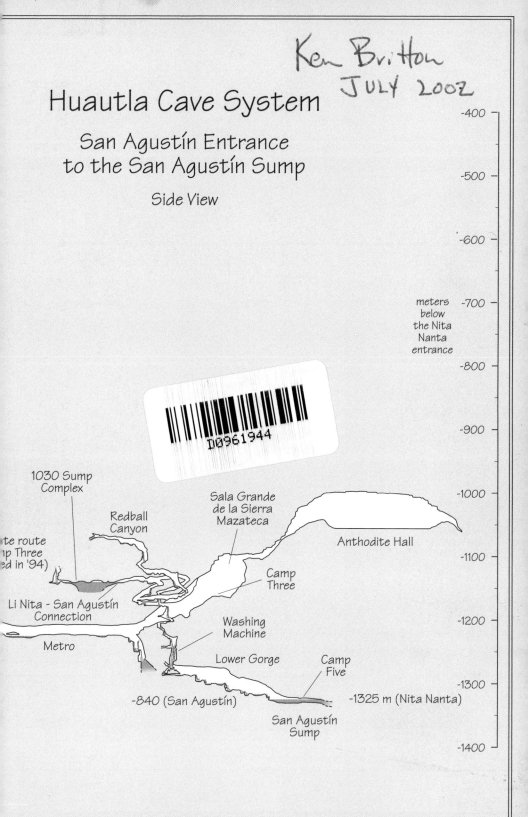

Huautla Cave System

San Agustín Entrance
to the San Agustín Sump

Side View

Ken Britton
JULY 2002

-400

-500

-600

meters
below
the Nita
Nanta
entrance

-700

-800

-900

D0961944

1030 Sump
Complex

-1000

Redball
Canyon

Sala Grande
de la Sierra
Mazateca

Anthodite Hall

...te route
...p Three
...d in '94)

-1100

Camp
Three

Li Nita - San Agustín
Connection

Washing
Machine

-1200

Metro

Lower Gorge

Camp
Five

-1300

-840 (San Agustín)

-1325 m (Nita Nanta)

San Agustín
Sump

-1400

drafted by Barbara Anne am Ende

BEYOND
The DEEP

BEYOND
The DEEP

THE DEADLY DESCENT INTO THE WORLD'S MOST TREACHEROUS CAVE

WILLIAM STONE AND BARBARA AM ENDE
WITH MONTE PAULSEN

WARNER BOOKS

An AOL Time Warner Company

Warner Books, Inc., 1271 Avenue of the Americas, New York, NY 10020
Visit our Web site at www.twbookmark.com.

 An AOL Time Warner Company

Printed in the United States of America
First Printing: June 2002
10 9 8 7 6 5 4 3 2 1

ISBN: 0-446-52709-2
LCCN: 2002101115

To Jim King and Roland Puton,
visionary patrons who saw this for what it was:
the exploration of the last terrestrial frontier.

To Rolf Adams and Ian Rolland,
who lived more in their brief time on earth
than most people ever will.

ACKNOWLEDGMENTS

The authors are deeply grateful to the members of the 1994 San Agustín Expedition, many of whom candidly shared their recollections in extensive interviews some six years after the events portrayed in this book. Their extraordinary openness made possible the reconstruction of the far-flung events and complicated human interactions of this story. Also deeply appreciated are the dozens of support team members who helped haul more than a ton of equipment and supplies in and out of the cave, and the more than sixty corporate sponsors who generously provided most of that matériel; their names are listed in the appendices. And the authors remain thankful for the generous assistance of no fewer than nine jurisdictions within the government of Mexico, without which this and so many other important expeditions would not have been possible. Special thanks are extended to Sergio Zambrano and Angel Soto Porrua, both of Mexico City, who provided invaluable and dedicated assistance in planning the expedition; and to Nigel Jones and Mike Stevens of the Cis-Lunar development team, whose endless 2:00 A.M. de-bug sessions made the rebreather a reality. Thanks to Wes Skiles for his photographs and to Linda Heslop for her illustrations. Thanks to Michael Carlisle and Neal Bascomb of Carlisle & Company, and Rick Horgan of Warner Books, for their consistently valuable advice. And finally, the authors are uniquely indebted to the earlier Huautla explorers—Jim Smith, Bill Steele, Mark Minton, and many others—whose work created a framework of exploration and mapping that paved the way for the 1994 expedition.

Bill Stone is grateful for the very early guidance of Ron Bergman of North Allegheny High School in Pittsburgh in learning the basics of cave exploration. He thanks his mother, Helen M. Stone, and father, Walter Curtis Stone, for their generous understanding, encouragement, and early financing of his involvement in this unusual pursuit. He is especially grateful to Sheck Exley, who taught him both how to survive underwater inside a cave and to understand the power of humility; and to Jim King, Roland Puton, and Bill Graves, who enabled him, over many expeditions, to think boldly in engineering design. And finally, Bill thanks the management of the National Institute of Standards and Technology, for their generous understanding that has allowed him to pursue the dual life of a scientist-engineer and explorer.

Barbara am Ende thanks her sister, Louise O'Connor, and brother, Fabio (oops, that's Gerald am Ende), for their advice. She hopes her father doesn't have a heart attack when he reads this detailed account of the expedition, and apologizes for the worry this will cause. She posthumously thanks her mom for chauffeuring her to caving events before she was old enough to drive, and wishes she were still alive to see the publication of this book and so she could say, "Mom, you were right!" Finally, Barbara thanks the community of cavers who helped her experience the best of times, and provided a shoulder to cry on during the worst.

Monte Paulsen thanks all the cavers—those who go on expeditions as well as those who just get muddy on the weekends—who generously shared both their skills and stories with the newcomer in their midst. Thanks also to Anna Mulrine for the mot juste, to Jason Vest for the happy wisdom buried in his grumpy counsel, and especially to Ron Williams and everyone at Dragonfly Media, without whose support this book would not have been completed. Monte extends his deepest appreciation to his family, who always accepted him, and to Sheila, who inspired his courage.

CONTENTS

LIST OF ILLUSTRATIONS

AUTHORS' NOTE

Beyond the Deep is the true story of the 1994 expedition into the heart of Mexico's Huautla Plateau, as told from the perspective of Bill Stone and Barbara am Ende. This story is drawn from their logbooks, diaries, and recollections, as well as from dozens of interviews conducted by co-author Monte Paulsen.

To weave so many individual stories into a cohesive narrative, we were forced to omit many great anecdotes, and to move others to dates or locations that vary from the times or places at which they actually occurred. Throughout the chapters in which we introduce the cave itself, for example, we deemed it less confusing to slightly alter the timeline than to leapfrog about the labyrinth. No incidents have been made up, however, and the major events of this story have been retold as accurately as possible.

Likewise, it was necessary to reconstruct dialogue. Putting words in another person's mouth is always fraught with danger; even more so seven years after the fact. We asked each of the core team members about dialogue, and used much of what they could recall. When crafting a speech, we sometimes drew words or phrases from later comments by the same speaker. This was the case with all of the Mazatec characters in the story, who kindly shared their recollections with us in Spanish.

Memory is inherently subjective. In most cases, when we discovered that team members disagreed in their recollection of events, we crafted a workable compromise. In a few instances, we simply told the incident from Bill's or Barbara's perspective.

We substituted common words for technical jargon wherever possible—there's also a glossary at the back of the book—and we tidied up a few salty phrases along the way. We were less successful in cleaning up the expedition's mishmash of English, metric, and other measurements. As scientists, Bill and Barbara prefer the precision of the metric system; unfortunately, most American and British divers don't talk that way. We compromised by providing the critical cave measurements in meters, and most day-to-day observations in the English units that are more familiar to American readers.

There are two increasingly common writers' tricks we did *not* employ anywhere in this book: We didn't add fictional events. And we didn't create fictional or composite characters. Everything in this book actually happened during the 1994 expedition (except for clearly noted historical references), and everyone whose name appears in this book is a real person.

The people whose stories fill this book are an amazing lot. For no reward other than the joy of discovery, they submit to incredible hardships and put their lives in one another's hands on a daily basis. They've earned our respect, and we trust they'll win yours.

Monte Paulsen	Bill Stone	Barbara am Ende
Baltimore,	Gaithersburg,	Germantown,
Maryland	Maryland	Maryland

February 2002

PROLOGUE March 19, 1979

Eight hundred and forty meters beneath the dark soil of a Mexican cornfield, Bill Stone crept timidly along the ceiling of the underwater tunnel. His knees scraped silently against the overhead rock.

Upside down at the bottom of the world, he grasped a pressure gauge bobbing near his chest. He tugged the hockey-puck-sized dial into view, and inhaled, slowly. Cool air flowed to his lungs. An eerie sound broke the silence: "Swhooo-oop." A thin black needle twitched ever so slightly across the glowing green gauge. When it came to rest, the needle showed how much air he had left: 2,700 pounds per square inch. In a pony tank like the one dangling from his hip—a metal cylinder about the size of a large bottle of wine—that meant maybe ten more minutes of breathing, if he kept a cool head. He exhaled: "Phooossh."

Silver blobs of air tumbled up his arms. A few lodged themselves within cracks in the ceiling. Most slithered away between his legs, like mercury on the lam. He watched his breath flee the cave, as if it knew better than he what lay ahead. He wanted to turn and scurry, too. But the same buoyant force that lured his breath out of the cave was holding his body in place. The thick neoprene fabric of his tattered black wetsuit was filled with air, and since he wasn't wearing a weight belt, that air's buoyancy kept him pinned to the ceiling. Rather than scraping his back as he slithered along, he had simply flipped over and crawled into this water-filled section of the cave with his hands and knees above him. The thought of the deep blue Mexican sky looming a half-mile beneath his belly was disorienting. He tried not to think about it.

Bill refilled his large lungs and skittered forward like a six-foot-four-inch spider. "Swhooo-oop." Atop his fraying wetsuit he wore a heavy nylon harness attached to a thick nylon rope. At the other end of the rope stood Hal Lloyd and Steve Zeman, ready to yank him back to the surface. All three expected he would need to be hauled back. Deep caves like this one were carved by subterranean rivers. As they surged through cracks in the rock, these rivers overflowed narrow passageways between larger underground chambers, creating flooded tunnels called sumps. Because he and his teammates were confident that the next air-filled room would be lower in elevation than the one where Lloyd and Zeman stood, they expected to find a waterfall at the other end of the sump, cascading violently down into the next chamber. Stone feared that a sudden current would develop, suck him over the falls, and hurl him to his death below. So he'd asked Lloyd and Zeman to pay out the line slowly, and watch for his signal: One jerk on the rope meant "Stop." Two or more meant "Reel me back, *right now.*"

More mercurylike bubbles fled the sump. Bill waited for the gurgling to stop, then drew still. He stuck a callused finger alongside his jaw, and loosened the neoprene hood he wore under his helmet, wondering whether he would be able to hear the waterfall before he saw it. Cold water surged into his ear, but he heard nothing. He shivered, rechecked the locking carabiner that secured him to the rope, and continued forward.

The marblelike ceiling continued to descend. Something glimmered up ahead. The small electric lights mounted on his fiberglass helmet weren't bright enough for him to make out what it was. He crept cautiously forward, ready to brace himself against the expected current. As he drew closer, he realized that he was looking not at the first ripples of a watery vortex, but at the silvery underside of a large puddle of air trapped in a rise along the ceiling. He waded into the airbell, and stuck his head up inside. The orange glow of his two-watt headlamps seemed brighter inside the dry alcove. He pushed the regulator halfway out of his mouth and exhaled normally. He drew in a tiny breath, then a full one. The air seemed okay. But he kept the scuba regulator ready just in case; three British cavers had died just a few years earlier after breathing bad air in a sealed chamber much like this one. He stuck the regulator back into his mouth, and descended back down into the dark water.

The vertigo of reimmersion twisted his sense of direction. In the airbell, up had been up. Back in the sump, up was down again. He felt as though the cave itself had rolled over, as if he were slithering through the bowels of some giant animal. The vision terrified him. His heart rate leapt. He started gulping down air: "Swhoo-ooo-ooo-oop." The thin black needle jerked violently.

Get a grip, man! he scolded himself. *Panic will kill you before the cave gets a chance.* Plenty of cave divers drowned once fear got the better of them. They sucked through their bottled air at four times their normal respiration rate, and deprived themselves of precious time to deal with whatever it was that had startled them. Bill reminded himself that he'd never actually heard of anyone dying as a result of being flung over a waterfall. He forced himself to relax. He recalled a joke his old friend Jim Smith often made in such circumstances. "Ol' buddy," the Georgia caver would drawl, "ya can't get buried no deeper for no cheaper."

The gallows humor settled his nerves. He exhaled calmly,

inhaled gently, and rechecked his air supply: 2,200 psi remaining.

He pressed forward. The ceiling descended rapidly. The tunnel was shaped like an inverted pear. The bulging upper section measured about three meters across; the gravel-lined trough was about five meters below the arched ceiling. The black limestone walls were coated with a velvety layer of ocher silt, lending the sump a warm feeling despite the chilling sixty-four-degree water.

Thirty-five meters into the sump, he checked his pressure again: 1,900 psi. He'd used a third of the air in his primary bottle. To keep a third in reserve, he'd best turn back. His black-rimmed diving mask had sharply restricted his peripheral vision. So before turning around, he gently pushed off the ceiling and rolled over to take one final look at what lay ahead. What he saw took his breath away.

While his attention had been narrowly focused on moving across the arched ceiling, the tunnel's floor had simply disappeared. In its place stretched a crystal clear sea of unfathomable depth. The water was so pure that the twin beams from his dim electric headlamps pierced down into the deep blue canyon and faded to black before revealing any hint of a bottom. He'd never seen anything like it. For one silent moment, he gazed longingly into the center of the earth.

"Phooossh." The release of his held breath broke his silent reverie and snapped his attention back to the present. He was only ten meters below the sump's surface, but even at that depth every breath he took was removing twice as much gas from his tiny tank as it would have on the surface.

"Swhooo-oop." The needle jerked noticeably across the gauge, resting at 1,600 psi. It was time to go. He spun around, and gave three hard tugs on his lifeline.

"Phooossh." Nothing happened.

"Swhooo-oop." 1,500 psi. Five minutes, max. He tugged again.

"Phooossh." Still nothing.

"Swhooo-oop." 1,400 psi. The thick nylon line went slack, and began to sink, curling like a long strand of spaghetti. *Lloyd! Aren't you paying attention?* he wondered. *And where the hell is Zeman?*

"Phooossh." Bill began to sink. The heavy link was dragging him down, like an anchor. The same rise in water pressure that compressed the air in his tank also compressed the air inside his wetsuit. With less volume came less buoyancy. No longer pinned to the ceiling, he was now sinking slowly into the deep blue abyss.

"Swhooo-oop." 1,300 psi. He kicked his feet, to little avail. In order to reduce the weight of the diving gear he and his teammates had painstakingly hauled down 840 grueling meters (a little more than half a mile) from the surface, he'd left his fins behind. Without them, his legs flailed in the water.

"Phooossh." He swam ferociously toward the pear-shaped tunnel above, gulping down air at an ever increasing rate.

"Swhooo-oop." 1,100 psi. His long arm managed to catch a lip in the limestone wall.

"Phooossh." He pulled himself up into the trough at the tunnel's base.

"Swhooo-oop." 900 psi. He resigned himself to the task of clawing his way back using small holds on the rock walls.

"Phooossh." The tunnel, which had been crystal-clear only a few moments earlier, was now a forest of fuzzy ocher columns. He played his lights across the ceiling. From each spot where he'd placed a hand or knee, and every place where the silvery bubbles of his exhaled breath had struck, a plume of orange silt now erupted. He'd loosened the sediment on the ceiling, and it was now raining down like a snowstorm.

"Swhooo-oop." 700 psi. The columns were quickly converging into one massive silt-out. By the time he'd crawled a few more meters, he couldn't see his hand in front of his mask.

"Phooossh." He felt about blindly for his lifeline. His whole plan had unraveled: lost buoyancy, zero visibility, soaring air consumption, and now a slack safety line. *Where are those guys?*

"Swhooo-oop." 500 psi. Almost time to switch to the backup bottle. He'd sucked through one bottle getting this far under good conditions. He'd have to keep a cool head if he were going to grope his way back on the same amount of air.

Then the line went taut. He could feel himself being pulled through the amber muck. *Yeah!* he thought. *It's about time.*

"Phooossh." He could feel himself accelerating, but saw nothing in the haze. "Whack!" His helmet smashed into a wall. *Or was it the ceiling?*

"Swhooo-oop." He rolled off the rock, and stuck his hands out in front of him. The visibility slowly began to improve.

"Phooossh." As his buoyancy returned, he flipped upside down again, and used his fingertips to keep himself off the ceiling. Breathing became more difficult as his tank ran dry, but he'd have to risk smashing into the rock again to reach down and find his second regulator. Before he'd decided what to do, he felt his head splash to the surface. He spat out the regulator and gasped at the cool cave air. Lloyd and Zeman kept pulling the line, until he was directly beneath them. Once he'd caught his breath, Bill flashed his friends a broad smile.

"Yo!" Lloyd called out. "Bro! We were really worried about you."

"Never saw a signal," Zeman added. "Too much friction, I guess."

Bill shivered, and nodded.

"Yeah, I thought I saw a jigger in the line," continued

Lloyd, "and we figured, hell, he's been down there too long anyways. And so we started pulling."

"You were right on time," Bill replied. He twisted the black rubber mask off his face and slid it down around his neck. Then he swung himself up to the ledge where Lloyd and Zeman were waiting.

"Man," he said, "you wouldn't believe it. That canyon is headed straight for the center of the earth."

The 1979 expedition wrapped up a month and a half later. The team of young explorers de-rigged the cave—called the Sótano de San Agustín—repacked their rusty pickup trucks, traversed the high Huautla Plateau (pronounced WOW-tla), streaked northward across Mexico, and were back home in Texas by the middle of May.

Those were the cowboy days of Mexican caving, when any determined soul with a miner's headlamp and a truckful of rope could find an unexplored cave and become the first to plumb its depths. Bill lived among a clique of such cavers, who shared a warren of low-rent duplexes in Austin. The Kirkwood Road crew spent most of their money—and all of their free time—exploring Mexican caves. Like long-haired refugees from a *Star Trek* backlot, they were addicted to the experience of boldly going where no one had gone before.

Bill's nervous dive into the San Agustín sump earned the lanky twenty-six-year-old an article in *Outside* magazine. He'd been caving throughout the U.S. and Mexico since he was a teenager, but had never seen anything like the gaping blue abyss at the heart of Huautla. Caves had previously divulged their secrets one dark crevice at a time, occasionally rewarding weeks of work with a deep canyon or large chamber. Such incremental progress was the essence of exploration; and for Stone, exploration was what distinguished caving from other outdoor pursuits, such as mountaineering. While high mountains were measured from the flatlands *before* they were climbed—Everest, for example, was named not for the brave men who first topped its summit, but for the colonial surveyor who determined its height—no one will know which cave is the deepest until explorers bottom them all.

But the consensus among the Kirkwood Cowboys was that his harrowing dive had been a failure. Because he'd found no route forward, his fellow "pit hippies" concluded that the Sótano de San Agustín simply didn't go any deeper. Bill tried to change their minds. During late-night parties that flowed from one crumbling stucco duplex to the next, he told again and again of that moment when the beckoning abyss revealed itself. To him, the fleeting vista was a revelation: Beyond this deep sump, he was certain, lay the bottom of the world. But to his fellow cavers, there were more promising holes to explore.

So when Bill and the other pit hippies returned to the Huautla Plateau in the spring of 1980, they turned their attention to a "going" cave called Li Nita. But after three months of grueling exploration, they found themselves at more or less the same place they'd been the year before: Like San Agustín, Li Nita bottomed in a sump. Bill strapped on his hip-mounted pony bottles, and waded in to take a look. Employing the same crawl-on-the-ceiling technique he'd pioneered the year before, he plodded through a couple of airbells and was about to turn back when he spotted the gleam of a surface. Through that silvery window he popped up into a large canyon. Shivering with excitement, he dropped his dive gear and ran down the wide-open passage before him. "Oh please," he shouted to the emptiness, "please be it." Two hundred meters ahead, he saw what he was looking for: Scrawled in black soot on the smooth limestone wall was a small circular target, and the letters "US10." It was a survey station, one of many markers cavers used to map their position underground. "Up-Stream, 10th survey mark," he mumbled. Then he let loose a long, happy howl. He was standing in East Redball

Canyon, a back alley of the Sótano de San Agustín. By connecting the two caves into one 1,220-meter deep abyss, the Kirkwood Cowboys had established the third deepest cave on earth.

With the Li Nita connection, the 1980 expedition accomplished something previously unimaginable: stealing the bronze medal of deep caving from the French, who practically invented caving. Frenchmen explored the first sump, established the first underground camp, and pioneered the use of mountaineering techniques below ground. A French team led by Pierre Chevalier first broke the 500-meter-deep barrier in 1944, and French cavers had claimed all of the depth records—until then. Over the next few years, the "deepest" title would change hands several times, and newly energized teams from Russia, Poland, and Australia all competed with the French for the record.

Bill and some of the other Austin pit hippies were swept into the race to the bottom of the world. Not since Roald Amundsen raced Robert Scott to the South Pole had explorers vied for such an obscure—and dangerous—prize. Led by hard-charging young cavers including Jim Smith and Bill Steele, the American explorers soon stopped describing the interconnected caves of the Huautla Plateau by individual names like San Agustín or Li Nita, and began thinking in terms of Sistema Huautla, a complex underground system with multiple entrances and myriad opportunities for exploration. And they calculated that for Sistema Huautla to battle its way back up the deep cave list, two fronts were required: First, in the same way that Li Nita had added height to San Agustín, they'd have to add more elevation by connecting a cave called Nita Nanta to the system. Second, they'd have to return to the San Agustín sump.

The job of organizing an assault on the sump fell to Bill. It was primarily a technological challenge. And besides having already pushed farther into the sump than anyone else, he was the science wonk among the Kirkwood Cowboys. The son of a onetime pro baseball player, Bill preferred his basement chemistry lab to the ball field. He'd long since forgotten who won the 1962 World Series, but readily recalled the sunny afternoon when he and his Catholic school buddies huddled around a tinny transister radio, listening to news of John Glenn's historic space flight. While most of the pit hippies worked odd jobs between expeditions, he completed a Ph.D. in engineering at the University of Texas. His fascination with the San Agustín sump led him to spend much of the next winter as an apprentice to the legendary Florida cave diver Sheck Exley, who taught him the discipline of technical diving.

The Kirkwood Cowboys returned to the mountain village of San Agustín Zaragoza in early 1981, toting twelve high-pressure scuba tanks, each of which packed enough air to stay in the sump for up to two hours at a stretch. Bill persuaded his teammates to help him carry down two complete sets of dive gear—including fins, weights, buoyancy control vests, and other tools to enable him to overcome the difficulties he'd survived two years before. But an unseasonably early spring rainstorm flushed through the cave, and the resulting turbulence stirred up the silt on the sump's floor. The entire underwater tunnel was filled with the thick murky ocher haze that had almost paralyzed Bill at the end of the 1979 dive. Refusing to be cowed by either the silt or the mythical killer falls, he made two long dives, ultimately reaching a distance of 285 meters from the sump's surface before turning back.

Stone was eager to return the following year, with better tanks and more divers. His teammates weren't. They'd lugged the heavy dive gear all the way down to the sump on two separate expeditions, with little progress to show for it: Altogether, the dives had only added twenty-eight meters of depth to Sistema Huautla. Newcomers to the team wanted no part of hauling tanks for Bill Stone. And even the tight-knit Kirkwood crew began to splinter, as Bill Steele shifted his fearsome focus to finding the Nita Nanta connection. Reciting an old bromide popular among Texas cavers, Steele warned Stone: "A sump is God's way of telling you that the cave ends there."

Bill's brief glimpse into the heart of Huautla haunted him for another thirteen years. He dreamed often of that fleeting moment when, floating peacefully beneath a half-mile of limestone, the bottomless azure blue sea revealed itself.

It wasn't the first time that a solitary image had changed the shape of Bill's life. In the fall of 1968, at the beginning of his junior year in high school, he was signing up to rejoin the chemistry club when the name of another after-school activity caught his attention: "Spelunking." He didn't know what the word meant, but he liked the sound of it, so he talked his mother into driving him back to school the next evening. There he found his trigonometry teacher, Ron Bergman, warning how it had come to his attention that some seniors had recently entered a nearby cave. Bergman stood before the class, and in a laborious high school math teacher tone of voice, explained that this was a dangerous thing to do on one's own. If there were North Allegheny High School students who wanted to explore caves, well then, he'd take it upon himself to see to it that they received the proper instruction. Toward this end he'd invited two local cavers to present a slide show. That's when Bill saw the picture. It showed a caver rappelling down into the dark shaft of Hellhole Cave in West Virginia. The man hung gracefully from a single strand of damp rope that glistened like gold in the sunlight. Bright green ferns and small patches of moss clung to the upper reaches of the fluted limestone walls. Only blackness lay below. Bill was hooked. He signed up for the caving club. And for the remainder of his life, the dueling dreams of finding the bottom of the earth and following John Glenn into outer space defined his ambitions as surely as the double helix of his DNA provided him with his father's athletic physique.

Without the Kirkwood Cowboys to haul tanks for him, Bill began searching for a new route to the sump. He went looking for the place where the underground river exited the Huautla Plateau. After a couple of scouting expeditions, he found it at the base of a deep gorge called Peña Colorada, or Redwall Canyon. And in the spring of 1984, he and Bob Jefferys co-led an expedition to penetrate the San Agustín sump from below.

They arrived at the rim of the canyon with a mountain of equipment, including seventy-two new composite-fiber scuba tanks. They hired 200 men and sixty burros from the village of San Miguel Huautepec to help haul it all down the steep red cliffs to their riverbed base camp. In the place of Bill's old Austin pals was an all-star team of divers. They'd spent less total time underground than the average pit hippie, but they had more experience diving in dangerous environments. The international team included the talented Mexican divers Angel Soto and Sergio Zambrano, British diving prodigy Rob Parker, a quirky Texas caver named Noel Sloan, and Dr. John Zumrick. The team established two underground camps—the first ever set beyond flooded tunnels—and broke through seven consecutive sumps leading toward San Agustín. But their four-month expedition was ultimately halted by the same logistics barrier that had defeated Bill and his crew in 1981: After expending so much of their time and supplies to get to the exploration frontier, there was not enough matériel with which to continue.

One afternoon late in the expedition, Bill staggered out of the cave entrance and slouched into the sultry riverside base camp with a load of five empty tanks. He lay down his burden and stumbled into the mess tent, where he found Noel Sloan and John Zumrick collapsed at the table. The setting sun cast a red glow across the tent's netting walls. Noel, a lanky young doctor, was quartering a lime with surgical precision.

"That," said Noel, waving a weary arm at the mountain of gear just beyond the tent, "that's the problem." He licked his salted wrist, bit into a lime slice, and tossed back a healthy slug of tequila. When he was done, he added, "The dives ain't so tough. It's the haulin' that's killin' us."

Bill sat down next to him, and agreed. "Our logistics are like a big pyramid. We start off with seventy-two tanks and eleven people. But by the time we get to Sump Seven, we're down to four tanks and two divers. That leaves us with one, maybe two dives to find our way through the maze. Same thing killed us at San Agustín." He swiped a lime, grabbed the bottle, and downed a shot. "If we could just squeeze more gas into the damned tanks, we'd be on the other side right now." He waved the bottle sullenly, watching the golden liquor swirl in the red light. "If we could just . . ."

"Change the laws of physics?" Noel asked, snatching back the bottle. He fastidiously prepared another shot.

"You know," Zumrick chimed in, "you aren't so far off about changing the laws of physics."

"Which laws do you propose changing?" Bill asked. He dispensed with the ritual and gulped down another throat-searing shot.

"Well, there are other ways to survive underwater," Zumrick began.

Bill looked up, squinting in the red light. "Okay, John, you've got my attention."

Zumrick was accustomed to commanding attention. Like Noel, he was a physician, but Zumrick also was a medical officer at the Navy's Experimental Diving Unit in Panama City, Florida, and a full captain. He'd seen many high-tech gadgets that civilians like Bill and Noel hadn't. Leaning forward in a whisper, he asked, "Have you ever heard of closed-cycle life support?"

As darkness overtook the canyon, Zumrick explained how, instead of lugging dozens of tanks into the cave, they could carry one tank, and breathe from it over and over again. Up to that point they'd been diving with scuba, the acronym for self-contained underwater breathing apparatus. The system—developed by a French naval officer in the 1930s, and perfected by Emile Gagnon and Jacques-Yves Cousteau with the 1942 introduction of the self-regulating Aqua-Lung—was almost foolproof: The diver inhaled from a bottle of compressed air, then exhaled into the water. The problem, as Zumrick explained, was that scuba was outrageously inefficient: Because the human lung can metabolize only about 5 percent of the oxygen available in any given breath, a scuba diver wastes the lion's share of his precious cargo. As anyone who has watched Cousteau's television show has seen, the wasted air flees the diver in a sparkling trail of bubbles. If a second diver were to capture those bubbles in a plastic trash bag, he could stick his head in that bag and rebreathe the scuba diver's wasted air—for a couple of minutes. After that, his lungs would have converted most of the oxygen into carbon dioxide, and he would pass out. But if there were something else in the bag, a device that could scrub the carbon dioxide out of the air and replace the tiny fraction of metabolized oxygen, then he could rebreathe from that same bag of air indefinitely.

"Close the metabolic loop," Captain Zumrick concluded. "That's the other way to survive underwater." He sized up his exhausted but enthusiastic audience, then dropped the bomb. "And," he added coyly, "such devices already exist."

The backpack-sized machines were called rebreathers. NASA was using them on space walks. And Navy SEALs were using them to slip in and out of hostile harbors without being detected. Rebreathers lacked the fail-safe simplicity of scuba. But because they consumed only a fraction of the supplies, rebreathers promised a technological solution to the logistical problems that had defeated both of Bill's attempts to crack the San Agustín sump.

Bill began studying rebreathers the day he returned from

the expedition, and devoted the next ten years of his life to the design and construction of what would become the most reliable rebreather ever manufactured. The long years of designing and building the new underwater breathing machine took their toll, however. By the end of 1993, he'd postponed his return to Huautla a half-dozen times. Alone and deeply in debt, he struggled to balance his roles as inventor, politician, salesman, accountant, and den mother to a highly eccentric pack of underwater explorers. By the time 1994 dawned, he was counting the days until he'd finally return to the dark heart of Huautla.

B arbara Anne am Ende watched the early morning sunlight stream through barren tree branches and speckle the walls of the large bedroom. A mere two weeks had passed since she'd packed up her life as a North Carolina graduate student and moved in with her new boyfriend, Bill Stone. She wasn't accustomed to either the icy Maryland winter or the rhythms of daily life within Bill's sparsely furnished suburban home. A cold blast of wind shook the high-sided tract house. The corner windows groaned. She tugged a blanket up under her chin and watched the shadows dance.

A small pulley swung wildly from one of the tree's thickest branches. Barbara recognized its outline, and that of the new nylon climbing rope that dangled through it to the ground below. She'd spent the better part of a day hanging from that rope, adjusting her new red and pink Petzl harness and tuning her climbing gear for the impending expedition. The pulley creaked as it bobbed about. The noise reminded her that she'd neglected to pack the rope. There was still an awful lot to pack, she thought, but if nothing else went wrong, she and Bill—and the five other team members sacked out about his house—might finally hit the road later today.

Barbara rolled over to face Bill, and watched him sleep. They'd met in the autumn of 1992 at a West Virginia camp popular among cavers. She'd been standing at the back of a friend's van assembling her gear in preparation for the rescue of an injured caver at a nearby hole called the Portal, when the voice of another caver, also hastily recruited for the rescue party, sounded behind her. "You're going?" he asked, without attempting to conceal his incredulity. Barbara spun around. It was Bill Stone. She knew who he was, as did everyone else in the camp. His expeditions and diving developments had made him a legend among cavers. She'd gone out of her way not to fawn over him. In return, there he stood, questioning her abilities as a caver. She was a little intimidated. But while she knew she wasn't the fastest or the strongest, she was competent. She stammered, "Well, I brought my vertical gear."

Annoyed at her verbal fumble as soon as the breath passed her lips, she sat in silence as the rescue team car-pooled to the cave entrance. As fate would have it, she and Bill reached the injured caver first. They put the man into a sling, lowered him to the others, and helped him out of the cave. Late the next morning, after the others left in search of coffee, she and Bill sat in their sleeping bags and chatted. He grilled her: "What are you studying?" (Ph.D. in geology.) "How do you get to school?" (Bicycle.) "How much do you exercise?" (Jog eight kilometers twice a week.) She was offended by his rapid-fire inquisition, but attracted to his intensity. He slipped his business card into her toiletries kit before he left. She'd passed the quiz.

Now he lay asleep beside her. He was separated from his wife and three young sons, but not yet divorced. He'd courted her long-distance for the past year and a half. They took turns making the long drive from Chapel Hill to Gaithersburg. This was their first Valentine's Day together. And it wasn't exactly shaping up like a scene from a Hallmark commercial. The expedition was already a month behind schedule. The team was restless after weeks of delay. And Bill was showing signs of stress: For the past several days, he'd leapt frenetically from task to task, completing nothing.

She got up quietly and padded into the bathroom, catching sight of herself in the mirror as she switched on the light. A memory of another mirror flickered through her sleepy mind. The youngest of three children, Barbara took an early interest in caving. After reading every book her local library had about caves, she began pestering her mother to take her to one. When she was about thirteen years old, her mother drove her to Maquoketa Caves State Park in Iowa. Near the entrance to Dancehall Cave she charged into a small opening that snaked into the rock. She slithered forward on her belly until the crawlway became too tight. When she came back out, she was covered in mud. And she was beaming. Her mother took a picture. On the way home, they stopped for dinner at a Kentucky Fried Chicken. Barbara went into the bathroom to wash up. She caught sight of herself in the mirror, and felt torn. She was embarrassed for being so dirty. But as a budding caver, she was proud of her first real caving trip—and wanted to continue wearing the mud as a badge of honor. Now she studied herself in Bill's mirror for a moment, and smiled. She was taller, and thinner, and thirty-four years old. She was headed to a much more serious cave. But her excitement about the expedition was exactly the same as it had been all those years ago.

She returned to the bedroom, and realized that she and Bill wouldn't find another moment together once they headed downstairs. So she rustled about as much as possible in the hope that he'd wake. It worked. He lifted his head and peered at her through one eye.

"Happy Valentine's Day, Guillermo," she said. She'd taken to using the Spanish version of his name as a term of endearment, or sometimes just "G." The Mexicans called him Guillermo Piedra—William Stone.

Bill propped himself up on one arm, and sighed. He disliked the holiday. He regarded it as part of an elaborate conspiracy to sell greeting cards. But he liked Barbara, so he played along for the sake of the budding relationship. She reached under the bed and dug out the gifts she'd hidden there: a can of macadamia nuts, a jar of jam, and a card. Guillermo produced one of the team polo shirts he'd printed for the expedition. No card. They lingered in bed for a few moments longer, savoring their shared sense of hope.

As they made their way down the open staircase into the high-ceilinged front room, the couple found Ian Rolland sitting amid scrupulously sorted rows of valves, hoses, connectors, and other parts for the rebreathers. A small, muscular man with wispy brown hair, Ian had been at work since well before dawn. He tossed the couple a disarming smile, and called up a cheery: "Mornin', mates!"

Bill's living room featured none of the items one would normally expect in a suburban American home: no sofa, easy chair, coffee table, or television. In their place was an assortment of makeshift workbenches surrounded by shelves crammed full of caving equipment. Ian sat atop a high stool at the largest bench. A veteran of the groundbreaking British Cave Diving Group, he was one of the most experienced cavers on the expedition. He'd already plumbed most of Europe's deep caves by the time he met Bill in 1985 on an experimental diving expedition at England's legendary Wookey Hole.

Bill matched Ian's infectious grin, and showed his appreciation for the young man's hard work by hamming his way through a dreadful imitation of a stiff British colonial accent. "Well, good day to you, too, Mr. Rolland," he said. "Care to join us for a spot of tea?"

Ian hopped down and joined them in the kitchen. On leave from his job as a Tornado jet engineer in the Royal Air

Force, the twenty-nine-year-old had arrived in mid-January with the expectation that the team would be leaving for Mexico within days. He missed his wife, Erica, and their "two girls and a little lad." And while he was willing to temporarily live apart from them to go exploring, he found it irksome to have spent a month sorting parts in a bland American suburb. So without ever being asked, the young RAF sergeant had begun organizing the expedition. Each morning he casually questioned Bill about the status of various projects. Afterward, with humor and tact that belied his age, he gently cajoled his fellow team members into attacking the jobs he considered most essential.

"So then, Bill," Ian began, "should we pressure-check the new tanks before we toss them on the lorry?"

As Ian's laundry list of concerns poured out, Bill and Barbara foraged for silverware among the carefully sorted piles of freeze-dried food that concealed the kitchen's faded yellow countertops. They were well into their corn flakes by the time Noel Sloan's bare feet staggered across the dingy linoleum.

Noel headed straight for the coffee pot. He dumped eight heaping tablespoons of sugar into a small cup, then topped it off with java. Ian ceased his interrogation to gaze in mock horror. Barbara stifled a laugh. Noel, oblivious to them both, loudly slurped down the first cup of syrup, then fixed himself another.

Bill had seen Noel's morning routine many times before. The two were like brothers separated at birth. They'd both been brainy kids who'd nearly blown off their hands in boyhood chemistry experiments. They'd both taken up caving while in high school, and gone to graduate school in Texas to live close to the Mexican caving grounds. And they'd become friends the moment they met outside a Florida dive shop. It was the fall of 1983, and Bill was sitting on the shop's lawn assembling a new type of high-pressure scuba tank. Noel hopped out of a sleek Mazda RX-7 sporting a cowboy hat and mirrored sunglasses. He strolled straight for Bill, studied him a moment, then blurted, "Hey, man. Very cool. How high can you pump those suckers?" Bill looked up at the tall stranger, then back down at the bright yellow fiberglass tank resting between his long legs. "Well," he said, "I figure they'll blow up at about 17,000 psi." Noel laughed, and extended a hand still scarred from childhood. They shook, and had been caving together ever since.

Noel pawed through the cupboard in search of a bowl. Then he poured himself some cereal, shoved aside a large pile of cardboard boxes, and joined the others at the table. Ian resumed questioning Bill, but Noel wasn't listening. He, too, was frustrated that the team was still in Gaithersburg; but unlike Ian, he wasn't the least bit surprised. All of Bill's expeditions had started this way. In fact, as Noel knew all too well, it was one of these prolonged refugee encampments that had broken the back of Bill's marriage. Noel studied Barbara as he sucked down his cereal. He was pleased Bill had found a girlfriend, and delighted she was a caver. He was glad to have a woman on the team, having noticed over the years that expeditions tended to be a bit more civil whenever women were around. But Barbara's presence had seriously altered the long-accustomed team dynamic. She'd replaced him as Bill's confidant, just as Ian had replaced him as Bill's de facto lieutenant. As he slurped down the milk at the bottom of his bowl, Noel realized that for the first expedition in memory, he didn't really know what his role would be. He set his bowl down and smiled. The mystery of his own concealed future excited him.

Ian was plodding through an oral inventory of the equipment stacked throughout the two-story house and adjacent garage. There were 106 tanks, nine rebreathers, compressors, camp supplies, two tons of food, and a seemingly unlimited supply of clothing donated by various outdoor suppliers. There was simply no way it was all going to fit into two small Toyota pickups and the Step Van delivery truck they'd borrowed for the trip.

"We've got a mountain of fleece, mate," Ian noted. "Maybe we could pare down the Patagonia pile a wee bit?"

After a half-hour of defending the necessity of every item Ian questioned, Bill was about to concede Ian's point when Noel, who'd just tuned in, leapt on the fleece thing. He stretched his neck out and tilted his head forward, confronting Ian with bulging blue eyes that looked as if they were about to pop out of their sockets. "So, what kind of underwear are you going to wear under your drysuit?" Noel objected, unconcerned that he was derailing Ian's effort to focus Bill. "I mean, the water in San Agustín is pretty damned cold, man."

Noel's face remained pointed at Ian while he waited for an answer. He tugged the edge of his mouth back toward one ear for an instant. The head tilt and jaw tick, along with his bulging eyes and prematurely receding hairline, lent him the look of a large iguana. Barbara choked back another laugh. She looked from the amiable iguana, to the frustrated inquisitor, to the hapless den mother. And she thought, *Maybe we won't make it on the road today after all.*

With a conciliatory smile, Ian was about to answer Noel when Kenny Broad slipped into the room.

"I'm going to wear the pink lacey undies you gave me, Noel," Kenny said. "You know, the ones without the crotch."

The room filled with laughter.

Besides being a compulsive wise-ass, Kenny was the most experienced diver on the team; he'd spent more time underwater than the rest of them put together. Slight of build with a leathery tan and a scraggly reddish beard, Kenny grew up in Miami Beach and had been diving since he was a boy. He'd worked all sorts of diving jobs—including gigs as a stunt diver for adventure shows—before moving to

New York City to study for a Ph.D. in anthropology at Columbia University. Behind the swashbuckling persona hid a remarkably methodical twenty-eight-year-old: He was a licensed captain, an emergency medical technician, and a hyperbaric chamber operator.

Kenny's relentless pranks helped bridge the cultural divide that separated the cavers from the divers. Bill, Barbara, Ian, and Noel were cavers who, after being stymied by one sump or another, had learned to dive through sumps as a means to push deeper into caves. Kenny was an ocean diver who hadn't started working in dry caves until 1993, and then only to transport himself down to remote sumps like the one at the bottom of the Sótano de San Agustín. Cavers who could dive were rare; divers who could cave were more so. Bill's long years of trying to find a way through the San Agustín sump made him one of the few expedition leaders with friends in both groups, and it had taken him years to assemble a team of interdisciplinary explorers. But as thoroughly cross-trained as the team was, their loyalties to their home tribes never completely faded. When tensions ran high, the cavers derided the divers as lazy and uncommitted, while the divers accused the cavers of being undisciplined.

Like Ian, Kenny was astonished by the lack of advance preparation. He was accustomed to working on well-funded research or filmmaking expeditions, not volunteer operations like Bill's nonprofit U.S. Deep Caving Team. So Kenny simply figured the chaos in Gaithersburg was just part and parcel of shoestring expedition life, and he adjusted his expectations accordingly. He concluded that one couldn't reasonably expect such a disorganized expedition to guard the well-being of each of its members, so he resolved to set his own safety boundaries, and stay within them.

The group hadn't finished laughing when Jim Brown strolled into the room. A childhood illness had left his hearing severely impaired. He fiddled with his hearing aid in an attempt to understand the confusing conversation, but it was too late: He'd missed the joke, and felt left out.

Jim's condition gave him an advantage underwater, where he was better able to discern which direction a noise came from. Among the nation's best sump divers, he'd met Bill in 1988 during the course of a gruesome body recovery operation at Arch Spring, near Johnstown, Pennsylvania. They'd spent four days probing the near-zero-visibility sump before finding the victim. It was a grim reminder of a tough truth: There are no *rescues* in cave diving, only body recoveries. A veteran diver with a cool head, Jim took an immediate interest in Bill's rebreather development project, and soon became the new rig's top test diver. By the time the expedition began, he'd racked up more than 200 hours of dive time on the machine; more than double anyone else. Bill secretly regarded Jim as his ace in the hole: If anyone could find their way through the San Agustín sump, he thought, it would be Jim.

But like a fish out of water, Jim was awkwardly uncomfortable around his teammates. One night the group had been headed over to the National Institute of Standards and Technology, where Bill worked, to jog up and down a tall flight of stairs with heavy packs as part of their conditioning. Jim heard a door close and looked up just in time to see the group drive away. They hadn't realized he wanted to come along. He took it personally, and after that his sense of being outside the group grew steadily.

Kenny and Noel were still talking about underwear when Steve Porter joined the breakfast gathering. Steve was having a hard time with the group, too, though for entirely different reasons. Like Kenny and Jim, Steve was a diver first. He'd spent years probing wrecks deep in the icy waters of Lake Superior before becoming one of the Midwest's most active sump divers. But while each of the others had joined the team through Bill's network of expedition buddies, Steve was an outsider who'd been forced to audition. After reading about Bill's earlier expeditions, he wrote and asked if he could join. Bill replied that Steve didn't have enough dry caving experience to be part of the team, but that he was welcome to come as a support member. Steve spent the next two years training. Bill was impressed, and after a 1993 shakedown expedition, made Steve a full-fledged member of the dive team.

Steve had found the chaotic weeks of preparation in Maryland both exhilarating and terrifying. He felt like a kid at Christmas every time the FedEx truck arrived with another box of exotic new gear; but he was shocked to discover how freewheeling the low-budget expedition really was. He wasn't close to Bill the way Noel and Barbara were, and he didn't have years of expedition experience to draw from the way Kenny and Ian did; he needed a team that would look out for him, and he knew it. He was particularly annoyed by Barbara's presence. He liked her, and recognized she was a hard worker who pulled more than her share of the weight. But having worked so hard to prove himself, it grated on Steve that Barbara had been invited without leaping the same hurdles.

It took the seven of them one more day to slip out of Maryland. They would pick up more team members in Florida and Texas before caravanning south to Mexico. After a tense morning of packing and repacking, their over-loaded trucks were rolling south by the afternoon of February 16. Noel, Steve, Ian, Kenny, and Jim headed straight for Florida, where they'd spend the next few days shaking down the rebreathers. Bill and Barbara cut inland to Georgia, where they rented a U-Haul and filled it with two kilometers of new PMI climbing rope. They caught up with the others at Ginnie Springs, a campground and dive site near Gainesville.

With names like Devil's Eye and Devil's Ear, the warm,

blue holes at Ginnie Springs are but a handful of the thousands of entrances to the largest underground river system
in the United States. Called the Floridan Aquifer, this fresh-
water labyrinth stretches from Orlando to the Panhandle.
The Floridan's passageways provide some of the best cave
diving in the world. Bill had spent most of the last decade
returning to the Floridan, as he refined his unique breathing
machine. After reviewing NASA's life-support backpack and
the SEAL rebreather, he'd concluded that neither rig was
rugged enough to survive the rough-and-tumble journey
into a deep cave. So he decided to invent and build his own.
He spent the next two years designing the parts: a breathing
bag, a miniature gas-processing plant to scrub out the
carbon dioxide, four waterproof computers to operate the
various systems, and a fiberglass backpack to carry it all. By
the end of 1987, he'd built a working prototype, which he
named FRED—Failsafe Rebreather for Exploration Diving.
FRED was the size of a kitchen table; one test diver compared donning the oversize rig to "strapping a Volkswagen
on your back." Once properly tuned, no bubbles escaped.
This gave the tester's diving buddies the willies. Accustomed to the familiar "swhooo-oop" and "phoooossh" of
open-circuit scuba, they were never sure whether FRED was
working properly—or the test diver had passed out.

After three years of development, Bill and Noel loaded
the prototype into a hand cart—at 205 pounds, FRED was
far too heavy to wear on one's back—and rolled it down the
dock at Wakulla Springs, also in Florida. Bill then entered
the water to determine whether FRED really did have the
range for which it was designed. He dropped down to a
sandy ledge about ten meters below the surface. Having no
other mission than to determine if FRED would really support him underwater for an entire day, he sat down on the
soft sandy bottom and read a book. The pulpy paperback
reminded him of the Doc Savage stories he'd reveled in

during his youth. The serial novels followed the adventures of a swashbuckling physician named Clark Savage, a man of "superhuman strength and protean genius." Savage traveled the globe with a team of "the five greatest brains ever assembled." The group's vigilante exploits usually involved destroying "evildoers" who frequently holed up in lavish caves. Within those pages of purple prose Bill found the piece he needed to complete his own life's puzzle: By becoming both the star athlete of his father's dreams as well as the uber-scientist of his own ambitions, he hoped to earn a role in the great adventures of his age. Like a Doc Savage sidekick, Noel floated down later that night, carrying an oversize set of scuba tanks. He took a seat next to Bill, and held up a white plastic slate on which he had penciled the words: "Got you covered till dawn, dude!" And sure enough, when Bill began to nod off about 4:00 A.M., Noel was there to kick him awake. Bill finally emerged from the spring the next afternoon, December 4, 1987. He'd broken the surface twenty-four hours after entering the water, smashing all previous records for self-contained diving equipment. A small crowd of reporters and divers erupted into applause.

He'd accomplished exactly what John Zumrick had described back at the Peña Colorada: He'd bent the laws of physics. But he was unable to slow the march of time. While he tested his rebreather near the water's surface, his team-mates explored 3.3 kilometers of Wakulla Springs. And while he refined the device, Bill's old caving buddies returned to Huautla; Jim Smith made a ten-meter dive linking San Agustín to Nita Nanta, and deepened Sistema Huautla to a depth of 1,353 meters.

Bill's life began to feel like a slow-motion version of the 1979 dive: His resources were quickly slipping away while he struggled to make his way back to the San Agustín sump. All of 1988 and most of 1989 bubbled away as he built the first field version of the rebreather. Dubbed the Cis-Lunar

Mk-II, it included two complete systems that weighed half what FRED did.

The way Bill saw it, redundancy made the Mk-II safe: If the first system failed, a diver could easily switch to the second; if both failed, he might be able to assemble a working system from the interchangeable components. That theory was proven wrong in November of 1989 when test diver Brad Pecel blacked out only twenty minutes into a test dive. Bill was swimming alongside when Pecel began convulsing. Bill quickly placed a backup scuba regulator in Pecel's mouth, and towed him to the surface. While Pecel was recovering, Bill discovered that the diver had mistakenly plugged his instrument panel into the system he wasn't using. With his display panel incorrectly indicating he wasn't receiving enough oxygen, Percel had overdosed. It was a mistake that could only have occurred on a fully redundant system. Pecel recovered, but left the team. The incident shook the others' confidence in the Mk-II, and the return to San Agustín was delayed.

Bill spent much of the next two years back at his drafting table. Meanwhile, a new Mexican cave called Cheve—seated just across the Peña Colorada from Huautla—was pushed to a depth of 1,386 meters, a mark that kicked Huautla out of its post as the Americas' deepest.

The Mk-III rig was finally ready for testing in the spring of 1992. It was lighter than its predecessor, and had greater range. To avoid any further accidents like the one that almost claimed Pecel, Bill took the team to a New York hyperbaric chamber for several weeks of dry testing before returning to Florida for another month of diving, all without mishap. By mid-April, Bill was laying plans to return to Huautla the following year. But on the last day of the Florida training exercise, Australian team member Rolf Adams decided to squeeze in some underwater sightseeing before flying home. He borrowed some scuba gear and plunged into a nearby spring called Hole in the Wall, where he panicked in a silt-out, and drowned. Though Adams's tragic death was unrelated to the rebreather, his passing shook the team's confidence, and the expedition was postponed once again. Adams's death also unleashed a barrage of attacks from Bill's critics—who overlooked the fact that Adams died on a recreational dive using traditional gear— and publicly accused Bill of sacrificing the life of a teammate to develop his rebreather.

Shortly after Bill returned from Adams's memorial service in Australia, Bill's wife, Pat—a college sweetheart he'd married in 1981—asked him for a divorce. She accused him of sacrificing his own life, and that of his young family, to his obsession with "that damned hole" in southern Mexico.

Living alone for the first time in years—and deeply in debt as a result of all the funds he'd poured into the various rebreathers—he somehow managed to produce several units of the Cis-Lunar Mk-IV, a significant evolution of the design based on team feedback collected during a two-month-long 1993 training mission. After ten years of development, the rebreather was finally ready to take on the sump.

But the divers who'd been the core of Bill's team at the outset were no longer part of the project. Rolf Adams was gone, and Huautla veteran Jim Smith gave up diving altogether after he'd nearly drowned trying to save Adams. Brad Pecel left the team after his accident. And Rob Parker, the young Brit who'd been a star of the 1984 Peña Colorada expedition and a stalwart of the rebreather development project, remained suspicious of the complex rig and focused his attention on his climbing business. So while the team assembled in Ginnie Springs possessed exemplary dive skills, they didn't have the level of deep caving experience Bill had initially sought.

The Gaithersburg gang was huddled about a picnic table as the tires of Bill's battered Toyota skidded to a stop at the edge of Ginnie Springs. Ian and Jim were dissecting a rebreather, its carcass spread across the table. Steve had felt something was wrong and surfaced after only five minutes. After five more minutes he came to the surface again, red-faced and panting, a clear sign he was inhaling too much carbon dioxide. The others helped him out of the water, and after confirming that he was okay, began ripping apart the machine. The inspection revealed that whoever had assembled the unit had neglected to install the essential canister of lithium hydroxide—a chemical that absorbs exhaled carbon dioxide. Like someone with a plastic trash bag taped around his neck, Steve had been underwater for ten minutes breathing nothing but his own exhaled breath.

Problems like this plagued the team for the rest of the week at Ginnie Springs. Bill felt vindicated that in every instance the problem turned out to be the result of some user error and not a malfunction of the machine itself. He responded to the problem by drafting a detailed pre-dive checklist, like pilots use. But the others were shaken by the string of minor mishaps. The divers began grumbling among themselves that the Mk-IV was too complex. They feared that the kinds of problems that were merely dangerous at Ginnie Springs could easily turn deadly in the dark depths of the Huautla Plateau.

By late Saturday afternoon, they'd managed to assemble, test-dive, and pack away five of the nine units. Bill felt they were over the hump and would soon be ready to go. In the last remnant of afternoon sunlight, he and Barbara and Jim started repacking them into the Step Van.

Steve watched in disbelief from across the campground. "What's he doing?" he asked Noel. "We haven't even put ten hours on those units. Not to mention that we don't have the operating procedures nailed."

"Ahhh, well, yeah." Noel was searching for an answer. He agreed with Steve that the team needed more practice with the rebreathers. But Noel also felt the team was way too stressed out. He thought it would be good for the group's karma if they got on the road. So he tilted his head at Steve and said, "Ya see, Bill's just got his own way of doin' things."

Kenny and Ian ambled alongside, wearing boots and climbing harnesses. They'd rigged a series of ropes up a nearby oak tree, and Ian had spent the afternoon teaching Kenny the finer points of a European rope-ascending technique called the Frog. The two were developing a close friendship. Kenny stared at Noel for a moment—the iguana thing still fascinated him—then turned his gaze back to Bill, who was passing the bright pink and lime green tanks up to Jim and Barb, for packing in the Step Van. Kenny shook his head, but said nothing.

Steve pressed Ian for his view. Ian had led the charge to get out of Gaithersburg. But he agreed that it was too soon to leave Ginnie Springs. "It's pointless," he said, "dragging gear all the way down into the cave if we're uncomfortable with it." Ian looked at the ground and kicked the sandy soil with one of his scruffy green Wellingtons. "And it's even more pointless dragging this stuff down to the sump if it turns out not to work." But the absurdity amused him. He looked at Steve, and smiled from ear to ear. "Pointless, mate."

Steve mistook Ian's observation for a marching order. He crossed the parking lot and told Bill that the team felt they needed more time to get comfortable with the rebreathers.

Bill didn't take it well. He knew the divers were grumbling behind his back, but figured Noel and the cavers were with him. He felt betrayed by all the bitching about the Mk-IV's complexity. He'd made each of the design changes in direct response to complaints these same divers had made about the previous version. Between the software, hardware, and custom tooling, those alterations alone had cost close to $100,000. His only hope for recovering all that

money had been a fee he'd expected to receive from a pro-
ducer who'd contracted to buy rights to film a documentary
about the expedition. Unbeknownst to the rest of the team,
Bill had received word earlier that afternoon that the film
deal was falling through. He hadn't taken that news well,
either. His long-delayed expedition was already a month
behind schedule, and the critical dry season—after which it
would be too dangerous to work in the cave—was slipping
away as swiftly as the evening sun. He feared that if they
didn't get to Huautla soon, the expedition might collapse
under its own weight.

He set down the tank he was carrying and glared at
Steve. A long breath snorted across his thick mustache. This
wasn't the first time Steve had come to him claiming to
speak for the group. The Minnesotan's touchy-feely way of
presenting things annoyed the hell out of Bill. He wanted
to unload on the man, but didn't know him well enough to
gauge how he'd react. He feared that if Steve quit, the
defection might start a chain reaction among the divers. So
Bill said nothing. He just picked up the pink tank at his feet
and went back to work. He brushed past Steve three times
without saying a word.

Steve didn't budge. He stood his ground, arms folded
across his chest.

On the fourth pass, Bill finally muttered, "Look, let's all
go to the party tonight and have a good time. We can talk
about this in the morning. Okay?"

Steve wasn't satisfied. But he could see that Bill was in no
mood to talk, so he decided not to push the matter. He
wanted Bill to understand that it wasn't only him, that the
others were feeling rushed, too. And he wanted Bill to
respect him. So without saying another word, he picked up
a tank and helped Bill finish loading the truck. Bill tossed
him a grin on the next pass.

After they finished, Bill sat in the cab of his pickup and
caught up on his daily logbook. *I guess one last thing is that*

I feel somewhat alone down here, the log entry concluded. *Barbara is extremely supportive, more supportive than I'd ever hoped . . . she keeps me from overstressing and gives me upbeat ideas to keep pressing on. But I have daily thoughts of my three boys: Dave, Rob, and Chris. Carry a picture of them in my wallet. I look at it and think, someday, I hope they'll be able to join me on some of these projects.*

The party was at Woody Jasper's house, just north of High Springs. Woody was a Mole. So were most of the rest of the guests at the barbecue.

The Moles, as the gang of middle-aged good ol' boys like to call themselves, were a fraternity of cave divers who'd spent much of their lives exploring the Floridan Aquifer. The Moles specialized in pressing their bodies through the minuscule water-filled crevices that connected one spring to the next. This usually involved stripping off their scuba units and pushing their tanks ahead of their bodies as they slithered through coffin-sized passageways. Because their tanks held a limited supply of air, the penalty for getting lost in the labyrinth or hung up on jagged limestone was death. What made the Moles so unique was that these fastidious rednecks had been diving—and surviving—together for more than two decades. When asked to explain how the Moles had beat the odds for so long, Woody liked to quote the escape artist Harry Houdini: "There's always slack somewhere."

Woody met Bill and Barbara at the front door and guided them through the small ranch house to a backyard patio, where the Moles were drinking beer. Tom Morris waved hello to Bill while listening to Wes Skiles tell a story. A middleweight man with unruly gray hair and bushy eyebrows, Morris had started cave diving when he was thirteen years old. He worked as a freelance biologist, and specialized in the study of bizarre little critters that found ways to survive deep within wet caves. The Smithsonian Institution named a blind crayfish after him, a tiny white animal called *Procambarus morrisi.*

Wes Skiles was ringleader of the Moles. A barrel-chested man with a deep Florida growl, Wes was among the world's best-known cave divers. He'd taught cave diving for years; Kenny Broad and Steve Porter were among his thousands of students. Wes had also distinguished himself as one of the world's top underwater photographers, and had landed an assignment to photograph the 1994 expedition for *National Geographic* magazine. He and Tom planned to drive down about a month behind the core team.

Bill spied a huge stack of raw chicken, and offered to barbecue the birds. Woody handed him a fork and a beer. Barbara wandered off to talk to the other divers. Then Sheck showed up.

Sheck Exley was among the first humans to begin exploring the Floridan, and pioneered most of modern cave diving's safety techniques. He'd personally taught Wes and Bill and most of the rest of the world's top cave divers how to stay alive in an underwater cave. At forty-four years of age, he ate a rigid diet that left almost no fat on his muscular body, and he'd studied meditation to slow his heart and breath rate. As a result of his discipline, Sheck could squeeze more time out of a tank of air than any other diver, and he could keep a clear head at depths that left other divers silly from the intoxicating effects of nitrogen narcosis. Standing a mere five and a half feet tall, he was cave diving's Babe Ruth, Michael Jordan, and Tiger Woods all rolled into one.

Bill worshipped Sheck as much as the Moles did. And Bill owed Sheck his life. Back in 1980, when Bill was training for his second assault on San Agustín, Sheck led him 230 feet down into Eagle's Nest sink. The dive was twice as deep as most scuba divers ever venture, and was Bill's deepest yet. Everything seemed to be going well, until Sheck gave the hand signal to end the dive. When Bill went to inflate his buoyancy control device, nothing happened. Then he realized that his hands weren't doing anything. Mesmerized by the overload of nitrogen in his head, he just gazed into space while his air supply bubbled away. The silt in the water and the nitrogen in his head created the illusion that he was sitting in a dark tunnel. Then a hand reached down through the tunnel. It was Sheck. He towed Bill back up to the 190-foot level, where the nitrogen narcosis cleared. The incident was over in a few moments, but Bill never forgot how Sheck's steady hand saved him.

Bill wasn't expecting to see Sheck at the party. But as soon as he did, he felt some of his own stress slip away. He felt like Sheck might be the only person alive who understood what he was going through.

"Ahh, Pierre," Bill exclaimed, a bit too loudly, in a clichéd French accent, "the world's greatest cave dive-air!" He'd been baiting Sheck with Pierre jokes for years. French cavers held nearly all of the cave records, except for the dozen or so held by Sheck, which at that time included the longest single cave dive (10,450 feet) and the deepest (868 feet). The Pierre jokes flowed from the twisted logic that since Sheck was the world's best cave diver, he must therefore be French.

Sheck let loose a deep, hoarse laugh. He and his longtime partner, Mary Ellen Eckhoff, strolled over to the grill. "Well, Bill, looks like ya got a real good team here." Sheck's swamp-country drawl was unmistakable. "Ya gonna crack her this time?"

Bill sipped his beer and thought for a moment while Sheck slathered barbecue sauce on the chicken. If anyone else had asked, Bill would have simply said, "Of course." But Sheck had known Bill since the dawn of his long crusade to break through the San Agustín sump, and had coached him through numerous previous attempts. "If it's less than a kilometer long, I think we'll nail it," Bill replied. "If it gets much longer we'll have to switch to dual rebreathers, and I can't predict what would happen. I doubt

I'll feel comfortable pushing beyond two kilometers." He took another sip of beer. "But man, it's gotta come up before that."

Sheck nodded.

Bill poked the chicken with his fork, then pointed it across the yard at his team. "Jim Brown, well, you know what he can do. And Ian . . ."—the young Brit had overcome his initial awe of the Moles and had begun to quiz them loudly on their techniques—". . . he can crack anything."

Sheck nodded.

"So," Bill continued, "I hear you and Bowden are headed back to that hole you've been working?"

Sheck nodded again. He could go all day without saying more than a dozen words. Bill, on the other hand, was prone to delivering stream-of-consciousness monologues on any subject that interested him, at any time, to anyone who happened to be around. Both found the contrast amusing.

"Yeah," Bill said, "what's the name of that place again?"

Sheck laughed. The cave Bill was asking about had been discovered in Mexico by a Texas diver named Jim Bowden, who showed it to Sheck. The two laconic Southerners agreed they'd keep the seemingly bottomless sinkhole's location a secret until they'd plumbed its depths themselves. So Sheck knew with absolute certainty that neither of them had told Bill where it was. And he found Bill's clumsy attempt to coax it out of him amusing.

"Well, ya know, Bill, I gave Jim my word on that," Sheck said. "I'd love to tell ya. I really would. But I promised Jim, so I just can't."

Both men laughed. Bill knew Sheck would never give it up, and Sheck knew that Bill knew. The low-key, low-budget expedition being mounted by Bowden and Exley stood in stark contract to Bill's expensive Huautla effort, which depended on publicity to attract financial support.

Yet theirs would undoubtedly be the two most memorable Mexican expeditions that year.

"So what are you aiming for?" Bill asked.

"Oh, I'm kinda shootin' for a nice round number."

Bill smiled. "One thousand feet?"

"It's there," Sheck replied, referring to the secret hole. "I think we're ready for it."

Bill drew another sip of beer. He was worried about his friend. Industrial divers routinely went to 1,000 feet, but they spent a full day in a hyperbaric transfer chamber to do it. To make their dives on conventional scuba gear, Sheck and Jim would have to plunge all the way down in a matter of minutes. That rate of compression would expose them to a bizarre condition called high-pressure nervous syndrome, or HPNS. Sheck had experienced the symptoms the year before in South Africa; his muscles had twitched uncontrollably and his eyes produced multiple images, like a bug's vision.

"I sure wish you guys would simulate your dive in a hyperbaric chamber beforehand," Bill said. "That stuff you described at Bushmangat scares the hell out of me."

"I think we'll have it under control this time," Sheck said. "I *have* to do this, you know. My age. I'm not as fit as I was. My respiratory capacity is deteriorating. This will be a good dive to retire on."

"Retire?" Bill asked.

Sheck shrugged. But before Bill could press him on the issue, they were distracted by the ruckus Ian was raising among the Moles.

"No way, mate. That's not the way to side-mount," Ian was loudly insisting. "You do it like this." The diminutive Welshman then demonstrated for Wes the method by which most British sump divers carried their tanks through tight passages. Wes shook his large, high-domed head. Woody, the Moles' chief tinkerer, tried to explain that the Florida style was more flexible. But his voice was drowned when all the Moles began arguing at once. Ian's lilting accent finally pierced through the melee. "Listen, mate," he yelled, "you Yanks may have landed on the moon, but we Brits invented side mounting."

The party wound down around 1:00 A.M., after Wes screened a spoof of a diving safety film he'd shot a few years earlier. The short video stars Kenny Broad as an overly cocky Frenchman who attempts to free dive the long passageway from Devil's Eye spring to Devil's Ear on one breath. He drowns trying. The final scene features Woody in the role of a drawling redneck sheriff who concludes, "It's a real shame. But it could have been worse. He was Fray-anch, after all."

The team was back on the Interstate within two days. They were bound for Texas, but Bill found himself stuck in Louisiana after his truck ran out of gas. The Toyota's gas gauge had been broken for years, and he'd trained himself to stop and refill his tank every 250 miles or so. But in the scramble to get out of Ginnie Springs, he'd failed to consider how much the U-Haul trailer filled with rope was reducing his gas mileage. So late one night, he and Barbara found themselves—and the precious rebreathers—stranded on a freeway overpass in a rough-and-tumble New Orleans neighborhood. The little blue truck shimmied as eighteen-wheelers whizzed past at sixty-five miles an hour. And all the stress Bill had bottled up for the past month finally erupted. He whacked the steering wheel and shouted: "We're gonna get creamed!" Barbara had never seen him so upset. She stayed with the truck and waved a flashlight at oncoming traffic while Bill ran off into the night looking for gas.

They rolled into San Antonio early on the morning of the following day, and found the rest of the team sacked out across Bill Steele's living room floor. A gregarious man of bearish build, Steele was a longtime expedition leader who'd lived on Kirkwood Road back in the 1970s. His spacious San Antonio home was nothing like the peeling stucco ghetto in Austin. But for a couple of days in early 1994, it had the same feel. Four-wheel-drive pickups lined the street like pack animals waiting to be loaded. The garage was filled with equipment, which spilled out of the yard and drew complaints from the neighbors. Steele's career with the Boy Scouts prevented him from joining Bill's 1994 expedition, however. Like Wes Skiles and Tom Morris, he'd drop in on the expedition later, and lend what support he could.

Waiting for the team at Steele's house was Don Broussard, who'd arrived a few days before in his weathered blue Ford crew cab, a beaten hulk of a truck affectionately dubbed "Big Dog." While not a diver, and therefore not technically part of the core team, Don was a Kirkwood veteran who'd been caving in Huautla since 1968. A small man of perhaps 120 pounds, he had wispy yellow-blond hair, dark eyes, and a thick blond mustache. He worked as a computer consultant in Austin and spoke slowly and directly in a fashion that placed the conclusions first. He had a reputation for sticking it out when the going got tough. This was fortunate, because the going had a way of getting tough when Don was around. He was legendary for being in the wrong place at the wrong time—like when his light plane crashed in the rugged Sierra de Guatemala, and it took him and his companions three days to machete their way out of the mountains. The Austin cavers called him "Nine Lives Broussard."

Don had been an insulin-dependent diabetic since he was eight years old. Ian was also a diabetic. He'd been diagnosed only a year before, and the Royal Air Force initially refused his request to participate in the expedition out of fear his diabetes would put him in jeopardy. When Don discovered they shared the disease, he took it upon himself to sit Ian down on a couch in the Steeles' living room and make sure he knew how to stay on top of the condition. They spread their insulin kits out before them on the coffee table, and Don quietly quizzed Ian on the secrets of managing insulin in situations where it's impossible to eat regular meals. He advised Ian to carry two insulin kits, as well as a personal supply of candy at all times. "You have to pay close attention to this," he said, in a voice just above a whisper. "When you feel you might be crashing, you can't shrug it off. You've got to be aggressive and act quickly. Okay?"

The short stay in San Antonio ended much as the week at Ginnie Springs had, with a barbecue. As Stone watched the team play trampoline dodge ball, he realized that Sheck had been right. This was a good crew. Ian and Kenny, Noel and Steve, Jim and Don, he and Barbara: Each brought special skills to the expedition. Bill chuckled to himself when he realized he was comparing them to the Doc Savage sidekicks. Mexican diver Angel Soto would join them in Huautla, and Bill knew he could count on several dozen experienced volunteers like Steele to show up for a week here or there to help ferry gear in and out of the cave. For the first time in a decade, he began to feel like it might just all come together.

Late in the evening, Steele strolled through the yard and announced: "The time has come, we're gonna go caving now, you're all gonna see Steele Caverns." No one had any idea what he was talking about. They could tell from the terrain that there were no significant caves nearby, but instinctively started rounding up their helmets and lights. Steele laughed. "Oh, you don't need a light for Steele Caverns," he told them. His sixth-grade daughter, Audrey, then led the curious through the backyard, out a small gate, and around the gully into a large storm drain. The group laughed when they saw that Steele had strung electric Christmas lights into the culvert. They crawled through the concrete box in single file, with Audrey in the lead. The culvert grew tight on the far end, requiring large men like Noel and Bill to flatten themselves in order to get out. Steele's wife, Janet, a lanky anthropologist with a sharp sense of humor, waited at the far end. She pointed to Bill as he struggled through the final squeeze and said loudly to her daughter, "Look there, honey. That old man thinks he's going to make it to the bottom of the world. But he can't hardly find his way out of a Texas sewer."

The Mexican officials at the Los Indios customs station took one look inside the Step Van stuffed with dive gear and refused to let the team enter Mexico without an import license. In Spanish, Bill spent half an hour explaining the expedition to the officials. He showed them his letters of permission from Oaxaca and Mexico City. He showed them magazine articles and scientific journals. He pulled out brochures and even team polo shirts. But the customs men couldn't care less. Defeated, he slunk out of the little office and past the team, which was lounging about out front. Barbara looked at him for an answer. He whispered back, "We're screwed."

Like a cave diver feeling his way through the darkness, the five-truck caravan spent the rest of the day probing one border crossing after another, hoping to find one that would let the commercial-looking truck through. By the time they pulled into Reynosa, it was *siesta* time and no customs agents were on duty. A woman from the visa office argued with her supervisor over what to tell the gringos. After a bit, they insisted that the white Step Van be opened. As the door rolled upward, they gazed in amazement at the box of wonders. Then they began demanding to know the value of the rebreathers, scuba tanks, compressors, gas boosters, and the other shiny gear stuffed inside.

Noel's voice sliced through the litany of questions. "*Cueveros*," he shouted. "We're just a bunch of cavers! This is personal equipment, *todo éste*." Noel flapped his long arms wildly as he flailed ahead in mangled Spanglish. "For *buceo* in *cuevas*, underground, *comprende?*" He gestured across the entire truck, then pointed to his chest as he repeated, "All of this—*todo éste*—personal equipmento!"

The visa officials could plainly see that the truck held enough inventory to stock one heck of a dive shop anywhere in the world. They asked several more questions in Spanish.

Bill, who spoke Spanish, stepped forward to answer; but Noel, who clearly did not, shoved him back. Noel continued shouting the same crazy phrases regardless of what questions they asked. Bill turned away so that the Mexicans wouldn't see him laugh. By the time he turned back, Noel had done it. Perhaps simply wishing to get rid of the annoying gringo, the woman marched over to the Step Van's cab, slapped a *turista* sticker on the window, and said "*Pásale.*"

"See," Noel said triumphantly as they hopped back in the trucks, "that's how you speaka da Spanish. Now let's get the hell outta here."

The convoy crawled across the coastal lowlands of eastern Mexico and arrived in steamy Tehuacán on Monday, February 28. They made their way to a bright, airy restaurant called the Peñafiel. Immediately across from the small city's lush central square, the Peñafiel had long been a favorite meeting place for cavers. While the others ordered tortillas and eggs, Bill made his way to the cashier's desk and retrieved a tattered ledger book that served as an unofficial roster of cavers bound for Huautla. Its pages were a testament to how Huautla had become the Katmandu of caving.

Bill thumbed through the log. His own entries dated back to 1976. The memories of entire expeditions unfolded beneath each scribbled entry. Before he and the others finished eating, another group of cavers stopped by. Led by the well-known Australian explorer Alan Warild, they were on their way *out* of the region. Their departure reminded Bill once again that February—the height of the dry season— was already gone.

CHAPTER TWO

In the morning, Bill and Barbara returned to the Peñafiel, where Angel Soto Porrua was waiting for them. Angel was among Mexico's best-known high-altitude mountaineers. And along with Noel, he was one of only two veterans of the Peña Colorada expedition who had stuck with Bill through ten long years of rebreather development and was back to help crack the sump. After breakfast, Angel climbed into his aging white Volkswagen, and followed Bill's battered blue Toyota south along the lush Tehuacán Valley. They slipped into the state of Oaxaca, and wound their way past the high adobe walls of the seventeenth-century Franciscan mission at Teotitlán del Camino before turning east toward Huautla de Jiménez.

Just past Teotitlán, the road began to climb. The lush lowlands of the river plain quickly gave way to a dusty desert of mesquite bushes and elephant cactus. The road began to wind mercilessly. The two-lane strip of asphalt soon became a narrow ledge carved precariously into the plateau's corrugated cliff. A wall of crumbling rock loomed above the uphill side, occasionally tossing down boulders. Nothing but desert sky bordered the downhill side: no shoulder, no guardrail, not even a thin white line. The road switched directions every few kilometers. The Toyota's tiny engine would howl as Bill geared down to negotiate another steep U-turn. By the time the howling stopped, earth and sky had swapped sides.

Ornate crosses marked most of the switchbacks and just about every other spot along the cliff road where there was enough shoulder to hammer a marker into the rocky ground. Some of the crosses were cast in cement, and stood atop shrines filled with photographs and candles. Others were intricately welded of wrought iron, with dusty plastic flowers tied to the metalwork. A few more were sparse wooden affairs, painted white with a name and date printed in block letters. Most were about waist-high. All marked places where some luckless motorist plunged off the narrow ribbon of road.

Bill had almost earned his own cross on a previous trek. It was back in 1979, the year he first dove the sump. An eighteen-wheeler passing on the left suddenly swerved back into the right-hand lane, forcing his old Ford onto the shoulder. The pickup flipped over and skidded down the highway on its roof for eighty meters before coming to a stop. He hung in his seatbelt for seconds that seemed like hours, watching asphalt grind metal and wondering where he and his fellow cavers would be when the sparky ride was over. Miraculously, everyone survived. But he had no desire to repeat the performance here, where an asphalt slide of even a few meters would carry the little Toyota over the cliff.

A civil engineer by trade, Bill made a joke to calm his nerves. "They've almost got enough material standing there to build a guardrail," he noted wryly. "I mean, for what all these families have spent on cement and cast iron crosses, the government could have strung up a post-and-rail safety barrier."

Barbara stuck her head out the window. During the first half-hour of the drive, she could spot the rusted carcasses of errant vehicles perched on the rocky cliffs below. But now the road had crept high up the side of the massive plateau, and the wrecks were too far below. She pulled her short blond bob back into the cab, and matched Bill's engineering quip with a geology joke.

"Yeah, but after a few million more trucks pile up, there won't be much need for a guardrail, will there?"

The limestone at the heart of the plateau they were climbing was itself created through a process much like the one she joked about—except instead of trucks piling up, it was sea shells.

Beginning about 144 million years ago, this whole region was submerged beneath the sea. The water was warm at this latitude, and shallow enough that the sunlight streamed all the way to the ocean floor in places. Tiny plants and animals flourished in warm water, and in turn these microscopic organisms provided food for an entire colony of Cretaceous Period marine life. Strange-looking fish swam about a growing mound of clamlike creatures called rudists. Like trucks piling up at the bottom of a cliff, each new calcium carbonate skeleton added to the ancient mound.

A lot of clams died. Over many millions of years, the colony grew into a high bank that somewhat resembled a modern reef, such as the Great Barrier Reef off Australia's eastern shore. All those shells and skeletons crumbled into calcium carbonate sludge, and recrystallized as limestone. The ancient clam bank grew so fast that it began to sink into the soft ocean floor. Fortunately for the clams—and the cavers who would come later—it settled at more or less the same rate it grew. Had it sunk more quickly, the clams would have perished below the sun's reach. Had it sunk more slowly, they would have died when the bank rose above the ocean's surface. But at Huautla, the bank sank at just the right speed. By the time extinction finally caught up with them, the rudist clams and their Cretaceous kin had left behind a big block of soft rock roughly 200 kilometers long.

The massive limestone slab was lifted out of the sea about 60 million years ago. During a geological event called the Laramide Orogeny, the Farallon Plate was forced under the North American continental plate. The Rocky Mountains were created, and to the south, the old slab of Cretaceous limestone was buried beneath the eastern ridge of a large plateau that stretched across what would later become known as central Mexico. Three small mountain ranges harbor the deepest slabs of soft limestone. Together, they are regarded as the Himalaya of caving.

"Look, there." Bill pointed to a distant mountain ridge that popped into view as they lurched around another switchback. "The Sierra Zongolica. Three deep cave systems, each more than 1,000 meters deep. One of those pits is so big you can still see daylight 300 meters down."

He started to point out another range at the next curve, but jerked his hand back to the wheel to yank the truck around a particularly tight U-turn. They were approaching the rim of the plateau, and the turns were coming close together. His steering grew rhythmic as he slalomed through the switchbacks: left, right, left, repeat.

"And over there," he nodded, "the Sierra Juárez." The mountains looked like cardboard cutouts against the hazy Mexican sky, each peak a shade less blue than the one beyond. "Sistema Cheve. That's the system that stole the depth record from Huautla."

Bill spun the tiny truck round another curve, and grumbled: "Thirty-three meters."

"Huh?" Barbara asked.

"Thirty-three meters," he repeated, raising his voice above the whine of the tiny engine, and adding a laugh. "That's what we're short in Huautla. After the 1980 expedition, Sistema Huautla was the third deepest cave in the world. It's slipped down the list several notches since, but at 1,353 meters it remained the deepest in this hemisphere. Until 1991. When John Schweyen dove the sump at the bottom of Cheve and pushed the Sierra Juárez to a depth of 1,386 meters," he said, waving his hand at an unassuming mountain range in the haze to the south.

Barbara did the math. Then she asked, "Is the Cheve sump still going?"

"Well, Schweyen was one of the best side-mount divers around—I carried tanks for him that year—and he couldn't find a way through," Bill said. "After a hundred meters, the sump splits into a bunch of one-meter-wide fingers. Most of those became too small to follow. So that sump is finished."

Bill flashed a grin. "That's the difference. When I turned around in San Agustín, I was looking at deep blue passage."

Still grinning, he turned his head to look at Barbara. "Maybe you'll get to see for yourself."

She smiled. Then she laughed out loud. She didn't have anywhere near as much experience as the other divers, and she didn't plan to be a part of the exploration. But if they marked a route through the sump, she'd follow. And she'd served on enough expeditions to know that with enough hard work—and a little luck—anyone could wind up scooping some booty. To herself, she thought: *If the chance comes, you're damned right I'm going to see the sump for myself.*

To Bill, she said, "Eyes on the road, Guillermo."

As they crested the rim of the plateau, the desert land-scape gave way to a pine forest. The road straightened for a few hundred meters at the pass, where a small cinder block store sold beer and snacks. Just past the store, the pines were overwhelmed by thick vegetation, and the Toyota plunged into a dense fog.

The truck dropped into a deep pothole. Barbara bumped against the cab's ceiling and squawked in surprise. Bill clung to the steering wheel as his right foot kicked about, searching for the gas pedal. Once he'd fallen back into his seat, he quipped, "Welcome to the Sierra Mazateca, Dr. am Ende."

"Thanks, G," she replied. He swerved around another pothole. "Think you could slow it down a bit?"

While falling rocks and frightening curves had been the navigational hazards during the long drive up the rim, potholes were the primary obstacles on the trek across the high Huautla Plateau. The Mazateca was a rain forest surrounded by desert lowlands, like a misty island in the sky. Clouds that formed over the steamy Gulf of Mexico drifted lazily westward until they collided with the high plateau, which held them captive and drained them of their watery cargo. But the rain that nurtured the alpine soil also destroyed the thinly paved road to Huautla de Jiménez. The fog drizzled relentlessly into tiny cracks in the asphalt, and trickled through to the loose gravel below. Small voids formed where the gravel eroded beneath the surface. When the voids grew large enough, the asphalt crust collapsed. Once a pothole had formed, it began collecting water, like a funnel, and accelerated the erosion.

The great caves of the Huautla Plateau were likewise formed by erosion. Had millions of years of rain fallen directly on the soft rock, the limestone would have eroded away eons ago, leaving dramatic valleys but few caves. But the Laramide Orogeny threw a thin blanket of hard, metamorphic cap rock over the ancient clam bank. The cap protected the limestone in much the same way the asphalt protected the gravel. Rain passed through cracks in the cap and eroded the softer rock below. The cap layer also eroded in places, creating deep shafts called *sótanos*—literally Spanish for basement—that selectively funneled the rain into the limestone layer. Over the last 250,000 years or so, small cracks in the rock beneath those funnels eroded into a dramatic limestone labyrinth with vertical shafts the height of skyscrapers and horizontal boreholes large enough to drive a train through.

Bill slowed the Toyota. The fog had grown so thick he could barely see the front of his own hood. Undaunted, he opened the driver's side window and crept onward by following the white line at the center of the road. He could hear Angel's Volkswagen grinding along behind him. The visibility improved steadily as soon as the road began descending from the rim of the plateau. He resumed his discourse on the Mexican Himalaya.

"There are sixteen deep caves in the Sierra Mazateca," he said. "Sixteen that we know of, that is. Three more than a kilometer deep, and two more within spitting distance of the minus-1,000-meter mark . . ." Bill's habit of reciting his knowledge of whatever subject was at hand to whoever happened to be within earshot had once prompted the slow-talking Moles to joke that Stone spoke without commas. Those predisposed not to like Bill sometimes found his extemporaneous lectures condescending. But Barbara had come to realize that it was just his way of showing his enthusiasm.

"How many have been connected?" she asked.

"The four big ones—Li Nita, La Grieta, Nita Nanta, and the Sótano de San Agustín—have been linked. That's the bulk of what people now refer to as Sistema Huautla. The length is presently around fifty-two kilometers, but I wouldn't be surprised if it breaks a hundred by the time we're through. There's a ton of borehole waiting to be scooped beyond the San Agustín sump."

Barbara gazed out the window. They'd emerged from the fog, and the transformation was overwhelming. A vertical landscape of green fields replaced the barren hillsides of the cliff road. Neatly planted rows of corn, beans, and squash stretched down the steep and treeless hillsides into the deep *dolinas* below. Tiny villages of small mud and straw houses clung to the narrow ridge tops. And looming atop a distant ridge, the city of Huautla de Jiménez looked like a fortress against the blue sky.

They crossed the Puente Fierro bridge and wound their way up to the city. As they came closer, Barbara could see that it was not a walled city after all. Huautla was built on ground so steep that even modest buildings standing a mere single story high at street-side often reached three or four stories on the downhill side. What looked like embattlements from a distance were just absurdly high foundations. They passed the first billboard they'd seen since Teotitlán, then the first power poles. A patchwork of brightly colored flags fluttered from thick twine strung between the poles.

Hung in celebration of a big local festival—la Fiesta del Señor de las Tres Caídas—the overhead jumble of flags and banners thickened as the truck wound its way up into the city, past bus depots and beer distributors, gas stations and tire shops, shoe stores and cantinas. The festival had spilled into every street. Huautla de Jiménez was home to some 30,000 souls, but many more of the roughly 170,000 surviving Mazatec from the surrounding area had swarmed into the ethnic capital for the celebration. The older women wore colorful dresses called *huipiles*, stitched together from pink and blue satin ribbon, and performed ritual dances with elaborate names like "Ring of Gold" and "Orange Blossom." The men wore white trousers and dusty sandals, and conversed in an odd mishmash of clicking and whistling sounds, mixed with occasional phrases in Spanish. Within a few more blocks, the dusty Toyota was frozen in traffic.

Bill pointed the truck down a side street in an attempt to skirt the traffic, and Angel followed. The smaller streets were narrow pedestrian walkways, lined with yellow-, pink- and lime-colored stucco structures that opened to the cobblestone alley via rows of heavy double doors. Barbara folded in the side-view mirrors, Bill leaned on his horn, and somehow they squeezed through. They found places to park both vehicles, and made their way toward the *zócalo* on foot, snaking their way through the mosaic of tables, tarps, and goods for sale. There were roots, vegetables, spices, a dozen varieties of chiles, as well as cauldrons of boiling chickens and racks of hanging cow halves. A butcher with a long knife and a bloodstained apron startled Barbara with a toothless smile.

Bill led them into a *tortillería* where a crew of women pulled hot, fresh tortillas off an assembly line belt and piled them on a blue and white tiled counter. The women— none of whom were much more than four and a half feet tall—giggled when the skyscraping *gringos* entered the shop. One of the older women whispered, "Guillermo Piedra." The younger women all nodded knowingly, and repeated Bill's Spanish name. Word of the *gringo*'s arrival passed into the tidy office at the back of the factory, and a portly man with wire rim glasses quickly emerged. He strode across the cool cement floor and extended a strong, weathered hand.

"Amigo Guillermo!" he said. *"Qué pasa?"*

"We are back, my old friend," Bill replied in Spanish. "And this time, we are going to make it through the sump!"

Renato García Dorantes laughed loudly, without letting go of Bill's hand. The two met back in 1976, on Bill's first trip to Huautla, and had remained friends. Renato had since become a prominent businessman and an unofficial curator of Mazatec culture. He laughed because he was happy to see his old friend again, and because he had lost count of how many of Guillermo's expeditions had begun with the pledge that "this time" he would crack through the sump.

"We are going next door to each lunch," Bill said, continuing in Spanish. "Can you join us?" Renato agreed, and ushered his guests out the side door of the *tortillería*. They crossed the narrow street, passed a bank where two shotgun-toting guards lingered lazily in the afternoon sun, and climbed the terra cotta steps to the Bellas Rosas. The proprietor led them across the restaurant's clean white tile floor, seated them at a large table beside the window, and served them a rich local coffee with an almost bitter taste.

Bill introduced Barbara and Angel, then pressed Renato for advice on how to handle the local politicians, from whom he needed to secure official permission for his expedition. "Who is *el presidente*?" Bill asked, referring to a local official somewhat akin to a mayor. "And how should I approach him?"

"Ahh, Guillermo," Renato replied, stroking his thick, black mustache. "You understand that there are now three mayors in Huautla."

"Tres presidentes?" asked Angel. He fished a crumpled Atlas cigarette from his shirt pocket, lit the smoke, and took a long drag.

Renato explained that after a contentious local election resulted in a three-way draw, the city's elders decided to resolve the dispute by allowing each of the three major political parties to appoint a mayor. Angel laughed. Such tripartisanship was unheard of in the Mexico of the early 1990s, where the Institutional Revolutionary Party had dominated electoral office for many decades.

"You're surprised?" Renato asked. Angel nodded. "Then you don't understand the way of the Mazatec." Renato watched the urban Mexican for a response.

"You see, my friend, the Mazatec were never conquered," Renato continued. "Never. Not by the Aztec. Not by the Mixtec. Not by the Spanish conquistadors, the Catholic missionaries, nor the Mexican federales. And we were not conquered by the PRI, either. Instead, we learned to accommodate."

Unable to follow the Spanish, Barbara studied the menu, which featured both traditional Oaxacan mole sauce, as well as American-style pizza.

Angel nodded. "I see," he said. "Walking through the *feria* today, I noticed that few Mazatec speak proper Spanish, the way you do."

"You're correct," Renato replied, relishing the cue to launch into one of his favorite subjects. "We're among the least Spanish-speaking people in Mexico. Roughly half of my people speak no Spanish at all, especially the elders . . . Spanish is a language that was imposed on my people for the benefit of your people. Yours is a fine language, my friend. But the language of your people does not contain words for the ideas of my people."

Angel leaned forward, and gestured for Renato to continue by gently waving the hand that clenched his cigarette. "Can you give me an example?"

"Absolutely," Renato said, smiling. "You're here to explore a cave, yes?"

Angel nodded.

"You call it *cueva*, yes?"

Angel waved the cigarette.

"In Mazatec, we call such a place *gui-jao*," Renato continued. "Literally, this means 'beneath the stone.' *Gui-jao*. Beneath the stone. But what we mean to say is another thing. *Gui-jao* is not the same as *cueva*." He paused to sip his dark coffee.

"*Gui-jao* represents something that is alive. *Gui-jao* is a living being. We Mazatec believe that the trees, the stones, the rivers—and in this case, the caves—these are all living beings. They are all connected to each other, and we Mazatec are connected to them. They don't belong to us; we belong to them."

Renato took another sip.

"So when we say *gui-jao*, we mean the life. But when we say *cueva*, that meaning is lost. Using Spanish confuses things, no? Are you with me more or less?"

"*Sí*," Angel said. "Tell me about this living cave."

Renato stroked his mustache again. He was far more willing to share the details of his complex spiritual culture than most of his fellow Mazatec. Besides running both the *tortillería* and a trucking company, he'd helped found a local museum called Casa de Cultura. But there were still topics he was reluctant to interpret to outsiders. And though he was a fellow Mexican, Angel was every bit as much an outsider in the Mazateca as Bill and Barb were.

"It's difficult to explain," Renato replied. "Perhaps one might say that the *cueva* is the entrance to *gui-jao*. We Mazatec believe that after we die, we will make a journey into the cave. So the labyrinth is the entrance to the afterlife. It's sacred to us because our ancestors have all gone there before us, and it's alive because we will go there one day ourselves. Also, we traditionally believe that there are spirits who guard these places. We call them *Chi Con Gui-Jao*, or He Who Knows What Lies Beneath the Stone."

Lunch arrived—white plates overflowing with rich, Oaxacan-style dishes—and Bill used the distraction to steer the discussion back to a less metaphysical topic: "So, Renato, which *presidente* should I approach first?"

Renato explained that two of the *presidentes* were schoolteachers. He said they were educated men, and that if Bill were to show his respect for their knowledge by making a brief presentation about the status of local exploration, they would surely approve his expedition. But the third *presidente* was quite traditional, Renato warned, and clung to old beliefs about *Chi Con Gui-Jao*.

"What sort of beliefs?" Bill asked.

"What we were speaking of before," Renato explained. "Spirits guard all of the important places of the Mazateca. There are spirits who live in the mountains, spirits who protect the rivers, spirits who dwell in the caves. The mountain lords, they are like saints. If you pray to them and make offerings, they will help you. But the cave lords, they are tricksters. It is unwise to taunt a trickster, no? So perhaps this third *presidente* will not think it a good thing that you propose to mess about in the trickster's cave."

Barbara leaned over and whispered in Bill's ear: "What did he say?" She knew a few Spanish words, enough to discern they weren't talking about ordinary paperwork.

Bill leaned back, rolled his eyes, and answered in English:

"He says we have to get permission from three mayors and a god."

After lunch, Bill brought the threesome back to the truck. He took a shortcut across the market, and led them down a long, dark alleyway that led toward the church. A thin gringo stepped into his path, and held up an old Samsonite briefcase. Bill almost tripped over the ghostlike American. He wore tattered blue jeans and a dirty leather jacket. His deep-set eyes peered up at Bill from between long strands of greasy hair as he muttered: *"Hongos?"*

Back in 1955, a Mazatec healer named María Sabina introduced amateur ethnobotanist R. Gordon Wasson to some hallucinogenic mushrooms. Wasson returned to New York and wrote an account of his "soul-shattering" trip for *Life* magazine. Titled "Seeking the Magic Mushrooms," the article spurred what eventually became a Huautla-bound stampede of trip-chasing hippies that continues to this day. Mushrooms, not caves, are the grail most Huautla-bound tourists seek.

"Mushrooms?" Bill laughed. "No way, man."

They wound their way out of the crowded city and up the narrow gravel road to San Agustín. He pointed out the curve where a local truck that Bill Steele and his wife, Janet, were riding in had slipped over the cliff. They were thrown free as the open *pasajero* rolled down the steep hillside, but an iron cross served notice that not all of their fellow passengers were as lucky.

In the distance, Barbara spied a hillside speckled with limestone pillars. The toothlike monoliths checkered the next valley, their sun-blackened surfaces contrasting sharply with the mossy green vegetation. "Karst," she said, absentmindedly voicing the geologist's term for the terrain. Cavers use the word less scientifically to refer to a whole system of disappearing surface streams and underground rivers. First identified in the former Yugoslavia, karst is German for "stony ground."

Bill wheeled the blue truck through the village of San Andrés Hidalgo, a long alley of a town where the houses cling to each side of a single ridge-top street. At the far end of the village, he pulled the truck over and pointed into the steep valley to the east.

"That's the village of San Agustín on the far ridge, and the *sótano* is right down there," he began. "William Russell was the first caver to find it." After spotting some promising sinkholes on a set of Mexican topographic maps at the UT geography department, Russell left Austin in the summer of 1966 with Tommy McGarrigle and John Kreidler. After wasting a few days in Huautla—everyone was trying to sell them *hongos*, too—they drove Russell's little yellow Corvair to the end of the road and started running down the *dolina*. "After surveying the entrance to the Sótano de San Agustín, they crossed that far ridge and found the Sótano del Río Iglesia. And on the way back through the village, they were shown the Cueva San Agustín. Amazing. In one afternoon, those guys discovered three of the deepest caves in the world."

Bill shifted into four-wheel drive and turned the truck back into the rocky path that passed for a road. He pointed out an even smaller road to the left. "That's the road to La Grieta," he said. "There were several expeditions to this valley in '68 and '69. But relations with the Mazatec were deteriorating quickly by then."

In the decade following R. Gordon Wasson's article, all sorts of rock stars came up to El Fortín to see María Sabina: Bob Dylan, Pete Townshend, the Beatles. Local legend holds that John and Paul wrote "The Long and Winding Road" on the road to Huautla. By 1968 the counterculture glitterati had moved on, and a flood of wannabe hippies had arrived. They were a motley bunch and it didn't take long for them to annoy the Mazatec. A line in the Donovan song "Mellow Yellow" summed up the relationship: *I'm just mad about Fortín; Fortín's mad about me.*

"Toward the end of the 1968 expedition," Bill resumed, "Don Broussard was up there, at La Grieta, with Meri Fish. Don was waiting at the top of the sixty-meter-deep entrance drop while Meri was still climbing up their rope. A dozen angry Mazatec showed up. They were coming home from the market in Huautla. Several were drunk. Some sort of altercation ensued, and a machete was brandished. Before Don could yell down to Meri, one of them chopped the rope! Don scrambled to the edge of the pit, certain she'd been murdered. The Mazatec bolted down the path toward Plan Carlota. To Don's amazement, Meri was clinging to a small ledge where she'd somehow managed to catch her fall. So Nine Lives Broussard raced back to base camp to retrieve a rope and recruit a posse. Meri survived. But she never came back."

Barbara watched the farmers hoeing their steep terraced fields in preparation for planting corn and black beans. They hid their leathery skin from the harsh, high-elevation sun with loose white cotton pants, white shirts, and wide straw hats.

"That was really just the beginning," Bill said. "Cavers were threatened in town. Boulders were rolled into entrances where they were working. And after a team in Cerro Rabón took refuge in a rented house, their drunken pursuers tore down the mud walls to come after them. Then the Nixon administration asked Mexico to evict the hippies from Huautla and other drug-prone areas. Of course, the Mexicans made no distinction between cavers and hippies. So the army established armed checkpoints on the road to Huautla, ordered the soldiers not to let any gringos pass."

By the end of 1970, Huautla was not only a foreboding place, but also a forbidden city.

Bill grew quiet as he steered the truck into the tiny village of San Agustín. The narrow gravel road clings to a steep hillside as it winds into town, with several houses set into the uphill bank on the left, and several more hanging out over the downhill side on the right. The road ends at the village square, which is surrounded on three sides by the municipal building, a two-room school, and a white stucco Catholic church. The fourth side opens to a magnificent view over the Río Iglesia *dolina*.

Ian met them on the road. He and Noel had arrived early that morning. Noel was too tired to negotiate for another house in his exquisite Spanglish, so they made their way to a stone house already rented by Jim Smith, the caver from whose garage Bill and Barbara had collected the trailerful of rope. Smith was away, and there was a combination padlock on the heavy wooden door. They tried "1353" first—the depth of the cave—and then Noel dialed up the street address of Smith's Georgia home. They were in. Smith apparently had a pretty good idea what Noel would do once he got inside. There was a note waiting for him on the chair, begging the new arrivals not to "booty-ize" their food.

"So where is Noel?" Barbara asked.

"Oh, he's inside, cooking up some of the food Smith left," Ian said. "You hungry?"

With Renato's assistance, the negotiations in Huautla went smoothly. Bill and Angel then ironed out a deal with the village leaders in San Agustín Zaragoza, and with a man who claimed to own the property on which the *sótano* was seated. Once the permissions were secured, Bill arranged to rent four houses: two for sleeping, both on the uphill side of the road; a lockable stone structure for use as a gear shed; and a small mud-walled house on the downhill side for use as a cookhouse.

Village of
San Agustín Zaragoza

Top View

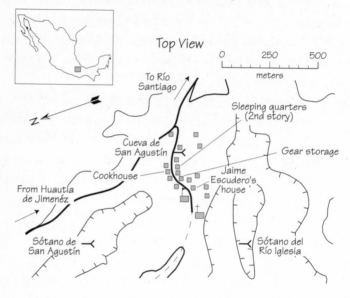

To Río Santiago

Sleeping quarters (2nd story)

Cueva de San Agustín

Gear storage

Cookhouse

Jaime Escudero's house

From Huautla de Jimenéz

Sótano de San Agustín

Sótano del Río Iglesia

0   250   500

meters

N

Side View

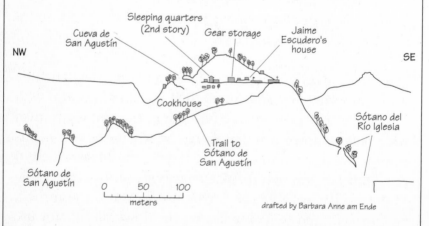

Sleeping quarters (2nd story)

Cueva de San Agustín

Gear storage

Jaime Escudero's house

NW

SE

Cookhouse

Sótano del Río Iglesia

Trail to Sótano de San Agustín

Sótano de San Agustín

0   50   100

meters

drafted by Barbara Anne am Ende

Jim Brown and Don Broussard arrived late that afternoon with the big trucks. The team spent the next several hours unloading gear. Much of it went into the ground floor of the stone-walled gear house owned by Epifanio Villega, where the rebreathers would be assembled and packed for hauling.

Two Mazatec villagers curled up on the steps of one of the bunkhouses to watch the spectacle. At sixty-four years of age, Bernardo Escudero was one of the oldest men in the village. His dark, leathery skin contrasted sharply with his thick white mustache and his bleached white *campesino*-style pants. Virgilio, his nine-year-old grandson, wore a faded Chicago Bulls T-shirt and no shoes.

Bill recognized Bernardo, and the two nodded in greeting as Bill walked by carrying two neon green oxygen cylinders. Virgilio's big brown eyes watched in awe as Bill and Noel—each of whom seemed nearly twice the height of an average Mazatec—strode back and forth, shouldering what looked to young Virgilio like superhuman loads.

"Grandfather, is that Guillermo Piedra?" the boy asked in Mazatec.

Bernardo nodded.

"Is he a *brujo*?"

"A *brujo*?" Bernardo sounded surprised. "No. No." The old man scowled. "Who told you he was a sorcerer?"

"The boys at school," Virgilio replied, sliding deeper under the colorful blanket Bernardo had draped over the two of them. "The boys from the next valley."

Bill strode past with another load. He suspected they were talking about him and the team, but because the conversation was in Mazatec, he followed none of it.

"Guillermo Piedra is no *brujo*," Bernardo repeated. "He's a man, just like you. Except taller, yes?"

Virgilio giggled. "Yes. And look at that one!" he said, pointing at Barbara, whose height was even more surprising because she was a woman.

"True. But look at those two," Bernardo said, pointing to Ian and Don, the smallest of the group. "They could be Mazatec."

"So why do people say he's a sorcerer?" Virgilio asked.

"Those people who say that are not good Catholics, like us."

"Why?" the boy asked.

The old man looked down at his grandson, who had reached that *Why? Why? Why?* phase. He tousled the boy's hair.

"Do you know the story about the Black Dog by the river?" Bernardo asked.

"Of course," Virgilio said. "The Black Dog waits by the Great River that runs through *gui-jao*. He meets you by the river. If you've been a good boy, he will pick you up by the scruff of your neck and carry you to the other side. There you can continue your journey into the afterlife."

Bernardo smiled. "That's right. You're a good storyteller. So do you believe that story is true?"

"No, Grandfather. I believe that I will go to heaven, like the Father says at the Spanish church."

"You're right. But your friends from the valley, they don't come to church with us, do they?" Virgilio shook his head. "So," Bernardo went on, "perhaps they still believe in the Black Dog, and the other old ways."

Virgilio didn't look satisfied. "Has Guillermo Piedra seen the Black Dog?" he asked.

"I don't think so," the old man said, laughing. "He looks pretty healthy to me."

"Then why does he go into the cave?" Virgilio asked.

"I don't know."

"Is there treasure in the cave?" the boy asked. "Are there riches there?"

Bernardo stroked his white mustache a moment. "I don't think so," he said. "I used to think so when I was younger. But these men have been coming to our village for many years. They've been coming since your father, Jaime, was little, like you. I think that if they were here to steal from us, they would have already done so."

Kenny made a funny face as he marched past Virgilio with a few more of the oxygen tanks.

"What are those bottles?" the boy asked.

"I have no idea," Bernardo said with a sigh.

"Why do they—" Virgilio started to ask again, but Bernardo pushed the boy off his lap and stood up.

The old man was tired. "No more questions," he said. "Come with me. It is time to put away the goats."

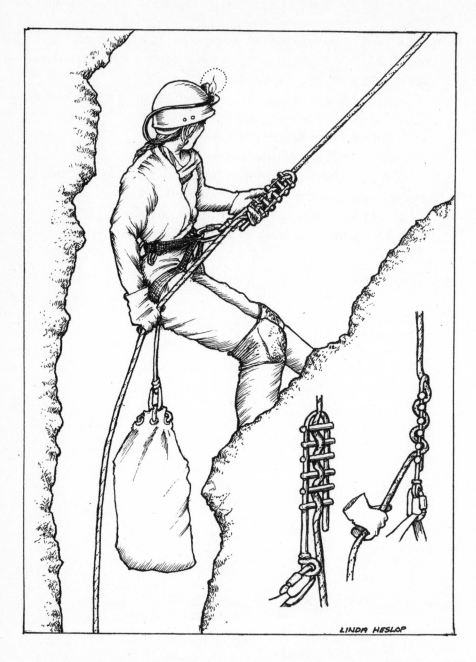

*Barbara rappels with a six-bar rack, which is attached
to her seat harness with a locking carabiner.
(Closeup of rack at lower right.)*

LINDA HESLOP

THREE _____

A couple of days later, Barbara was crouching on a small rock balcony at the lip of the abyss. She checked to be sure the thick nylon rope was threaded through the sliding aluminum bars of her rappel rack. Then she checked again. Once she was absolutely sure her rack was rigged correctly, she stepped nervously backward, until the rope had taken all of her weight from her boots. The first step of a long rappel was always the hardest for Barbara, who'd struggled to overcome a lifelong fear of heights.

The first step into the Sótano de San Agustín was more dramatic than most. The verdant sinkhole was a steep-sided funnel that plunged straight down as far as a football field. Using the bars of her rappel rack as brakes, she slid down the Jungle Drop past lush ferns and native begonias. A waterfall trickled down the other side of the canyon, a sunlit thread of water that mimicked the strand of nylon rope on which she hung. By the time she reached the base of the funnel, she'd dropped more than ninety-three meters from the lip of the sinkhole. At the bottom, she unthreaded her rack and yelled: "Off rope!"

Kenny threaded his rack as soon as Barbara was clear.

Developed by Alabama caver John Cole in the 1960s, the rappel rack is a foot-long steel U-bolt fitted with a series of four to six sliding horizontal bars. The rope threads down the U, passing over one horizontal bar, under the next, over the next, and so forth. By adjusting the number of bars in contact with the rope, a caver using a rack can control his descent more precisely than one using the lightweight descenders commonly employed by climbers and mountaineers. Ian followed Kenny, and Bill zipped down in the rear.

Once assembled on the sinkhole floor, the foursome fired up their helmet-mounted carbide lamps—called ceiling burners in recognition of what the bright acetylene flame would likely do if worn indoors—and rappelled down the second drop into the cave's yawning mouth. Beyond the reach of direct sunlight, the second drop was devoid of leafy vegetation; in its place was a watery layer of green algae that made the footing treacherous. Noel dubbed it the Slip-n-Slide.

At the bottom of the Slip-n-Slide, the stream turned to the left and wound its way into a dramatic underground chamber larger than two football fields placed end-to-end. Explorers dubbed this stadium-sized hall the Sala Grande in 1966, and considered it the main route into the cave until 1987. "That was the year Broussard bruised his ribs," Bill explained, as he led the group away from the obvious eastward route forward and up a steep dirt slope to the right. "Don was in a world of hurt. But he was too stubborn an *hombre* to let the others carry him out. So he took, like, four hours to haul himself up those two drops. Bill Steele and Mark Minton were waiting for him at the bottom. They were bored out of their minds. So they started poking around up here."

The soft, loamy soil poured into Bill's low-cut rubber boots as he led the group up the hill. When he'd reached the top, he stopped to shake some of it out. Barbara and Kenny did the same. Ian just pointed to his high-top

Wellingtons, and smiled at Bill, who'd repeatedly urged the Brit to abandon the distinctive British rubber boots for something with a sole better suited for climbing. Bill grinned at Ian's silent protest.

"Back here on the other side of this breakdown," Bill continued, "Minton and Steele found a former riverbed, long ago displaced by the Sala Grande. While Nine Lives Broussard inched his way up the Jungle Drop, they uncovered a new route that completely bypassed Camps One and Two, and slashed by half the travel time to the sump. Because the shortcut was such a total surprise, and because of the date on which it was discovered—April 1, 1987—they called it the Fools' Day Extension."

Bill led the foursome over the mound of boulders—a common cave feature called a breakdown because the mounds appear wherever a layer of the sedimentary rock breaks from the ceiling—and down the far slope to a slot between three of the largest boulders. He took off his pack, and dropped it through the hole. Then he slid through himself.

As Kenny and Barbara followed, Ian studied a large rock above the slot. About the size of a sofa, the slab served as a bulkhead that prevented hundreds of tons of rock from filling the slot. A small V-shaped fracture cut across the width of it. Ian worried that if the sofa-slab split apart, it would crush whoever happened to be in the chute below. When his turn came, he slid under the Cracked Slab quickly, without touching the sofa.

The route continued down an even tighter slot called the Dust Devil. Fine, loose soil made the squeeze easy enough, but wind howled through the narrow passage, extinguished the cavers' carbide lamps, and threw dust in their faces. The wind roared through the Dust Devil because the air within the cavernous Sistema Huautla rushed to equalize with the continually changing air pressure above. On clear mornings when a low pressure front was moving through, the warm, moist air stored in the cave would rise up and meet the cold air that hung in the *dolina*. There the sudden temperature drop would precipitate a dense fog that would fill the *dolina* like a bowl of milk. It was as if the cave itself was giving breath to a cloud. The effect was not lost on the superstitious Mazatec, who took each morning fog as a warning from *Chi Con Gui-Jao*.

Ian finished the sand crawlway to find Bill tugging at a dust-coated rope secured to even dustier bolts. The small rappel had been rigged seven years before, and left in place. Bill's rack let out a "creeek-creeek-creeek" noise as the dry line jerked through. When his boots finally reached the floor, they crushed brittle plates of dried mud. It sounded as if he was stomping around on fine china. Still within sight of the ledge, he didn't have to raise his voice to call: "Off rope."

The route continued down a series of twenty-three such small rappels. Together, these nuisance drops formed the Stairway to Hell. The dry, upper drops were already rigged. But a small stream entered the stairs a third of the way down. Though throughout the spring it provided no more water than a typical kitchen faucet, water levels entering this passage could expand a hundred-fold in the rainy season and destroy the ropes below. To prevent this, the ropes had been pulled up, coiled, and located in places that appeared certain to be above flood levels. The group spread out and began the arduous task of rigging each drop anew. Ian and Kenny set the heavy bolts from which each rope would be hung, while Bill and Barbara began carrying forward massive coils of new rope.

Before long, the electric drill Ian was using lost its charge. Undeterred, he and Kenny continued setting bolts by hand, using a hammer and bit to pound them into the limestone walls. As he worked his way down to them, Bill could hear the pinging of their hammers long before he could see them. They were both laughing at some joke Kenny had made when Bill finally arrived, bearing fresh batteries. Rappelling suddenly into the space between them, he grinned, held out the batteries, and announced: "The Cavalry has arrived."

The group managed to rig halfway down the Stairway to Hell before calling it a day. Each subsequent trip would stretch a bit deeper, and require more rope. Weeks would pass before they'd finish rigging the ninety-two vertical drops between the surface and the sump, a task that would require more than three kilometers of heavy nylon line.

The grueling but inescapable truth about day tripping into deep caves is that the hardest part of the journey always comes at the end, after fatigue has already begun to chip away at will. Climbing back up the Stairway to Hell, the Slip-n-Slide, and the Jungle Drop was much harder than rappelling down.

Ian led the way. He pulled himself up the eleven-millimeter nylon rope using a pair of lightweight ascenders and a sling. Each ascender—sometimes called a Jumar, after the first brand widely used—was basically a metal handle wrapped around a toothed cam. The spring-loaded cam was positioned at an angle, so that it swung loose when the handle was lifted, but engaged the rope firmly when the handle was pulled down. Ian's upper ascender was tied to a hanging foot-loop, while his lower ascender—a unique, handle-free design called a Croll—was affixed to his seat harness. He slid the upper ascender as far up the rope as he could reach, then stood up in the foot-loop. As he rose, the ascender attached at his waist slid up the rope, and his seat harness slid up along with it. Ian then sat down, shifting his weight from the foot-loop to the seat harness. He was then free to begin the cycle again by advancing the upper ascender further up the line. Cavers call this sit-stand technique the Frog because it originated in France, and because the process of crouching and standing and crouching again causes the climber to look and feel an awful lot like the amphibian of the same name. Most of the expedition's younger cavers—and all of the divers—used the sit-stand Frog system, while Bill, Barb, and a few of the old-timers rigged their ascenders in traditional American systems.

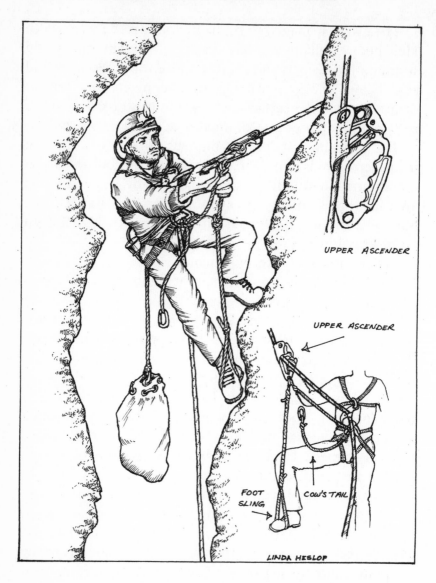

UPPER ASCENDER

UPPER ASCENDER

FOOT
SLING

COW'S TAIL

LINDA HESLOP

*Ian ascends using the Frog system. His Cow's Tail safety
tether can be seen dangling over his right thigh,
ready to snap into the next rebelay.*

It took the group until 2:00 A.M. to return to the balcony above the Jungle Drop. They were exhausted. The work of traveling down from the village, into the cave, halfway down the Stairway to Hell, and back up to the village again was roughly akin to climbing hand-over-hand from the top of the Eiffel Tower, down to the base, and back up again— if the Eiffel Tower were standing in Denver. The thin mountain air made the grueling physical labor of hauling oneself up a rope that much more difficult. Kenny and Barbara were so tired after that first day they could barely walk against the wind blowing through the village. They crawled up the stone steps to the hillside bunkhouse, and fell into their beds without even bothering to wash the mud off themselves.

Ian and Bill lingered in the moonlight. They were tired, too, but also invigorated by having finally made their way underground. They stood gazing across the *dolina*. It was almost 3:00 A.M. Every home in the village had been dark for hours. They each knew the group would use up all the rope they had to rig the Stairway to Hell, and that before anyone returned to the Sótano de San Agustín, someone was going to have to make a run to the Depot Hole, a deep shaft just outside the village where the team had hidden its cache of expensive nylon line from the locals.

Ian looked up at Bill. Their eyes locked for a moment. First Ian, then Bill realized they were going to make the three-hour trek, in spite of being tired, in spite of the hour.

"Well, mate?" Ian began. He smiled, then laughed.

"Okay," Bill replied, relishing the bond of insanity. "Let's do it."

The two men chuckled as they walked out of the village. The wind howled at their backs as they hiked down Tenango Gap and up the rocky hillside beyond. Cirrus clouds sped past overhead, and the bright moonlight flashed through at rapid intervals. The strobelike moon sent shadows dancing about the jagged limestone obelisks that studded the karst hillside. Bill and Ian clambered through the maze of rock like children playing in some prehistoric graveyard.

As Ian rigged a rope around one of the karst spires at the mouth of the secret Depot Hole, Bill scanned the ridges to see if any of the local farmers had watched them. While the Mazatec had little use for bottled oxygen, they had no end of uses for good rope. Over the years he'd been returning to San Agustín, he noticed that sooner or later, every cow, goat, and pig in the valley was tethered with expensive eleven-millimeter static climbing line. He joked that his longtime hosts had the best-tethered livestock in all of Mexico; and did what he could to reduce his losses. When he was satisfied that no one else was around, he followed Ian down the secret hole.

They rounded up four 100-meter coils of rope, tied them into a bundle, rigged a pulley system, and returned to the surface. Together they began pulling up the load. The awkward bundle became entangled on an overhang near the mouth of the fifty-meter-deep pit, so Ian rappelled back down to push the bundle clear with his feet while Bill pulled.

"Damn," Bill groaned, straining to lift the heavy bundle by himself, "this mother just doesn't want to come."

Ian's wry voice echoed up the shaft. "Just call it a challenge, mate. How often do you get to haul your own weight in rope?" The Royal Air Force mechanic twisted his muscular body sideways, and when he finally managed to kick the bundle completely free of the obstruction, he shouted up, "Chocks away!"

Bill pulled the bundle free of the lip, and tied off the line. Ian frogged back to the surface, and together they gave it a big tug. The load popped over the lip and the two men tumbled backward.

"There you go," Ian said, feet in the air. "Victory for the Crown!"

Bill lay on his back laughing for a moment. By the time he sat up, Ian was already separating the 100-meter coils. Bill admired Ian's spirit. And as he watched the young Brit work, he realized that he had been roughly Ian's age back in '76 when San Agustín first put its spell on him. He hoped Ian would grow to love the place as much as he did.

They de-rigged the drop and started back for the village. With two large coils of rope slung over his neck, Ian could barely see where he was going. Bill felt like he was conversing with a bundle of rope as the two of them hiked into the bitter wind. Bill was towering, socially awkward, and liked to transform even the simplest of inquiries into a scientific discussion. Ian was eye-level, charmingly easygoing, and always got to the point. Ian's role as Bill's lieutenant was well established. Several team members had taken to communicating with Bill through Ian, who took advantage of the short hike back to San Agustín to relay some thoughts.

"Noel's not in such good shape, you know," Ian observed. "He and Steve might lag a bit until they tone up."

"Yeah, Noel always shows up with his gut hangin' over his belt," Bill replied. "But he always shapes up once he's here. We should see some reinforcements from the Cheve and Cerro Rabón crews soon. He'll be up to speed by the time they leave."

Ian nodded, and the large coil over his head shifted.

"You see that crack in the slab just above the Fools' Day Extension?" the voice from the coil asked.

"The Cracked Slab. That's been there awhile," Bill replied.

"It's got Noel spooked. I'm not so keen on it either."

Bill launched into a short exposition about the mathematical formula for shear strength of compressed rock. It was his way of suggesting that even if the rock split, he didn't think it would fall. Ian cut his lecture short.

"Listen, mate," the voice from the coil interrupted, "why

don't we just suggest that everyone keep their weight off the bloody rock?"

Bill was still thinking about how to calculate all the variables affecting the slab. It took him a moment to see Ian's point. He conceded with a simple, "Okay."

It was almost six by the time they stashed the rope in the gear shed and made their way up the narrow stairs to the sleeping bags at the fieldstone bunkhouse. Barbara woke up when the two of them came in. Unable to get back to sleep, she went down to the cookhouse, made some tea, and sat by herself watching *Chi Con Gui-Jao* blow a cloud into the valley at sunrise.

Each day for the next two weeks, the team worked its way a bit deeper into the cave. At first they carried only rope and rigging supplies. Then, once each section was rigged, they began the arduous task of lugging in the more than 1,800 pounds of dive gear and supplies they'd need to establish a series of underground camps. Their lungs slowly acclimatized to the altitude, and their muscles slowly adapted to the rope work. Each trip stretched a bit deeper than the last, and each day's pack weighed a bit more than the one before.

Fortunately, dozens of volunteers arrived to help ferry the gear toward the sump. The Sótano de San Agustín was among the most famous caves in the world, but since the brunt of Mexican exploration had shifted to other systems, the San Agustín entrance had not been rigged for seven years. By bolting more than three kilometers of heavy rope into the cave, Bill's team provided a nylon highway that made it possible for other expedition-level cavers to "tour" the fabled hole. It was as if the expedition was offering elevator rides to the bottom of the Grand Canyon in exchange for a price: Each visiting caver was expected to haul in a load or two. Almost three dozen such volunteers showed up during the weeks Bill's team spent ferrying gear into the cave, most of whom were on their way home from expeditions at Cerro Rabón and Sistema Cheve. Most were long-time friends of one team member or another, and for the few weeks they were around, their presence buoyed the dive team's spirits.

Bill hung a small scale from a rafter in the cookhouse, beneath a handwritten note suggesting each caver carry at least thirty pounds per trip. A friendly contest soon began as several of the more macho-minded cavers competed with one another to see who could haul the most. A California caver named Bill Farr was especially zealous. Farr had driven down with the team from Texas, but didn't plan to stay for the whole expedition. Nonetheless, over big breakfasts of pancakes and coffee, he chided the new arrivals into upping their loads. Ian quietly frowned on the competition, and privately counseled the newcomers to carry no more than what felt comfortable. The game ended after Ian discovered that Farr had abandoned a load prematurely. He picked up Farr's jettisoned gear and carried it forward to the designated staging area. The next morning, when Farr started heckling others about the weight of their packs, Ian lashed out at him. "What the hell are you doing, mate?" he asked. "We picked up your piddlin' little pile and took it down to where you were supposed to." He then stomped across the cookhouse, snatched down the scale, and tossed it onto a shelf stuffed with tins of dried food. "Enough of this macho thing," he warned. "Someone's going to get hurt."

The rebreathers were among the few loads that simply couldn't be lightened. By transferring some of the components to other packs, Bill managed to reduce the total weight to forty-three bulky pounds, still a sizable haul on rope. A visiting caver named Mike Frazier graciously volunteered to lug one of the beasts down by himself. Frazier was from Colorado and was less affected by the altitude than the others. But he was unable to prevent the awkward load from swinging on its tether—and banging against the hard limestone walls—as he worked his way down the Stairway to

Hell. When he crossed paths with Ian at the base, he shared his concern that he might have seriously damaged the life-support equipment.

"Look, I'm being as careful as I can," Frazier apologized, "but I gotta level with you: I'm thrashing this sucker good and hard."

Realizing there was nothing to be done at that point—and impressed that one of the touring cavers had volunteered to carry a rebreather in the first place—Ian consoled him.

"No worries, mate," Ian said, grinning. "It's a rental."

That cracked Frazier up. He repeated the line to himself as he rappelled down the next drop—a gaping 110-meter shaft—and managed to crack himself up over and over again. A good-natured guy who liked to write and sing his own campfire ditties, Frazier started humming a "rebreather song." By the time he reached the deck below, he was singing at the top of his lungs: "Stone said this rig could take it, he said she could take it all; so how was I to know, she wouldn't take the blow, of a 110-meter fall?"

The One-Ten was the first of six deep shafts that plunged below the Stairway to Hell. Collectively, they were known as the Bowl Hole Series. The One-Ten was the deepest shaft any of the divers had ever seen. A stream flowed gently down the smooth, tan-colored travertine walls of this breathtaking drop. Rappelling down the center felt like descending into an oversize section of pipe.

Here the consequences of even a minor mistake grew exponentially larger. Whereas a fall from any of the twenty-three house-sized drops along the Stairway to Hell would have broken bones and led to an extremely difficult rescue, a fall within a shaft like the One-Ten would have resulted in certain death. To reduce the likelihood of such a catastrophe, Bill and Ian bolted the rappel line to the wall in several places along the way down long shafts such as the One-Ten. Called rebelays, these mid-route attachment points reduced abrasion on the line, and enabled two or more team members to travel up or down the long rope at the same time, albeit in different sections. Altogether, there were close to fifty rebelays throughout the ninety-two drops between the surface and the sump. With so many visiting cavers willing to haul loads into San Agustín, the One-Ten soon resembled a human mule train.

The Bowl Hole Series continued below the dramatic One-Ten with an equally harrowing sixty-meter shaft. The rebelays required each caver to unthread and rethread his or her rappel rack several times while traveling down and up the nylon highway. So while the mid-drop attachments provided a measure of added security for the experienced cavers, they also provided a dangerous obstacle—and therefore an additional opportunity to make a mistake—for divers Jim, Steve, and Kenny, who were still fairly new to the art of rappelling and frogging in the dark.

The procedure was also new to Angel Soto Porrua. Angel had climbed many of the world's major peaks, and had topped Mexico's Mount Popocatépetl some 300 times. He was a star gymnast—at fifty years old, Angel still enjoyed showing off for the other cavers by cranking out one-arm pull-ups—and an accomplished cave diver. But despite his high-altitude climbing skills and his superior fitness, Angel was, like the other divers, relatively new to racks, rebelays, and the finer points of traveling on rope underground.

On March 14, Angel had successfully negotiated some fifteen rebelays before reaching the sixty-meter shaft. He racked in at the top, carefully lowered his heavy duffel below him until it drew taught against his harness, then unclipped his Cow's Tail—a stiff, foot-long rope with a carabiner at the end that, when covered with mud, looks much like its namesake. He rappelled smoothly for nearly fifteen meters, and adjusted his stance as he approached the first rebelay. There he clipped the carabiner at the end of his

Cow's Tail into a small metal hanger attached to the bolt in the wall. With his weight temporarily suspended from the short Cow's Tail, he unthreaded his rack from the upper line leading to the bolt, rethreaded it on the lower line leading down, unclipped the Cow's Tail, and started down the shaft.

But he was unable to descend. He'd neglected to steer his hanging duffel clear on the way down, and now the tether was hung up and over the line coming from the pitch above. He looked up in dismay. His tether went up and over the loop of rope, and the pack now hung in front of his eyes, counterbalancing his own weight. He tried to push the duffel up with one arm, but it was useless. He was stuck. Grumbling to himself, he put his ascenders on the line and began to work his way back up. Back at the rebelay, he clipped his Cow's Tail safety line into the hanger, and then swung the duffel free. It dangled below him like a forty-pound sausage.

"Okay," he muttered to himself. "Now get back on rappel, and get on with it."

He put away his ascenders and had begun to rethread his rappel rack when a few drops from the waterfall above landed directly on his carbide headlamp. The water extinguished the flame. He reached up and struck the piezo ignitor, but nothing happened. Again. Nothing. The tip was too wet to light. Again. So he switched on his backup electric. Out poured a dim, amber glow. He'd failed to replace the batteries after his last trip. He could barely see his own hand. He shook his head. Barbara was waiting for him at the base of the drop; maybe she'd have spare batteries with her.

"Are you okay?" she shouted up.

Angel took this as a prompt. He'd been moving slowly and he knew it. He thought he was being told to hurry up—by a woman! This grated his Latin sense of dignity. He'd summited several of the world's highest mountains;

and had dived many of Mexico's deepest caves. And now he was being told to hurry along, like a child. Told by a *gringa*, no less. A woman who, he admitted to himself, was more proficient at this style of rope work than he.

"Ahh," he groped for the words in English, "ah, please, give me . . . more minutes. The rebelay. Is a problem."

His awkward English left Barbara wondering if he needed help. She looked at Nancy Pistole, a hauling volunteer from the Cheve project, to see what she thought. Pistole shrugged. A few small rocks tumbled down the shaft, and the two women leapt out of the way. They could see he was in the dark up there, but neither wanted to make the climb unless he really needed help.

Angel's electric died quickly. He rethreaded his rack in the dark, detached his Cow's Tail, and eased back into a rappel position.

"Click."

The loud snap of aluminum against steel riveted his attention. He froze. "Shit!" It couldn't possibly be . . .

"Click."

. . . no doubt now. None at all. Amid all the confusion— the hanging duffel, the sputtering carbide, the dead electric—he'd threaded the rappel rack backward. And now, instead of compressing the aluminum brake bars together, his own weight was popping them off the U-shaped steel frame. Two of the five had already unzipped. He didn't have much time.

He grasped the three remaining brake bars with his left hand, and clenched them in his fist. Tendons leapt out of his wrists. With his right hand, he tried to jam the remaining bars together, to add braking friction. His hand began to shake, as he held his entire body weight, plus that of a forty-pound duffel, on just three bars. If he let go, he'd plummet thirty meters to the rock floor below, and die at the feet of two *gringas*.

"Click."

Three down. This wasn't working. *Got to try something else. Fast.*

Angel slid his right hand over the rack, and gripped it as tight as he could. He then thrust his left arm upward, searching for the loop of rope hanging from the upper pitch. His left hand found it, grasped it, and wrapped it around his wrist a couple times for security.

"Click," snapped the fourth brake bar. With the fifth and final bar unable to provide any friction by itself, the rack was free.

Angel hung in the darkness, swinging gently in the open shaft, connected to life only by a left wrist that was screaming in pain. Had anyone else on the expedition made the same mistake, it would have been fatal. Their last desperate grasp would have been insufficient to answer the inexorable pull of gravity. But Angel's years of gymnastics—and all those macho one-armed pull-ups—gave him a chance.

"Are you okay?" Barbara yelled up again. "Angel?"

"Am I okay?" Angel mumbled to himself. "What is *with* those women!"

He was unable to lift both his weight and that of the duffel on one arm. So he flung his right hand up to the loop, and pulled himself up to where he could throw his left arm over the rope. With his right hand, he then fished around his harness for an ascender. He couldn't find one, but did find the Cow's Tail. It wasn't ideal, but would work. He raised the carabiner to his face in the darkness, and stuck it in his mouth to determine which way the gate opened. Then he snapped it into the same loop he was still hanging on to by his left arm. He relaxed cautiously, and let his weight transfer to the Cow's Tail. It held. He then attached his ascenders, and rested in the darkness.

"Angel?" Barb and Nancy yelled up again. "You okay?"

"*Sí,*" he finally replied, after catching his breath. "*No problema.*"

• • •

Diana Lowrey

The first attempt to crack the San Agustín sump nearly met with disaster when a large truck ran Bill Stone's overloaded pickup off the rugged Mexican highway in 1979. Hal Lloyd poses atop the scattered gear; one of the small scuba tanks used on the first dive can be seen to the right of the coiled ropes. Two years later, Bill returned to San Agustín with a team of veteran deep cavers to help haul his high-pressure scuba gear down to the flooded tunnel. The 1981 team included (from left to right): Ron Simmons, Chris Kerr, Bill Stone, Neil Hickson, Bob Jefferys, Tony White, Alan Warild, and Tommy Shifflett.

Bill Stone

British cave diver Rob Parker swims a sled of eight high-pressure fiberglass scuba tanks through the Peña Colorada (at right). The 1984 expedition reached a point more than four kilometers from the entrance before being exhausted by the overwhelming logistics of ferrying 72 open-circuit scuba tanks forward through six flooded tunnels; during the de-rig, closed-circuit rebreathers were proposed as a means to crack the open-circuit barrier. Three years later Bill Stone tested the ungainly prototype Cis-Lunar rebreather at Wakulla Springs, Florida. On December 3 and 4, 1987, (below) he remained underwater for 24 hours, breathing nothing but his own recycled air.

Bill Stone

Wes Skile

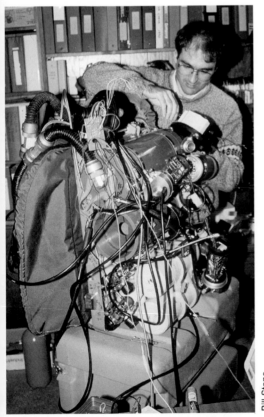

Team members Ian Rolland, Rob Parker, and Noel Sloan (above, left to right) prepare to "test-dive" the Cis-Lunar Mk-II in a pressurized chamber at the North American Hyperbaric Research Center on City Island, New York. Computer designer Nigel Jones (at left) helped Bill halve the size of the Mk-II rig, which utilized six onboard computers. In 1992, the international team trained for two months before deciding to postpone the San Agustín expedition.

By the spring of 1993, the team began testing the Cis-Lunar Mk-IV. Ian Rolland (right), a sergeant in Britain's Royal Air Force, brought organization and drive to the project. Bill Stone (below) trains on the gas-sipping rebreather, which was nearly 200 times more efficient than traditional scuba gear.

Bill Stone

Stone

Barbara am Ende (above) joined the expedition as part of the support team after meeting Bill Stone on a cave rescue in the fall of 1992.

Software engineer Jim Brown (left), the rebreathers' primary test diver, sometimes seemed more at ease underwater than on dry land. Cave diving pioneer

Bill Stone

Sheck Exley (inset) planned a parallel expedition to Mexico in 1994; he and Jim Bowden would dive the abyss at Zacaton.

Veteran diver Kenny Broad samples coc
milk (left) with team newcomer Steve Po

The 1994
expedition
was team
leader Bill
Stone's
(right)
fourteenth
trek to the
Huautla
Plateau.
Kneeling
with the
Explorers
Club flag
(below) are
old friends
Noel Sloan
and Bill
Stone;

Barbara am E

standing behind them are, left to right:
Barbara am Ende, Paul Smith, Tom Morr
Wes Skiles, Kenny Broad, Steve Porter,
Jim Brown.

Bill Stone

Bill Stone

The team rented several houses in the tiny village of San Agustín Zaragoza, one of which was used as a cookhouse (above); from left to right: Barbara am Ende, Kenny Broad, Jim Brown, Steve Porter, Angel Soto, Ian Rolland, Noel Sloan, Bill Farr, and Don Broussard. Steve, a newcomer, and Noel, the team physician, occasionally entertained the team with antics (at left) including a "bongo brothers" routine.

Perched on the craterlike rim dividing the massive San Agustín and Río Iglesia sinkholes, the village of San Agustín Zaragoza (above) served as the expedition's base camp. The village is one of hundreds of Mazatec settlements scattered across the high Huautla Plateau (below), which soars 2,300 meters above Mexico's coastal plain. The Oaxacan highland is riddled with dramatic sinkholes - some plunging hundreds of meters below the surface - and has come to be known as the Himalaya of deep caving.

The Bowl Hole Series presented three more drops below the sixty-meter shaft: a thirty-seven-meter pitch, a twelve-meter shaft, and a seventy-seven-meter free-hanging rappel. The 77 started down a steep flowstone wall alongside a waterfall. About a third of the way down, the wall pulled away from the rope as the shaft opened into a giant dome-shaped room. No longer able to touch the wall with their feet, the cavers were unable to avoid swinging into the waterfall. Though the stream was not strong, it was often sufficient to extinguish the flames of their carbide lamps, leaving them to rappel in the dim glow of their electric backup lights. Worse, cave maps suggested that the water flowed from a small sinkhole below the village of San Andrés, which meant that the water trickling down the back of their necks and into their PVC suits almost certainly contained human waste.

Most of the core team and the cast of volunteers loathed the water torture of the seventy-seven-meter drop. But not Bill. He relished each trip through the infinite darkness of the room. Gliding down a thin nylon highway, unable to see the floor, ceiling, or distant walls in the gloom, he felt like he was rappelling through space.

He'd been fascinated by space ever since that sunny 1962 afternoon when he and his nerdy school friends lay in the grass and listened to John Glenn's space flight. Glenn and the Apollo astronauts gradually replaced Doc Savage as the heroes of his youth, and he laid plans to follow them on the exploration of the cosmos. After earning his Ph.D. and a private pilot's license, Bill applied for NASA's astronaut training program. Rebuffed at first, he added another expedition to his résumé and applied again. And so it continued for nearly a decade, as he enriched each succeeding application with more exploration and invention. He even dubbed his rebreather company Cis-Lunar lest anyone miss the point that the device was ultimately intended for an extraterrestrial market.

By the fall of 1989, he'd just about given up on NASA. He was hunched over his drafting table, working on plans for the next-generation rebreather, when the call came. A voice on the other end of the phone asked if he'd like to come to Houston for an interview. Bill was certain it was Noel or one of his other caving buddies playing a practical joke. But as the voice patiently outlined the details of his flights and accommodations, excitement overwhelmed him. Out of roughly 10,000 applications that year, he was one of about eighty being interviewed for perhaps two dozen openings.

Bill flew to Houston and enjoyed a couple days of physical and psychological exams. He found the game show–like stress tests relatively easy, especially when compared to the actual stress of camping below ground for weeks at a time in tight quarters with cavers whom NASA probably wouldn't admit into their visitors center. When his turn came for *the* interview, he screwed on a necktie and paced into a conference room packed with well-known astronauts. They sat around a long table, wearing khakis and polo shirts. Bill felt self-conscious in his suit. He folded his large hands together atop the brown table. Then he thought that might look too stiff, so he leaned back in his chair. In that position he noticed that one of his socks was drooping, so he bent forward to tug it up.

After a round of questions that most expedition cavers would regard as softballs—Do you have any fears about traveling into space? How would you feel about being crowded with six others in something the size of a small Winnebago for ten days?—Guy Bluford asked Bill, "Is there anything you regret about your life?"

"Not really. I've led a fairly privileged life," Bill began, "I've had the opportunity to pursue both science and exploration all over the world."

"Yes," Bluford persisted, "but surely you must have some regrets?"

"Yeah," Bill replied finally, "my financial status."

Bluford raised his thick eyebrows. The senior astronauts at the far end of the table craned their heads forward at the unexpected answer. Don Puddy broke the ice with his thick Texas accent and asked, "How's that?"

"Well," Bill continued, "I need about $2 billion." He was pleased they'd taken the bait, and he was preparing to reel them in.

"What would you do with $2 billion?" Bluford asked.

"I'd land a private exploration team on the moon," Bill replied. He went on to explain that he wasn't all that interested in flying a glorified 747 in orbit; what he wanted to do was to establish a permanent base on the moon. By sealing off the mouths of cavernous lava tubes, he could construct a dwelling with superior thermal protection and minimal cost—

Puddy cut him off with a squint: "It's unlikely that NASA will return to the moon during your tenure as an astronaut."

Bill couldn't believe what he was hearing. How could NASA—NASA!—say such a thing in public? Then it hit him: They weren't saying this in public. Puddy was telling him in private what the real deal was, without all the sugarcoating NASA feeds to Congress and the taxpayers.

Before he'd recovered from the vertigo of witnessing his boyhood dream plummet to earth, Bill opened his mouth. Words came out. They weren't well chosen.

"Well sir," he blurted, "then God help the United States of America."

There were more questions. Bill answered them. But the assembled astronauts had all seen Bill's promising candidacy blow up quicker than the *Challenger* shuttle. He could tell from their faces that they were only watching him out of morbid curiosity, the way motorists stare at car crashes.

Almost five years later, as he rappelled down the seventy-seven-meter drop, he could still recall those faces as though it were yesterday. He knew on the spot that he wasn't the kind of "Right Stuff" the shuttle-era NASA wanted. And by the time the gracious rejection letter reached Gaithersburg a few weeks later, it had sunk in that NASA wasn't doing the kind of stuff he wanted, either.

Bill's rack hummed lightly as he slid into the black abyss. He thought of the 77 as the Space Drop, though others had less flattering names for it. The waterfall widened and he soon felt the drops pelting down on him. His carbide head-lamp sputtered out, so he turned on his electric. Soon he could see the boulders below. As they approached, he pulled the rope up into his rack, compressing the brake bars and slowing his descent. He squeaked to a stop just as his duffel touched the rocks.

He unthreaded his rack, snapped its bars shut, and stowed it on the side of his harness, along with his Jumars. If NASA were building the rebreather, he mused, they would have declared the mission a success after the twenty-four-hour dive at Wakulla Springs. But to his way of thinking, the rebreather hadn't really accomplished any-thing until it enabled an explorer to discover previously unreachable terrain. NASA had reduced itself to a bureau-cracy that built impressive ships, but only flew them in cir-cles around the earth. He couldn't care less about orbit. He wanted one thing, and one thing only: to explore virgin territory. To place his own boot where no one had before.

That's why he was here. That's why every member of the team was here. They'd made enormous personal sacrifices in the pursuit of this elusive grail. They'd left family behind for a third of a year; had trained relentlessly for two years just to get here; had gone deeply into debt; and were subjecting themselves daily to physical hardship. And that's why, Bill reminded himself as he shouldered his duffel and began walking, he needed to do everything possible to provide each of the core team members with an opportunity to step into the unknown depths of the Huautla Plateau.

Not far down the large canyon—dubbed Tommy's Borehole in honor of Tommy Shifflett, the caver who first discovered this bit of virgin territory—Bill came to a rock as big as a small house. The rock had a flat top, which provided a tidy place to stack supplies. Located 620 meters below the surface, the convenient storage site became known simply as the 620 Depot. Bill added his load to the mountain of duffel bags, bottles stuffed with freeze-dried food, wetsuits, oxygen, heliox, and argon tanks and rebreathers already piled there.

Volunteer Nancy Pistole dropped in a few minutes later, with Ian not far behind. They added their loads to the depot. Bill took stock of the swelling pile, and realized for the first time since leaving Maryland that it was finally happening. They were winning the war of logistics. They finally had enough people and supplies in the cave to push the sump.

"Hey," he asked cheerily. "We've got all this stuff here. You two want something to drink? Something to eat?"

"Well, yeah," Nancy said. "That would be nice."

Ian agreed: "Righto, mate."

Bill whistled as he scrabbled about among the plastic bags and Nalgene bottles of food. Within a few minutes, he produced a pot, some water, and a single-burner stove. He whipped up some hot chocolate and served the two of them where they sat, politely bowing at the waist as if he were a waiter, and they were sitting in some fine restaurant.

Once his guests at the 620 diner had been served, he sat down and poured himself a cup. "I think it's all coming together," he said.

Pistole, who'd worked with Bill on several previous expe-

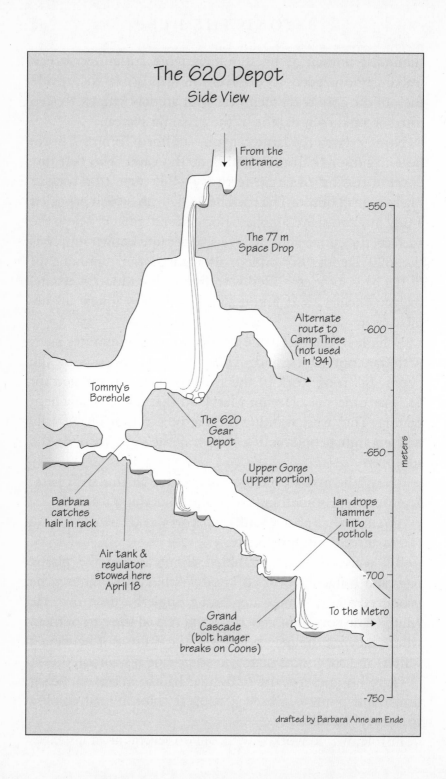

The 620 Depot
Side View

From the entrance

The 77 m Space Drop

Alternate route to Camp Three (not used in '94)

-550

-600

Tommy's Borehole

The 620 Gear Depot

-650

Barbara catches hair in rack

Upper Gorge (upper portion)

Ian drops hammer into pothole

Air tank & regulator stowed here April 18

-700

Grand Cascade (bolt hanger breaks on Coons)

To the Metro

-750

meters

drafted by Barbara Anne am Ende

ditions, was amused by the sea change in his temperament. She'd caved alongside Barbara all morning, and had heard her concern about how stressed out Bill had been throughout the long trek south. But here—620 meters below the surface—he seemed totally comfortable; here—deeper than the height of the Sears Tower in Chicago, the Petronas Towers in Kuala Lumpur, or any other man-made structure—he was behaving normally, even graciously, as if he were serving tea and cookies in his own living room. *Bill's himself again*, she thought. *This is the turning point. This is good*.

"So, what was the fuss up there at the base of the sixty?" he asked.

Pistole rocked her head from side to side. Finally, she said, "We almost had another Yeager up there."

"What are you talking about?"

"Angel," she said, "he nearly bought it on the rebelay."

Bill shuddered as Pistole described the incident. His head filled with fears that the other divers still might not be adequately trained for such unforgiving vertical work. Kenny was clearly enjoying Ian's tutelage, and Steve seemed to gain a pound of confidence for each pound of flab Noel lost; but Jim Brown was working without the benefit of a daily caving partner, and had taken to busying himself with work on the surface. Bill feared that his best rebreather diver had become intimidated by the rope work.

"Almost like Yeager," Bill mumbled. Chris Yeager was a young caver who died in 1991 after making a similar mistake in Sistema Cheve. Like Angel, Yeager hadn't bothered to attach an ascender safety to the line below the rebelay. Unlike Soto, he failed to lock his rappel rack carabiner. When he disconnected his Cow's Tail, the carabiner simply snapped away from the rappel rack. It was still hanging on the rope as Yeager fell to his death.

"Uh-huh," said Pistole, a co-leader of several Cheve

expeditions. She and Bill had spent an unforgettably gruesome week dealing with Yeager's corpse.

"And Cuber," Bill added, recalling a Polish caver who
severed his spinal column during an accident-plagued European expedition to Huautla in 1980. The Poles arrived early
that year, hoping to scoop the elusive San Agustín–La
Grieta connection before the American team arrived. After
touring down to the sump—and allegedly installing a brass
plaque to rub their presence in the American team's faces—
the Poles suffered two serious accidents. First, Jerzy Musiol
broke his leg while traversing a canyon. Then Josef Cuber
fell down a twenty-five-meter shaft. "Cuber was on his way
to help Musiol," Bill said. "The rope broke. The Poles were
using this really cheap rope; all sheath, no core." Teams
from throughout the Sierra Mazateca dropped what they
were doing to converge on San Agustín and assist with the
rescue. "The Belgians got here first, and their team doctor
saved Cuber's life. Steele and I and the rest of that year's
group showed up next. It took a week to haul those guys
out of the cave."

Bill looked up again, and added, "Cuber still can't walk.
He's paralyzed."

The three of them sat in silence for several moments.
Finally, Bill asked Ian if he'd take some time on the surface
to drill Angel on rebelay technique. Ian readily agreed. But
privately, Bill figured that would be the last trip Angel
would make below the One-Ten, and wondered how long
it would be before Jim would make it to the Depot. *We
haven't even made it to the sump*, he fretted, *and already
we're losing divers.*

CHAPTER FOUR

The dive team and the supporting volunteers continued lugging gear down to the 620 Depot. To carry a load beyond that point was too far for a day trip. So on March 16, Bill and Barb were among the first to begin camping underground. They rappelled the entrance drops, crawled through the Dust Devil, popped down the Stairway to Hell, dropped the Bowl Hole Series, rested at the depot, and then started working their way down the Upper Gorge.

The Upper Gorge is a five-meter-wide river canyon carved through hard limestone. Streams from the La Grieta, Nita Nanta, and Agua de Carrizo cave systems all join forces at the kilometer-long gorge. The combined flow carries a tremendous volume of water, and is prone to flash flooding. A single rainstorm on the surface could turn the Upper Gorge into an impassable, aquatic nightmare for days. Even at low levels the river crashes down through a series of twenty powerful waterfalls, each terminating in a frothing plunge pool. Traveling through churning water underground is more art than science. If one knows how to move with it, it becomes a playground. If not, it can be the most dangerous place on earth.

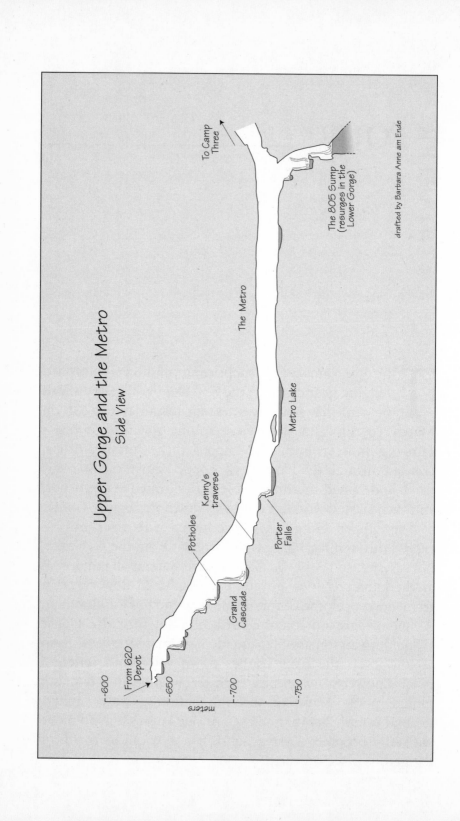

Upper Gorge and the Metro
Side View

From 620 Depot

Potholes

Kenny's traverse

Grand Cascade

Porter Falls

Metro Lake

The Metro

To Camp Three

The 805 Sump
(resurges in the
Lower Gorge)

meters

—600
—650
—700
—750

drafted by Barbara Anne am Ende

Barbara racked into the first drop and began rappelling into the Upper Gorge. Bill waited on a rock above the drop, sucking on a piece of Jolly Rancher candy he'd found in one of the food bottles at the 620 Depot. One of the basic rules of safe caving is to always travel in pairs, so that if one person gets hurt, the other can assist. Bill was able to move at his own natural pace when traveling with Ian, but he had to slow himself down when caving with Barbara or the others. When he led the way with Barb, he tended to shoot ahead, then stop and wait. She would catch up with him, exhausted, only to watch him shoot off again. This annoyed her. So after weeks of hauling loads, he finally learned that when traveling with Barb, he had to let her go first and set the pace. He'd loaded a few extra pounds into his pack to slow himself down.

She cleared the first drop, and he started down while she headed toward the second. Rather than unclip, shoulder, and reclip her duffel bag, she just dragged it over to the top of the next pitch by its strap, as though she were taking a reluctant dog for a walk. Cavers rarely travel with loads as heavy as those the San Agustín team was hauling daily, and the bulging bags complicated even the simplest of on-rope maneuvers. While Barbara was racking into the next pitch, her muddy duffel slid along the smooth wet wall and slipped into a narrow slot in the limestone. She reached down and tried to pull the bag free, but from the position she was in, the forty-pound duffel was too heavy to lift with one arm. So she grabbed the tether with both hands and tugged.

The bag popped loose from the rift, dropped, and its weight snapped taut to her harness. The shock load bounced her rack, and the extra turn of line she'd looped around the U-shaped device popped free. Without that lock-off loop, she began to slide down the line. She leaned far forward to grab the rope, caught it. But she had to lean unusually far forward to do so. And before she was able to arrest her descent, her short blond hair was sucked up into the rack, along with the nylon line. As the muddy rope slipped slowly through her raised hand, the rack pulled tighter against her scalp.

She hung silently for a moment, and considered her situation: If she let go, a good patch of the surface area of her scalp would be mercilessly ripped from her head. Full-size rappel racks were voracious machines, and this sort of thing happened often enough that the National Cave Rescue Commission had developed procedures for it. One option, euphemistically referred to as "self-extraction," involved producing a knife and freeing herself by cutting off her own hair. She rejected this alternative, however, because she couldn't see the area she would have to cut. Under tension, nylon rope sliced like butter. If she mishandled the knife even slightly, she'd sever the rope and plummet to the rock floor six meters below. So she moved on to option two, which, though embarrassing, was clearly a better choice: Seek external assistance.

"Help!" she yelled. She measured her tone carefully. She wanted to sound loud enough for Bill to hear her over the roar of the water below, but not so loud that he'd think she was panicking.

He heard at once. He whizzed off the first pitch, unclipped his duffel, and hopped to the top of the second. Looking over the lip, he shouted, "Hey? You okay?"

"No!"

He couldn't quite see what had happened, but he could tell from her tone that she was in pain.

"All right. Hold your position. I'll Jumar down."

Descending a weighted rope is a difficult maneuver. Racks and other rappel devices are nearly impossible to affix to heavily loaded line, and wouldn't descend against all that friction anyway. So the only way to descend was to affix two handheld ascending devices—such as Bill's worn yellow Jumars—and climb downward by cracking the cams and carefully sliding them down the line one at a time. He'd had years of practice, however, and was on top of her within seconds.

"Okay," he said, once he saw that she was trapped in her rack. "I'm going to reach down and clip my Cow's Tail to your harness. We might bounce. It might hurt."

"Do it," she gritted, still holding on in the same awkward position.

He snapped the carabiner at the end of his Cow's Tail safety line into the metal D-link on the front of her harness. He readjusted his ascender and gently sat down in his harness. He took a deep breath and prepared himself mentally for his next move: lifting his weight, and hers, and that of the fat duffel below, all on one leg. He slipped his muddy rubber boot into the nylon web foot-sling attached to his lower Jumar, cocked himself into position, and with a yell he pushed on the sling with his foot while pulling on the rope above with both hands.

It worked. Barb and the bag were now suspended from Bill's harness, and her rack had gone slack.

"Okay. That was the tough part," he panted.

"Thanks, G."

"Let's put that rack back on," he added, helping her thread it, "without the hair this time." He could see she was more embarrassed than shaken. "Look," he said, "shit happens."

Privately, he began to wonder once again whether he was pushing Barb and the divers too hard. Mistakes like this and Angel's self-rescue seemed to be happening almost daily. And little mistakes had a way of becoming big mistakes when people were tired. Only the day before Steve and Noel had suggested they all take a short break. He'd squelched the idea, suggesting they wait to take a break once they'd struck the first underground camp. *But maybe they were right.*

He released Barbara, and watched her deftly rappel down the rest of the drop. He feared the expedition was becoming dangerously strung out. But he feared the approaching rainy season even more.

The seventh drop of the Upper Gorge was unlike any other in the cave. Over untold thousands of years, the river had eroded deep potholes in the floor of the river just upstream of the cascade. Bowling-ball-sized boulders had found their way into several of these potholes. The round rocks churned about in the swirling water, and gradually carved the potholes into hourglass shapes. Eventually, the hole closest to the cliff eroded all the way through, and the river began pouring out. The result was a powerful vortex through which the entire force of the underground river shot out and formed a spectacular eight-meter arch.

Bill was on the 1976 expedition that first discovered the awesome horsetail falls, which even during low-water conditions flowed with the force of a dozen fire hydrants. He was one of the slow ones on that trip, struggling to keep pace with caving prodigy Jim Smith, who—under the pretense of "scouting ahead"—sped past the group and personally scooped nearly all of the spectacular booty that is the Upper Gorge. The Texans caught up wih the Georgia dynamo waiting for them atop the horsetail falls. They all gazed in awe. Twenty meters below, the plume crashed into a violent plunge pool; anyone sucked into that maelstrom would be thrashed against the walls until drowned. Bill suggested it might be a good spot to turn back. Smith wouldn't hear it. "You gonna wimp out over a little cascade like this?" he bellowed atop the thunder. Bill didn't twitch a muscle, but his ashen face betrayed him. Smith charged to the lip and looked over again. He'd intended to show them up by pointing out some easy way to rig the drop; but after another look at the water torture below, even he felt some hesitation. By the time he turned around, a sheepish Southern smile had crept across his bearded face. "Well," Smith said, "maybe she's a bit *grander* than I first thought."

And ever since, the dramatic horsetail falls had been known as the Grand Cascade.

The Grand Cascade demanded a pound of flesh from every team that passed. The 1994 expedition paid its fare early. On March 15, while the core team was still muling duffels down to the 620 Depot, a group of unusually experienced visitors pushed ahead and started rigging beyond the Cascade. The veteran group included Don Coons, Patty Kambesis, Doug Strait, Shirley Sotona, Carol Vesely, and Cheve project co-leader Matt Oliphant.

Coons was in the lead. He rappelled alongside the falls and pendulumed out to set a route along the west wall. Eight meters from the lip of the falls he spotted a bolt and hanger exactly where he would have placed one himself. He eyed the aging steel suspiciously. The stainless steel hanger was an older type—possibly dating back to the original exploration in 1976—and needed to be replaced. But his group was traveling light, with just enough gear to make it down for a quick tour of the dramatic lower cave. So he clipped in and gave the bolt a light tug. Seemed okay. From there he rappelled another twelve meters down to the edge of the plunge pool below. There he shouted up to the group: "Off rope!" But no one heard him over the roar of the Grand Cascade. So he climbed back up to let them know the drop was rigged. He rested at the top while the others played through.

The route he'd set was a tension traverse, what climbers call a Tyrolean. Patty Kambesis went next. She placed her feet on the wall itself, and leaned back into her harness, which was attached to the horizontal line. She could feel the horsetail plume surging behind her back. After everyone else had worked their way around the horsetail cascade, Coons slung a heavy coil of wet line over his shoulder and followed them down. But while the old bolt and hanger had held his weight on the first trip down, it wasn't sufficient to hold the extra weight of the wet rope and the additional stress he applied to the hanger leaning farther out as he struggled to balance that weight. Microscopic cracks began creeping silently through the hanger as he threaded his rack on the down line. When he swung up to disconnect his Cow's Tail, he heard a high-pitched "ting." The hanger had split in two.

Coons's Cow's Tail fell away from the wall in slow motion, the shiny stainless hanger flopping about like a fishing lure at its end. His body followed, somersaulting backward into the black void below. His electric helmet lamp illuminated swirls of white mist as he spun down toward the rumbling horsetail plume.

The line leading to the bolt above the falls snapped taut. The violent jerk arrested his fall, then swung him sideways into the path of the powerful cascade. There his body slammed into a limestone pendant that projected out from somewhere behind the horsetail.

"Bam!"

The pain of the impact was all-consuming. He hung upside down in the thick, wind-driven mist of the churning falls. He was still in his harness, and, amazingly, still conscious. His entire right side was numb. He couldn't move his right arm. His head whirled. And the massive coil of rope slung round his neck was scooping up the torrential flow of water, adding that much more stress to the lone remaining bolt.

Coons started to yell for help, but stopped. *What would be the point?* he wondered. *No one will hear you anyway. You're going to have to get out of this one on your own.*

He righted himself groggily. Then, using his one good arm, he slipped on an ascender and somehow managed to slowly drag himself back up to the top of the drop. There he collapsed, and tried to regain his composure. The pain was almost unbearable, and now that he'd stopped exerting so much effort, he'd begun to shiver. He checked himself over. With the exception of his chest and right arm he was operational. Working with one arm, he threaded his rappel rack and dropped back down the shaft.

Patty Kambesis met him by the plunge pool, and helped him rejoin the others. He was diagnosed with several broken ribs and a badly bruised arm. The group set up camp for the night, and in the morning Coons began a marathon twenty-one-hour self-rescue, hauling himself up all of the long drops. He and Kambesis did not reach the cookhouse until early the next morning. Ever the early riser, Ian caught them staggering up the cornfield. "Tougher caving than planned?" he asked hesitantly.

Coons smiled weakly. "Umm. Yeah. You might say that."

Bill and Barbara reached the Grand Cascade a day later. Ian and Kenny arrived shortly thereafter. Bill could see that they'd have to rig the wall heavily to avoid another fall.

"You up for fixing this rigging, mate?" Ian asked.

Bill laughed. "Anything would be better than what we have."

While Barbara and Kenny headed back to the Depot to pick up two more loads, Ian took off his duffel and hooked it to the bolt above the pothole. As he gingerly began pulling things out, his hammer shot out of the bag. And without a sound it disappeared into a water-filled pothole.

"For the luck of St. Peter!" Ian shouted. "Do you believe that?"

Bill shrugged. He'd done it before. Pulling anything out of your bag in a place like this was fraught with risk. "Guess that's the end of that idea," he said.

"Oh, we're not dead yet, mate," Ian said. He dug into his bag again, more carefully this time. Several seconds later, he produced a dive mask.

"You're kidding?" Bill said. "You're not really going in there, are you?"

But before Bill could stop him, Ian had strapped on the mask and climbed down to the tiny opening. "Turn on your dive light," he yelled, "and shine it down here so I can see how to get back out." He took a deep breath, and was gone.

Bill was stunned. *Didn't Ian realize that the lower chamber was also the source of the Grand Cascade? Didn't he know about the bowling balls?* But there was no time to fret. He hastily detached the electric light from his helmet. The floor they were standing on was like Swiss cheese, with many small potholes opening up into what looked like a chamber below. Only one of these appeared humanly passable. He stuck the light down that hole hoping Ian would take the cue.

Bill grew impatient, and began counting the seconds. As ten passed, he looked over his shoulder, wondering if he'd even be able to tell if Ian's small body were fired out over the horsetail falls. As twenty slipped by, he remembered how, way back in '79, he'd feared that he'd be shot out of the San Agustín sump in just such a plume. As thirty seconds passed, he grew truly nervous, and began to regret he hadn't grabbed Ian and stopped him back when he had the chance.

A fist erupted out of the foaming froth. Clenched within it was the hammer.

Ian's head followed a split second later. He gasped for air. Then he fell back into the pool to his shoulders, and reached up to the edge.

"If I have to do that again," he spat out. "I'm going to bring a tank."

Below the Grand Cascade stood a deep canal. A hand line was rigged across the ceiling, to which most of the team clipped their duffel bags while they swam across. But Kenny found another way to do it, which wasn't surprising considering his ability to see pretty much anything in a different light. Bill and Ian were already halfway across when they saw his light on the other side. Kenny racked off the rappel, clipped nothing but his Cow's Tail into the quasi-Tyrolean hand line, and . . . jumped.

Bill watched in horror as Kenny whizzed down the line, ducked his head to clear a low-hanging rock, buzzed right past Bill and Ian in a blur of motion, and glided most of the way across the canal before landing with a loud splash.

"God, I love this place," he said, flashing a sinister grin. His bright eyes and wet goatee, in concert with the wild bits of hair protruding from his helmet, leant him a look akin to Nicolas Cage in *Raising Arizona*.

Bill shook his head and laughed. Now that he'd seen the whole stunt, it was obvious Kenny had previously calculated that the line was just low enough so that he'd hit the water before he hit the rock wall on the far side. "Classic Kenny," Bill yelled to Ian as they paddled harder to catch up. "He's got to be the most cautious crazy person I know." Ian nodded.

After another dozen short pitches and traverse lines, the Upper Gorge concluded in Metro Lake. Until the 1994 expedition, it had been customary to simply jump in the lake and swim down to the end. But Bill changed his thinking during the 1981 expedition, after a load of carbide sank.

The load was dropped, surprisingly enough, by Alan Warild, the Australian caver Bill and Barbara had run across in Teotitlán on their way up to Huautla. Warild was a legendary caver, and one of a handful of expedition leaders regarded as a serious contender in the gentlemanly hunt for the bottom of the world. He started across into Metro Lake wearing little more than his wetsuit and harness, just as he'd done on many previous supply runs. But this time, the sealed drum of calcium carbide he was toting in his duffel bag proved heavier than the buoyancy in his wetsuit. The twenty-kilogram drum began sinking, dragging Warild down with it. He stroked as hard as he could. But within a minute he was fully underwater. Fumbling about in the icy darkness, he slipped out of the pack-style duffel, and let it fall into the black depths.

Warild popped to the surface, swam to the end, and ran to tell the others. The situation was serious. For one thing, the carbide in that resupply drum was all that remained in the cave, beyond what each caver was carrying personally. Unless they could recover the carbide, the entire team would be forced to head for the surface the next day. For another, there was the simple fact that carbide reacts with water to make acetylene gas. That's how carbide lamps work: Water drips slowly from a small reservoir down into a chamber filled with gravel-sized chunks of carbide. As the water drips, acetylene gas rises from the carbide chamber, up to a small metal nozzle, where it fuels a bright and steady flame. All carbide lamps—both the traditional miners'-style cap lamps as well as the modern two-part ceiling burners made by Petzl and other caving suppliers—include a small valve that regulates the amount of water to reach the carbide. Warild's duffel had no such valve. Once the water in Metro Lake found its way past the plastic barrier and into the drum of carbide, a sizable cloud of flammable acetylene gas was soon to follow.

So Warild returned to Metro Lake the next day, with a mask, a few diving weights, and a flashlight. The entire team turned out to watch the spectacle, since they were all headed for the surface anyway should the Aussie come back empty-handed. They staked out seats on an irregular ledge that ran along the east wall. Warild finally found his pack at a depth of six meters, and hauled it to the surface. As the '81 group cheered, Bill quietly resolved to himself that next time—if there ever were a next time—he'd rig a long traverse line along the ledge they'd used as a spectators gallery. Sure enough, in 1994, a forty-meter-long hand line enabled the team to skirt the east wall of Metro Lake.

Just beyond the lake was the grand Metro Junction, where the Upper Gorge flowed into a massive river tunnel called the

Metro, so named because its twelve-meter-wide arched roof was reminiscent of a subway tube headed straight for the center of the earth. The Metro also featured a bizarrely eroded floor. The ever-shifting river had left bulbous totems of limestone standing about. Polished and shining like lab specimens from *The X Files*, the strange statuettes seemed organic, as though some shy species of cave creature had elected to momentarily freeze in place rather than interact with the invading humans.

Another 300 meters downstream, the Metro opened up into the great hall at the heart of the Huautla plateau. Dubbed the Sala Grande de la Sierra Mazateca, this massive chamber opened out along the south side of the river. It was here, atop a series of smooth flowstone mounds, that the 1994 expedition pitched its first underground camp, Camp Three.

Cavers working in Mexico's deep systems began using subterranean camps in the 1960s. Like the camps mountaineers utilize during assaults on high peaks such as Everest, underground camps were established after exploration extended beyond roughly fifteen hours of round-trip travel time from the surface. John Fish set the first camp in San Agustín in 1968; situated along the original route, Camp One was about 250 meters down. Camp Two was set in 1976 at a depth of 530 meters, also along the old route. And Camp Three, at minus 760 meters, was at least three full days travel time from the village. But the discovery of the dramatic Fools' Day Extension changed everything. By descending via the deep shafts of the Bowl Hole Series, the 1994 expedition bypassed Camps One and Two entirely. Once the long drops and wet chutes were fully rigged—and the team was fully conditioned—they were able to travel all the way from the village to Camp Three in a single hellacious day.

Bill arrived exhausted. After leading the way up the smooth flowstone steps to a long-established camp circle, he

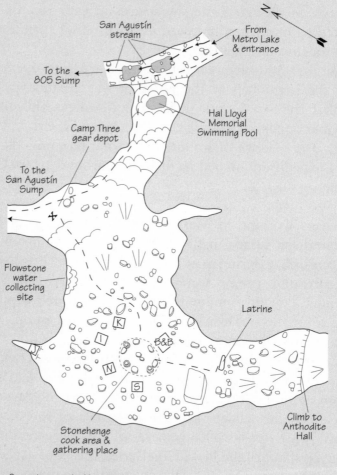

Camp Three
Sala Grande de la Sierra Mazateca
Top View

N

San Agustín stream

From Metro Lake & entrance

To the 805 Sump

Hal Lloyd Memorial Swimming Pool

Camp Three gear depot

To the San Agustín Sump

Flowstone water collecting site

Latrine

K

B&B

I

N

S

Climb to Anthodite Hall

Stonehenge cook area & gathering place

Campsites marked by initial:
Kenny, Ian, Noel, Steve, Jim, Barbara, Bill

Trails marked by dashed lines

0   50
meters

drafted by Barbara Anne am Ende

began emptying his bulging pack. In addition to his personal camp kit—Holofill sleeping bag, Therm-a-rest pad, and Mylar ground cloth; Capilene pants, sweater, and balaclava; plastic spoon, bowl, and cup—he was also lugging an assortment of heavy photo gear, including two Nikonos Vs, a pair of large Ikelite strobes, film, batteries, and sundry accessories. All told his pack weighed close to eighty pounds.

"Ahwaaooo—waaooo—waaoooah."

The massive chamber echoed with bizarre howling noises, like the chants West African women make. The eerie howls were capped by the sparkling arrival of an orange flare, which landed just outside the camp circle and touched off a tiny mushroom cloud of dust.

"Cool!" Bill exclaimed, after the Swiss flare burned out.

A group of volunteer cavers strolled into camp a few minutes later. They'd arrived a couple hours earlier and had hiked up to the massive Anthodite Hall—so named because it's filled with spectacular crystals—seated just above the Camp Three chamber. When they heard Bill, Barb, Ian, and Kenny arrive, they'd blown out their carbide lights and waited in the darkness, then Karlin Meyers shot off the flare as a surprise.

The touring crew mingled with the core team as they unpacked for their first night in camp. Compared to most underground bivouacs, Camp Three was the Ritz. It was located on a hilltop near the edge of a well-ventilated room so massive that the ceiling was too far away to see with a carbide lamp. The pleasant effect was the opposite of claustrophobic. Sleeping at Camp Three was like sleeping outside on a starless spring night.

But Camp Three's crown jewel was a circle of massive stone chairs assembled during the 1981 expedition. While Bill and Tommy Shifflett were exploring the San Agustín sump, Alan Warild and the other tank-haulers spent several days dragging massive slabs of rock from a breakdown pile and constructing four remarkably comfortable limestone thrones, around which they arranged three high rock cairns on which to place carbide lamps. Warild dubbed the inviting circle of rock Stonehenge.

Noel and Steve arrived shortly thereafter, and for the first time since their arrival in San Agustín, most of the dive team was in one place at one time. Bill was in an upbeat mood. He greeted Steve by walking right up to him, grabbing his head, and examining his eyes.

"Well," he announced, "I can see you don't have the Rapture."

"The Rapture?" Steve asked, looking to Noel for some clue as to what was going on. Noel just rolled his eyes.

"Yeah," Bill replied, giving the newcomer a welcoming smack on the shoulder. "Some guys get down here below 700 meters and they sorta lose it. Start getting twitchy and claustrophobic. Can't wait to get out. Their eyes give them away every time. Their eyes, they're like THIS BIG!" he exclaimed, bulging his own eyes out as large as he could for emphasis.

Noel leaned forward and stuck his own naturally bulging eyes in Bill's face. The comparison cracked everyone up.

"Anyway, you look fine," Bill told Steve. "Welcome to Camp Three."

The last group of volunteers said goodbye, and headed back up the Metro. They were among the most helpful of the touring volunteers: Cheve expedition co-leaders Matt Oliphant and Nancy Pistole, Cerro Rabón veteran Karlin Meyers, and Mike Frazier, composer of the rebreather ditty. Bill sorely wished they weren't leaving so soon. Ian hastily scribbled postcards to his wife and kids, and gave them to Frazier to mail. "I love you kids," he wrote. "I'll be home soon."

Barbara put a pot of water on the stove, and the dive team settled in around Stonehenge. Noel put away his Petzl ceiling burner, and installed small brass cap lamps on each of the stone towers. The quaint devices were nearly antiques; the best of them—the legendary AutoLite— hadn't been manufactured in sixty years. Most cavers had long since switched to the French ceiling burners or newer, all-electric designs. But what made the old cap lamps ideal for Huautla was their efficiency: The cap lamps produced three hours of light on a half-handful of carbide gravel. In a place where everything had to be hauled from the surface, every ounce mattered.

They'd nearly finished a big meal of freeze-dried stroganoff when Jim stumbled into camp. They greeted him loudly, but he said nothing. While the rest of the dive team had been hauling load after load of gear into the cave, he'd joined Don Broussard in tackling the more technically minded challenge of stringing a fiber-optic line into the cave. With ten kilometers of fiber-optic line donated by AT&T, the team had hoped to establish a communications link between the village and Camp Three. Jim and Don spent a week stringing the thin cable over the cornfields, into the *sótano*, and down as far as the Stairway to Hell. But when they tried to test the system, they discovered that one of the Mazatec had cut the cable with a machete. They carefully spliced the high-tech line back together, only to find it hacked apart again the next day. Another fix; another cut. After several such defeats, they abandoned the plan and joined the others in ferrying gear into the cave. But by that point, the other divers had been humping duffels for almost three weeks, and had grown mentally and physically conditioned to life on rope. Jim couldn't keep up. Making matters worse, the others grumbled about hauling his share while he'd been "tinkering on the surface." Disappointed over the failure to establish a communications line and rejected by his fellow divers, Jim's attitude sank quickly from his predisposed sense of isolation into a full-fledged depression. He avoided the group at Stonehenge that night, and staked out a private camp spot far away from the others.

While Kenny spun a bizarre tale about some anthropological fieldwork he'd recently completed, Bill worried about Jim. He could see that his ace rebreather diver was suffering, but had no clue how to perk up his spirits. After enjoying both the assistance and the enthusiasm of the visiting volunteers for so many weeks, Bill realized once again how thinly stretched his dive team really was. Until the last few days, he'd still hoped that Rob Parker—the British diver who'd been the star of the Peña Colorada expedition and who'd played such an integral role in developing the rebreather—might somehow peel away from his burgeoning climbing business and show up at the last minute. And he'd banked on Angel Soto joining the dive team; but after his dramatic mishap in the sixty-meter shaft, he would come no deeper into the cave. Now Jim was sinking into a funk.

"I wish we had more manpower," Bill declared to the circle, somewhat abruptly. "We're finding out quickly who can be counted on. Look around. See the six of us sitting here? You're the ones who are going to make or break this expedition."

Though the San Agustín sump lay only 121 vertical meters deeper, the route below Camp Three traversed what was undisputedly the most difficult kilometer of the system. After a few more days of ferrying gear from the 620 Depot down to Camp Three, Bill and Ian finally began rigging toward the sump on March 19. Wearing farmer john wetsuit bottoms over navy blue Capilene fleece, they made their way down the flowstone slope below Camp Three and followed the Sala Grande de la Sierra Mazateca down to a large waterfall at the lower end. Bill paused and looked up at the falls; it was in that overhead tunnel that he'd connected Li Nita to San Agustín in 1980. He and Ian then crawled into the breakdown pile at the base of the twelve-meter-high Li Nita falls. Behind a pickup-sized slab they entered an obscure one-meter-high slot. The awkwardly shaped passage had been considered a dead end until 1977, when Bill Steele slithered through and discovered the route to what came to be known as the Lower Gorge.

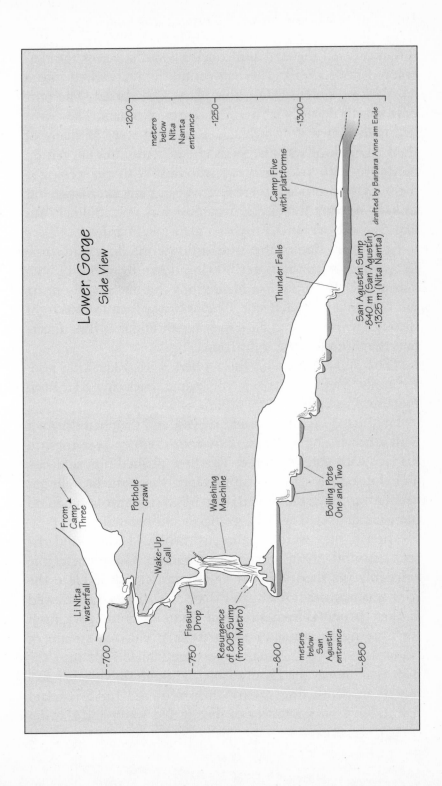

Lower Gorge
Side View

Li Nita waterfall

From Camp Three

Pothole crawl

Wake-Up Call

Fissure Drop

Resurgence of 805 Sump (from Metro)

Washing Machine

Boiling Pots One and Two

Thunder Falls

Camp Five with platforms

San Agustin Sump
-840 m (San Agustin)
-1325 m (Nita Nanta)

meters below Nita Nanta entrance

meters below San Agustin entrance

-700

-750

-800

-850

-1200

-1250

-1300

drafted by Barbara Anne am Ende

Ian crawled forward and rolled his duffel across the tan-colored floor ahead. The bag promptly disappeared into a jet-black pothole. "Damn this place," he cursed. The pothole wasn't deep. Nor were the scores of others. They were less than a meter, on average. But there were so many of them. The floor was like Swiss cheese. And they sucked up hardware with relentless repeatability. With the ceiling a mere meter overhead, there really wasn't any alternative but to keep moving forward in whatever way one could. It was like crawling across the top of a giant pegboard.

At the far edge of the eroded flowstone floor, Ian came face-to-face with the water flowing down from the Li Nita falls above. It erupted suddenly into the passage, shooting out of a hole in the left side. The only way forward was right through it. He looked back over his shoulder at Bill, uncertain they were on the right route.

"The Wake-Up Call," Bill replied, with a knowing nod. "Tommy Shifflett gave it the name back in '81. Keep moving. I'm cold."

Ian pursed his lips, closed his eyes, and dropped through with a howl. The numbing sixty-four-degree water cut into his face with stinging force. The flow pushed him sideways and doused his carbide lamp. Once through, he relit his ceiling burner just in time to watch Bill pass through behind him. He chuckled at Bill's grimace, and pressed on.

The rift they were shimmying through turned, and the rock around them changed character. Gone were the smoothly polished surfaces under the waterfall. Here the rock was fractured, fresh, and sharp. Its sharp edges clawed at their helmets, harnesses, and boots as if the rock itself were trying to convince them to turn back. A stream of water arced into the shaft below, and hissed off into the depths. This was the Fissure Drop. Though only twenty-five meters in depth, the narrow drop required three rebelays just to keep the route free of the cutting water and clawing rock.

Ian was digging through his pack when Bill caught up with him at the base of the fissure. He was fishing frantically.

"Believe it or not, that was the easy part," Bill said. "You ready to face the Washing Machine?"

"Actually," Ian responded, "I have to leave."

Bill was caught off guard. Ian wasn't one to bail in the middle of a mission, even one as miserable as rigging territory like this. The promise of something really gnarly usually fired him up.

"I don't know how this happened. I've lost my bloody chocolate bar," Ian explained. "I've got to go up. Now."

At first it sounded ludicrous. Bill had all but forgotten that Ian was diabetic. Then he remembered how sternly Don Broussard had lectured Ian about being aggressive in keeping on top of his blood sugar levels. Ian had been working nonstop since breakfast, and had been exposed to hypothermic conditions most of that time. If he didn't refuel, now, he could keel over from hypoglycemic blackout. This was no place to do that.

"Okay, man," Bill replied. "See you back in camp."

Ian returned to Camp Three alone—after so many weeks in the cave, the core team had grown a bit cavalier about traveling without buddies—while Bill pushed ahead on his own, and spent several hours rigging the infamous Washing Machine. The chamber had been rigged lightly by Matt Oliphant a few days before, so that he and Karlin Meyers could tour down to the sump. Bill beefed up the route as best he could. About the time he reached the bottom, Noel dropped down.

"Hey, dude," Noel greeted. "Got a bag of poles for ya." He leaned out and looked into a canal below, wondering if that was where they'd assemble the aluminum tubes into a dive platform. "Cool. Is that the sump?"

Bill frowned. "No, we're only about halfway."

"Wait a minute, man," Noel said impatiently. "You told us it was a one-hour trip."

"Well, once properly rigged, once you have the route wired, then, yeah, you'll probably be able to nail it in an hour," Bill explained.

Now Noel frowned. He was well aware of Bill's habit of over- or underestimating times and distances, based only on how the going seemed to Bill. He wondered if Bill was aware that his recent tendency to understate the difficulty of each cave segment was angering Steve and Kenny, who, lacking rope experience, found that everything took far more time and effort than predicted. Only a few days earlier, Bill had made plans to run from Camp Three to the 620 Depot and back in four hours. As soon as Bill passed, Kenny smirked at Noel and said, "Yeah, right. See you in eight." Bill's tendency to keep push-push-pushing the team didn't bother Noel. But because Bill was spending most of his time with Ian, who moved as fast as Bill did, and Barbara, who never complained, Noel feared that Bill had no inkling of the resentments that were taking root among the others.

"The thing is," Noel began, "I didn't bring any spare carbide 'cause I thought this trip was just gonna be a walk in the park, you know?"

Damn, Bill thought. *Doesn't anybody want to cave today?*

"Sorry," he finally said. "Leave your load here. We'll head back up—"

His apology was cut short by the ominous sound of clanking aluminum.

Even before she reached the head of the next pitch—and even though she'd never been there before—Barbara knew right where she was. The rumbling gave it away. Proceeding at her own safe but slow pace behind Noel, she'd reached the most legendary shaft in all of Huautla: the Washing Machine.

The narrow slot leading from the base of the Fissure Drop widened, and the floor fell away in an overhung pitch some twenty-five meters deep. The walls belled away from the drop, like some giant chemist's twisted flask. It would have been an awkward climb even if dry. But the flask was nothing remotely close to dry.

The full force of the Li Nita drainage horsetailed out into the void in a thunderous arc much like the Grand Cascade. And an equally forceful cylinder of water shot in just below. The second sluice blasted all the way across the flask, ricocheted off the far wall, and scattered into the black void below. Near the center of the flask, the two surging jets collided in a spectacular explosion that set the walls trembling, and completely deluged every corner of the chamber below.

On her hands and knees, Barbara peered down. She shook her head slowly from side to side, and thought, *You've got to be joking.*

Bill had scoped out a gymnastic rope route that gripped the right-hand wall, skirted the first crossing of the new stream, swung down under the overhung ceiling, then pendulumed away from the torrential nexus, and inched down through the drenching spray in a series of completely overhung rebelays. It was an even more audacious bit of rigging than the route around the Grand Cascade. Barbara leaned out to study the route one more time.

The trick was to hug the right wall. There was a thin ledge that could then be traversed out to the first bolt, ten meters away. Standard procedure would have been to tether her pack below. But the Washing Machine would fill her bag with water like a fire hydrant filling a bathtub, and within seconds she'd have an extra 100 pounds tugging at her harness. To shimmy out the ledge she'd have to wear the pack on her back.

Barb tightened the drawstring atop her bright orange duffel. The bag, made of urethane-coated nylon, was three feet tall. The aluminum tubes crammed inside, which would be assembled at the sump to create a platform on which to set Camp Five, were four feet long. And every time she moved, the poles inched a bit farther out the top, as if they were trying to escape. She shoved them in one more time, and inserted her arms through the shoulder straps.

She took a deep breath and clipped both her Cow's Tail and one Jumar into the traverse line. Easing out onto the ledge, she spanned a boulder with one arm on each side. She held tightly to the edges while her toes worked across the tan-colored rock. The waterfall had eroded the flow-stone, and the friction was good.

She leaned out looking for a hold on the far wall. Nothing. Her fingers slid down the smooth rock in a futile search. She couldn't hang here forever. She could feel the strain in her wrist tendons. She glanced at the rope, and realized she was now far enough around the boulder so that the line was straight to the bolt. She slid the Jumar out toward the bolt, and then leaned on it. The line drew taut. Using the rope and her right hand for balance, she stepped out onto the ledge, then leaned into the wall. Sigh of relief. She continued shuffling her feet slowly, one toe at a time, with her chest pressed against the wall. The ledge was not even as wide as her boot. She knew better than to look down. She didn't have to. She could feel the maelstrom trembling in her bones.

The traverse was agonizingly slow. When the bolt was finally within reach, she clipped her Cow's Tail carabiner into the hanger so fast that she startled herself. Although she was able to rest, she was still hanging in space. All that effort had merely allowed her to exchange sides of the shaft.

The first two rappels went like clockwork. She was soon clipped into the final roof bolt. She reached up and switched on one of her electric lights—there was no way the carbide would stay lit through the deluge to come—then leaned back away from her rack. This was no place to get her hair caught: She'd have wound up hung in the maelstrom, battered by the dueling falls while the ice water sucked away her body heat.

"Scccrretch."

She tried to turn and see what had made the strange noise. Something scraped against the ceiling, then fell away. Bright and glimmering, it tumbled end over end into the shaft. It was swallowed up in the vortex, gone like a fleeting dream. Before she could piece together the puzzle, she heard a "CLANG" deep below. The high-pitched ring of rebounding tube somehow managed to cut through the noise of the falls. And it continued. "CLANG . . . CLANG . . . CLANK."

Damn, she thought. She felt behind her head: one, two, three . . . one tube missing. Not good. There were no spares.

Okay, she thought, *got to go find it*. She leaned back, unclipped her safety Jumar, and let the wet line slip through her rack.

The passage through the nexus only took a few seconds. But the impact of the water was shuddering, cold, and hard. Barb kicked off the floor and swung out of the main force of the falls, though it was raining hard everywhere.

She was searching for the lost tube when a light appeared from below. It was Noel. He'd heard the tube clank down, and had come back to investigate.

"Hey! You okay?" he shouted.

She looked at him ruefully. "I lost a pole."

He grinned. "You mean that one right there," he said, pointing to a glimmering gray object projecting above the surface of the shallow plunge pool below them.

She felt incredibly lucky. Had it tumbled just a meter or two farther it would have gone over the next pitch and there would have been no chance of recovering it. She climbed down, took hold of the prize, and followed Noel out of the maelstrom.

Stonehenge basked in the warm glow of carbide light that evening. Steve was stretched out on a rock lounge. Noel, Bill, and Barbara occupied the other three chairs. Ian sat atop an overturned bag of rope. And Kenny tended the two small isobutane cookstoves at the center of the circle, cheerily passing out water to those with freeze dried dinners.

Noel was elated. "I tell ya, we are working like clockwork now."

Bill agreed. "I've been thinking," he said, "about the first dives."

The scraping of plastic spoons stopped instantly.

Bill looked around the circle. Noel. Steve. Ian. Kenny. Barb. *Who could be counted on to crack the sump quickly?* He'd expected to be here a month ago. Instead there'd been six weeks of delays in getting out of the States. They'd finally made it here. But still they had to find a route through the dark sump and make it out before the rains came. If they didn't manage to crack through within the wisp of time remaining, how many more years would he spend wondering how he'd let it slip away after having come so far? It was the substance of recurring nightmares he'd been having for the past few weeks: He'd wake up to find that the rainy season had arrived, but they hadn't yet begun to dive the sump. With each passing day, his reality seemed to be marching one step closer to his nightmare. He'd shared this with no one. Nor would he.

"Beginning the day after tomorrow, we'll have room for three divers at Camp Five," he said. In keeping with a philosophy he'd adopted in 1984, Bill removed himself from consideration for the first team. He wanted the others to whet their appetites with a little virgin booty first. "This would be a good time to discuss who we want to have down there on the first push."

Until just a few weeks before, Jim would have been his first choice. But Jim's funk had worsened to the point that he'd become surly, and his teammates had begun responding in kind. Maintaining a calm and sober mind was essential to safe cave diving. Jim's foul mood would hurt the push more than his technical precision and diving experience would help. *He's caught the Rapture*, Bill thought. *He might as well be on the moon.*

Steve lowered his food packet and looked up. "You know, I'd really like to have a crack at that sump."

"I figured you would," Bill said. Any newcomer willing to speak first must have a pretty strong fire to dive.

Bill looked over at Noel. Their eyes locked. Bill looked back at the center of the circle. He wanted Noel on the first dive team, but didn't want to appear to be playing favorites. Noel was the only one from the 1984 expedition to have made it this far. "What are your feelings on this, Noel?"

"Count me in," Noel said, eyes bulging, teeth grinning. "It's about time we scooped some booty. I wanna dive!"

That's two out of three, Bill thought. Now came the delicate part. Kenny and Ian had become nearly inseparable. Kenny certainly preferred to be working with his mentor. Ian was his own man and, aside from Bill, was the most driven individual on the team. Kenny was a crackerjack cave diver, possibly the best pure cave diver—on open circuit—sitting at the circle. *Who would be better to have down there? A joker to keep the crew lively? Or a sergeant to keep them moving?*

Kenny preempted the decision. He turned and put his hand on Ian's shoulder. "Oh, honey, why don't you go?" he said. "I'll stay here and watch the kids."

When the laughter subsided, Ian conceded.

"Right, well, that settles that, eh, mates? Now, I've got this list we should discuss about gear that has to go down tomorrow . . ." He produced his logbook and flipped to the next inventory.

Bill and Ian returned to the Lower Gorge the next morning, and continued rigging toward the sump. A turbulent canal where the flow from the Washing Machine's two powerful streams joined forces with the mighty Metro River, the Lower Gorge made its upper cousin seem easy. The water churned so loudly that from here down, they had to shout to be heard, even when standing next to each other.

They rigged their way along the canal, and around two whitewater sections that Bill thought of as Boiling Pot One and Boiling Pot Two. *Lose control here,* he thought, *and you'll be shot out over the drop into a Class 6 hydraulic cauldron. You'll drown before you can claw your way back to the surface.* Like the Washing Machine, the rope route around the Pots was difficult, but doable.

Below the Boiling Pots stood another deep canal, where two large boulders had fallen out of the ceiling and wedged across the canyon. They guarded the way forward like two giant Dragon's Teeth. Going over the hanging stones was out of the question. Ian rappelled down to the base of the teeth, and swam a line through to the other side. There he pulled up the slack and tied it off. "Try that!" he bellowed back to Bill at the top of his lungs. Bill clipped a carabiner directly from his harness, and whizzed down Ian's line, Kenny-style. He flew right between the Dragon's Teeth, with the water never rising above his farmer john. "Perfect!" he mumbled.

A bit farther along, he found Ian leaning out over a deep shaft filled with white spray.

"Listen, mate," Ian yelled over the roaring cascade. "Thought you said the sump was just around the corner?"

"I . . . I thought it was," Bill shouted back. "Guess that's what thirteen years does to your memory. Any rope left?"

Ian scowled, but removed his pack and withdrew the last coil of new nylon line. He held it up. Then he gestured back to the drop. "This is it, right?"

"This is Thunder Falls," Bill shouted hoarsely. "Got to be." While no more fearsome than either of the Boiling Pots, Thunder Falls was far louder. So he figured they had to be nearing the end of the air-filled canyon. "Last one. I'm pretty sure."

There was a piece of rope hanging over the lip, but it wasn't anything like the rope they'd been using. Ian pulled it over to inspect. The line had a sheath but no core. And the end was wildly frayed.

"Polish," Bill bellowed. "Cheap Polish rope. Left over from their 1980 expedition. Must have been the one Oliphant told us about." A few days earlier, volunteers Matt Oliphant and Karlin Meyers had pushed their tour of San Agustín to the limit by attempting a quick dash to the sump. Bill had piqued their curiosity by passing along the rumor about how the Poles had affixed a brass plaque claiming the sump as theirs. The two young climbers figured the plaque would make an awesome souvenir, so they carried a hammer and crowbar down with them. They ran out of rope far before reaching the sump, and started scavenging bits and pieces of the discarded Polish line. By using the salvaged line sparingly, they made it all the way to Thunder Falls. Oliphant celebrated with a pun: "Hey man, this stuff is good to the last drop!" At that instant, the coreless rope separated at his descender, and Oliphant fell into the plunge pool below. He pulled his way to the surface, looked sheepishly at Meyers, and added, "Well, maybe not the last drop."

Meyers shook his head: "You idiot," he said. "You better not be hurt!" The two friends made it to the sump corridor, and spent nearly an hour searching for the marker. It was nowhere to be found. Frustrated, Oliphant banged the rock with his crowbar. Meyers laughed: "You didn't really think there'd be one here?"

Sheepish again, Oliphant mused, "I thought there might be a chance."

By the time Bill finished telling the story, Ian had set a new bolt atop the final drop. They rappelled down Thunder Falls, removed their vertical gear, and waded into the cold clear water.

"Welcome to the San Agustín sump, Mr. Rolland," Bill said as he floated down the two-meter-wide canal.

"Thank you, Mr. Stone," Ian replied with a wide grin. "It *is* good to be here, finally!"

Together, they began constructing the platform that would become Camp Five. There was no dry land at the sump. So Bill had designed and built an ultra-light scaffolding comprised of decks of urethane-coated nylon stretched over grids of hollow aluminum tubing. Ian and Bill assembled the first square—the dive deck—and swam it down the tunnel. Unable to find any natural rigging points to suspend it from, they began setting bolts in the canyon's smooth limestone walls. While Ian was tapping away with the hammer drill, something caught Bill's eye near the water level.

"Well, I'll be damned," he said.

"What?" Ian asked.

"Look." Bill pointed to a rusted eight-millimeter bolt and hanger set in the wall.

"You guys set that in '81?" Ian asked.

"No. That's the point." Bill fingered the bolt hanger, a curved metal plate with two holes in it. The bolt passed through one, and the rapide or carabiner to which a rope would be attached passed through the other. Then he smiled, nodded, and smiled again.

"We found it!" he said, laughing.

"Found what?" Ian pressed, annoyed at the diversion. Much work remained.

"The Polish plaque," Bill exclaimed, inexplicably proud.

"It's just a bolt, mate," Ian reminded.

"Precisely!" Bill replied. "That's precisely it. There never was a brass plaque. That's not what the Poles said. They told the Belgian doctor that they'd placed a *plaqueta* down there to mark the deepest point they reached. Do you know what *plaqueta* means in Spanish?"

"Ahhh, no." Ian was growing frustrated. These bolts weren't going to set themselves.

"It means 'bolt hanger,'" Bill proclaimed. "*Plaqueta.* Bolt hanger. The Poles told the Belgians they'd set a bolt at the sump. It was a spur-of-the-moment thing, a mark of pride for having made it this far; quite an accomplishment given that only two other teams in the world had ever been here. But we Texans misunderstood. No wonder Oliphant couldn't find it! He didn't know what to look for."

Ian shrugged. Bill enjoyed the drama of international competition. Ian couldn't care less. He snatched a carabiner and sling from his harness, and snapped it into the old Polish bolt hanger. "That's what *I'm* looking for, mate." He smiled. "One less bolt we have to drill today."

Two spindly orange platforms were soon in place. The upper deck was constructed from three of the modular trampolines lashed together, and was hung close to the narrow canyon's ceiling to create a safe haven in the event of a flood. The lower platform was inches above the sump itself, for use as a dive deck. A ladder sewn of nylon webbing connected the two. The team spent the whole day ferrying gear down from Camp Three in an antlike procession through the Fissure Drop, the Washing Machine, the Boiling Pots, and Thunder Falls. By dinnertime three hammocks were in place over the upper deck, and a fully assembled rebreather hung from a pulley rigged alongside the dive deck. A kitchen was set up in a nearby alcove, and a head was established at one end of the upper platform—though the facility consisted of nothing more than a pile of one-gallon Ziploc bags, into which one deposited one's waste before stowing it in a vinyl duffel for later removal.

By late evening, Steve was quite cold and had begun to shiver. While the others had worn their wetsuits all the way down through the soaking Lower Gorge, he'd stuck to a dry caving outfit: Capilene underwear under a jump suit. He spread his sleeping bag out in the middle hammock, and was in the process of changing into dry clothes when Bill warned him to beware the puddles that were forming in the urethane decks.

"I should have installed drains in these things," Bill shouted over the incessant roar of Thunder Falls. "Best be careful there or you're going to get your dry clothes wet, too."

"Yeah, well. It's this or head back to Camp Three. That it?" Steve shot back. He was growing tired of being pushed by Bill—told what to do, what not to do—as though he were a child.

Bill was startled by the latent anger. He put up his hand, as if to say, *Whoa, back off a notch*. He figured Steve was just cold and tired.

Ian fixed hot chocolate for everyone, and before long Steve and Noel were both cocooned in their hammocks, enjoying the relative warmth of the sleeping bags. Noel surveyed the bizarre household. He looked over to Bill, who was repacking his duffel for the trip back up, and yelled, "Brother, you can't get any deeper in this cave without dive gear."

"You got that, partner," Bill replied. He then shook each of their hands—Ian, Steve, and Noel—before shouldering his bag for the last time that day. "You guys kick some ass and scoop some booty, all right?"

And with that he waded back to the base of Thunder Falls, and began climbing back to Camp Three. Without a heavy load, he moved quickly through the Lower Gorge, the Washing Machine, and the Fissure Drop. He slowed down on his way though the Wake-Up Call, and let the full flow of the Li Nita river cool him off. Back at the Metro, he ditched his well-rinsed pack, wetsuit, and vertical gear, and hiked up to Camp Three in his skivvies. Kenny seemed surprised to see Bill stroll into camp in nothing but his underwear. He opened his mouth to say something, but Bill beat him to the wisecrack.

"I've been refining my energy-to-weight ratio," he joked. He tugged at his shorts. "Once I lose a few more grams, I'll achieve peak performance."

He was expecting a laugh, but Kenny only stared. Bill guessed the same sort of fatigue that'd infected Steve's attitude had hit Kenny, too. *It'll pass*, he thought. He settled into Stonehenge, and fixed himself two freeze-dried dinners. Barbara came over to join him. She watched him wolf down first one meal, then another.

"Isn't it ironic," she said. "After ten years of effort, the lead team is down there, and here you sit: wet, hungry, and half-naked at Camp Three."

CHAPTER FIVE _____

I an slept in the hammock closest to the waterfall. Its red and yellow nylon strings clung to his sleeping bag, and when he rolled in his sleep they kept the mist-covered bag from rolling with him. By the time his head was fully exposed to the incessant spray and jackhammer pounding, he was wide awake. He slid to the edge of his hammock, unzipped the bag, and relieved himself in the general direction of the noise. His hammock tipped a bit during the maneuver, and with his arms trapped inside the mummy bag, he found it awkward to regain his balance. He couldn't hear the splash of his tinkle over the falls' roar. As he inched back into the center of the hammock, he pondered whether anyone would have heard him fall if he'd tumbled into the cold sump three meters below.

As he zipped himself back into the bag's warmth, he wondered whether he'd slept long enough to fire a carbide lamp and call it morning. He fished around in his bag until he found a small furry lump near his feet. He pulled the well-worn teddy bear up next to his unshaven face, and smiled. The bear belonged to his kids. It had been sent along to protect him on an earlier expedition, and brought him safely back to Scotland. So Conner, Carly, and Leonie agreed their little brown bear should accompany their father on future expeditions as well. He'd even taken the bear diving during the rebreather training exercises in Florida, where he warned Bill: "Keep an eye on the bear, mate. If he gets *narked* it's time for us to come up." He held the bear tightly in the deafening darkness. He thought of his children, and of his high school sweetheart, Erica, to whom he'd been married ten years. He hated being so far away for so long. He tiptoed along the precipice of his emotions for a few minutes more, then stowed the bear in his bag and lit the carbide lamp clipped to a carabiner at the end of his hammock.

He set his bare feet down into the cold puddle that had collected on the nylon deck, ducked under Steve's hammock, and padded gingerly toward the kitchen alcove. He filled the stainless steel pot with water, fired up the butane stove, then reached over and tapped on Noel's shoulder.

"Time to get up, mate. We've got a cave to explore," Ian said, shouting to be heard.

Noel mumbled something, opened his eyes, and fixed on Ian's face. "Yeah," he grumbled, "I was getting up already."

Ian smiled, then turned back to the stove. He sifted through the pile of Nalgene bottles in the alcove. It seemed as though an inordinate proportion of the food stowed at Camp Five was labeled "potatoes." Finally he found one labeled: "oatmeal: peaches & cream." He unscrewed the white nylon lid and set it down gingerly; anything that fell off the kitchen ledge had a nasty habit of disappearing into the drink below. He spooned the oatmeal into a purple plastic cup, then added hot water. Noel fired his carbide lamp, and Steve sat up groggily in his hammock.

"You ready for some exploration?" Ian greeted Steve.

"I don't know," Steve said, "why don't you see where the hole goes?"

Ian turned to Noel: "Right. And you, mate? Up for a swim?"

Still lying in his hammock, Noel passed his cup to Ian. "What I'd really like now is something hot to drink."

After slurping down his first cup of the day, Noel suggested that Ian make the first dive. Steve agreed. The process of having disassembled and reassembled each of the rebreathers several times that spring—at Bill's house, at Ginnie Springs, on the long drive south, and for the trek into the cave—left Noel and Steve feeling uneasy about the machines. They were far more accustomed to working with simple open-circuit scuba gear, with far fewer components and no onboard computers. But Ian, who maintained fighter jets when he wasn't caving, was unruffled by the thought of trusting his life to a piece of high-tech gear he'd assembled himself only the day before.

So with a load of oatmeal in his belly, Ian stuffed his sleeping bag in a plastic trash sack and stowed the bundle in Steve's hammock. Sitting crosswise in his hammock, he then began the laborious process of kitting up. On top of his expedition-weight Capilene camp fleece, he layered on thick Warm Wind pile pants, jacket, hood, and socks. Over all that went the jet-black urethane drysuit, a waterproof diving suit with tight rubber seals around the neck and wrists to keep the cold water out. Around his waist he fastened a small hip pouch stocked with high-energy candy bars. Last on were his trademark Wellingtons: He wore caving boots instead of diving booties because the objective was to find dry terrain on the far side of the sump.

While Ian suited up, Noel climbed down the rope ladder from the camp platform to the small dive deck suspended just above the sump's surface. There he readied the rebreather by rechecking the waterproof canister of lithium hydroxide that absorbed the carbon dioxide exhaled by the diver, carefully loaded it into the machine, and turned the latches. He installed two small green aluminum tanks filled with pure oxygen, checked the gas sensors and computers that monitored the release of that oxygen, and latched the orange fiberglass clamshell case closed. Outside the case, Noel mounted two long pink tanks filled with Heliox 86/14—a breathing gas designed for deep diving that contained 86 percent helium and 14 percent oxygen—used to dilute the pure oxygen that was supplied by the small inboard tanks, and to eliminate the possibility of nitrogen narcosis. Also, these tanks could be breathed directly in open-circuit mode in an emergency.

Ian joined Noel on the dive platform, and the two of them methodically worked their way through the detailed pre-dive checklist that Bill and Ian devised to fend off operator errors like the one that Steve suffered in Florida. Then Noel reached into the fiberglass clamshell and threw a waterproof switch. A half-dozen LED lamps began glowing and blinking.

"Okay," he said, "we are powered up and into the checklist. Oxygen running one-point-zero?"

"Correct," Ian replied, "oxygen partial pressure control set at one-point-zero atmospheres."

"Diluent select, onboard helium?"

"Right-o," Ian said.

They continued in this fashion until they'd completed the three-page procedure. Once the checklist was complete, Ian pulled a set of fins over his Wellingtons, slid his mask down over his neck, donned his helmet, and slid into the frigid water.

There Noel handed him a large yellow scuba cylinder— one of the high-pressure composite fiberglass tanks developed for the 1984 Peña Colorada expedition—with another 105 cubic feet of spare breathing gas. Ian clipped the tank to two stainless D-rings mounted on his harness so that the tank rode sideways, across his butt. This large cylinder would become the main bailout tank in the event of a complete failure of the rebreather.

Noel handed Ian two plastic reels, each filled with 120 meters of three-millimeter nylon parachute cord. The dive reel is a cave diver's most essential tool. By laying a line into the cave as he goes, the diver is able to find his way out again quickly in the event he becomes lost, loses his lights, loses visibility in a silt-out, runs low on air, or all of the above. There were knots tied every ten feet along the length of the line for estimating distances.

Finally, Noel passed a gap reel—a smaller reel with thirty meters of one-millimeter cord used to relocate the main line in an emergency—two dive knives, a backup decompression computer, and several plastic slates for writing on underwater. One by one Ian clipped these to various attachment points on the harness. He then floated around to face Noel and Steve, who were crouched down on the deck. Holding the deck with one hand and removing his mouthpiece with the other, Ian grunted: "Ready."

Noel gave Ian a thumbs-up, grinned, and said: "Scoop us some tube, bro."

Ian pulled the dump valve on his buoyancy compensator and sank slowly into the black water. He twisted the handle of his quartz halogen light and a laser-like beam punched out into the distance, revealing the walls of the underwater tunnel. He twisted the locking screw on the first reel and the parachute cord—the end of which was tied to the platform behind him—began to spool out freely.

Now, he said to himself, *we see what awaits.*

He started slowly kicking his way into the tunnel while he was still sinking. He kept his knees bent and made small kicks—like a tadpole—in order to keep his fins from stirring up the silt on the cave's floor.

About two meters from the bottom, he added a bit more gas to his buoyancy compensator. The inflator valve sounded a comforting "pop" as gas entered the horseshoe-shaped urethane bladder. He reached across his chest and similarly added a shot of gas to his drysuit. When he had achieved neutral buoyancy—neither heavier nor lighter

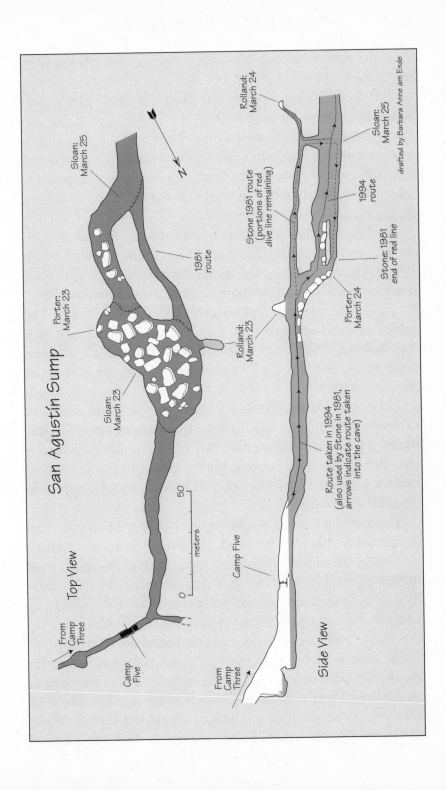

San Agustín Sump

Top View

From Camp Three

Camp Five

Sloan: March 23

Porter: March 23

Sloan: March 25

1981 route

Rolland: March 23

N

0   50
meters

Side View

From Camp Three

Camp Five

Route taken in 1994 (also used by Stone in 1981, arrows indicate route taken into the cave)

Porter: March 24

Stone: 1981 end of red line

1994 route

Stone 1981 route (portions of red dive line remaining)

Rolland: March 24

Sloan: March 25

drafted by Barbara Anne am Ende

than the water around him—he returned his attention to the terrain.

The long tunnel was about three meters across, and about five meters in height from the wider top to the narrower base. It had a coarse gravel floor and a few boulders scattered about. The walls were coated with a layer of ocher silt. The visibility was excellent: Ian's handheld primary light easily illuminated everything for twenty meters or more.

No one had passed this way—still shaped like an upside-down pear—since Bill had laid 285 meters of line here in 1981. Open-circuit scuba gear restricted that dive to a ninety-minute dash. But there were no loud "swhooo-oop" inhales, and no long "phooossh" exhales this time. The rebreather changed all that. Silence meant efficiency. Not one atom of oxygen was being wasted this time. The loudest noise Ian heard was the cyclic rasping of the line reel as the spool turned.

He finned slowly forward along the right-hand wall, and explored the ceiling carefully with his beam of light. He was looking for an airbell—a shortcut up to walking passage—that Bill might have missed. He spotted a jug hole—a natural loop eroded into the solid limestone—and stopped to tie off the dive line.

There was a natural alcove near where he'd stopped, and he decided that was a good place to secure the yellow bailout bottle. Filled with pure oxygen, the fiberglass tank would be available for use as a decompression station or— in the unlikely event of the failure of both the rebreather and the backup open-circuit system—a diver could pick up the bottle and carry it back out as a last-chance gas supply.

He aimed the big light back into the darkness, and swam along the path cut by its beckoning beam. The tunnel, which had been descending slowly since he left the dive platform, leveled off at a depth of about ten meters below the surface of the sump. The knots on his dive line spun off his reel as he finned his way forward through the cold, clear water at about twenty meters per minute. The entire passage was smooth and scalloped, like polished rock. *Yes, you lovely,* he said to the cave, *you do pump through here something fierce during the rainy season, don't you?*

The reel seized suddenly, jerking him back. He looked down with a grimace, expecting to see a jammed reel. He was surprised to see an empty spool. The first 120 meters of line had already run out. He was making quick progress.

He unclipped the second reel from his harness. There was a large loop at the end of the first line that allowed it to be detached from the first spool. He fed the second reel through the loop at the end of the first line, creating a Lark's Head knot. With the empty reel reclipped to his harness, he began running out more line.

About 140 meters from the dive platform, he found a vertical shaft leading down into what appeared to be a large breakdown room. Overhead was another tunnel, curving off to his right. *Well, well,* he thought, *which one of you is going to lead me to the booty?* Ever the optimist, he finned upward.

Up, up, up, the tunnel went. And his light soon bounced back to him off a silvery surface. He headed for the mirror and shortly broke through into a large airbell. He added air to his buoyancy compensator, lifting his head up higher out of the water. The air-filled chamber was about ten meters long by six wide. It was filled with warm, moist, breathable air. But there were no tunnels above the surface.

What about underneath? he wondered. With no natural tie-offs in sight, he used a lead weight to anchor his dive line, then reeled it out horizontally across the airbell. He hoped to find a continuing underwater tunnel on the far side, as if the airbell were like an oxbow in a river. But the floor came up quickly and he was soon up to his knees in muck. *Well, Mr. Rolland, that didn't work. Back to the junction.*

The retreat was not as orderly as the ascent. He'd kicked up a lot of muck while wading around in the airbell, and a dense cloud of ocher silt billowed down the tunnel toward the main shaft. By the time he returned to his primary dive line, he was working in zero visibility. He retied the line at the junction, and began descending down the shaft toward the breakdown boulders he'd seen before. But the silt-out was so thick he never saw the boulders. After descending twelve meters and seeing nothing, he turned back. Rather than leave the spool hanging in the shaft he reeled back in to the junction, locked off the reel, and left it clipped there for the next diver.

"You see that?" Noel bellowed, pointing at a flicker of light deep within the tunnel. It pulsed a few more times, like heat lightning on a summer evening, then focused into a steady beam that lit up the sump with an eerie blue-green glow, and lent Camp Five the look of a cut-rate science fiction flick. "Ian!" Noel hooted, fully awake and shouting a mile a minute as he leapt out of his hammock and threaded his way down the ladder to the lower platform.

Ian's head broke the surface. He grinned and grabbed hold of the lower platform. He unbuckled his helmet, and locked off his mouthpiece, to avoid flooding the rebreather.

"Well?" Steve asked.

Ian's lips moved, but neither Steve nor Noel could hear what he said. Ian couldn't even hear himself. After fifty-one minutes in the silence of the sump, Camp Five seemed louder than ever. He raised his voice and started again: "I dove to a junction, then followed the right-hand wall up to a large airbell. I placed a drop weight, then waded around the bell. There was no way on."

Noel reached down to help him up. When his bulging eyes met Ian's, he added: "So why are you back so soon?"

"When I reeled back to that junction, I tried to go down the shaft, but the silt followed me down. I gave her a go, but it was pretty thick. After the silt settles a bit, you guys will be able to take a fresh whack at it. It's opening up below."

Steve and Noel helped him out of the gear. Discovering that the urine bag inside the drysuit had leaked, they ribbed Ian mercilessly about the smell. After rinsing out the suit as best they could, Steve led Noel through the kitting up checklist, and watched him fade into the cold sump.

Noel followed Ian's line until he found the second reel hanging on the wall above the shaft. He picked up the reel and descended into the breakdown chamber, where he found stacked limestone blocks the size of large dining tables at about twenty meters depth. After decades caving, he knew there'd likely be an open passage somewhere at the bottom of the breakdown slope. The visibility was less than two body lengths—nowhere near enough to see across the large shaft—so Noel tied off the line and swept his way along the perimeter of the room, working from right to left. When he reached the end of Ian's reel, he tied it off and followed the line back to where he began the sweep. There he tied on a new reel, and started sweeping the left wall, working in the opposite direction.

During this second sweep, he spotted what looked like a piece of Bill's distinctive red 1981 line leading down through the breakdown. *That's it!* When he turned to look closer, one of his fins became entangled in the line he was laying. He had to stop and remove the fin to unwrap the line. While struggling with that, he lost control of his buoyancy—he was still learning to balance the drysuit's buoyancy against that of the rebreather's built-in bladder—and stirred up the ankle-deep layer of silt that coated the breakdown blocks. The silt billowed forth into a cloud, and after that, there wasn't enough visibility to continue the sweep.

He was caught in a silt-out. He hovered, and made each remaining move carefully. The concept seemed simple enough: Reel back in. But the thin nylon line was like a rubber band. It stretched this way and that, and provided only the vaguest orientation. Noel reeled gently. He knew that the line invariably stretched across a sharp limestone edge or two; if he tugged too hard, the rubber band would snap and he'd be left with no clue as to which way to swim out of the cave. Strings of minor events like these—a silt-out, a line break—killed a Florida cave diver every few years. He meditated to calm himself down, and cautiously reeled the line back up through the murky haze. Only forty-seven minutes after departing, he was back at Camp Five.

Noel was shivering as Steve and Ian helped him out of the water. Unlike Ian, he'd only worn one layer of fleece under the now damp drysuit. He climbed to the upper platform and tried to dry himself off while standing in the puddle of water, but it wasn't working. He then sat down in his hammock and wick-dried while briskly rubbing his feet. He finally put his feet into his sleeping bag in a pruned state. They took an hour to dry fully. Ian fixed Noel a cup of hot Crystal Light lemonade—a sour concoction that, when spiked with several tablespoons of sugar, had became an expedition favorite—then returned to the lower platform to lead Steve through his kit-up.

Because Ian and Noel had left such poor visibility in the main tunnel, Steve began by exploring a side tunnel on the right-hand wall near where Ian had stowed the bailout bottle. But after only seven meters or so, the floor rose sharply, and the passage near the ceiling was too narrow for the bulky Cis-Lunar Mk-IV rebreather to pass through. So he followed the main line down to the breakdown chamber and retraced the route of Noel's first sweep, continuing past where Noel had turned back. But even after forty minutes into his dive, clouds of silt were still rolling down from where Ian had stirred up the muck overhead. Believing that the way ahead was straight over a large boulder, he tightened the nut on the reel and left it on the breakdown. He returned to Camp Five after forty-eight minutes in the sump.

They dried Steve off and inventoried their gear. They'd emptied three reels over three dives. One of the rebreather's two tiny oxygen tanks had 490 psi remaining, and the other was full. Whatever else, the Mk-IV was already proving its efficiency: After 146 minutes underwater, they'd used less than a tenth of a single standard scuba tank. An open-circuit diver making the same dives would have already sucked through five or more full tanks.

The three explorers shared a large dinner of powdered, freeze-dried beef Stroganoff—though Noel doubted anyone would have been able to guess the meal's identity were the waterproof Nalgene bottle not so labeled—and did their best to relax within the deafening confines of Camp Five. As if the noise and the spray weren't sufficiently intimidating, they were stuck with nothing to wear but foul-smelling fleece, as a result of the urine bag leak. Ian produced a card game called Pigs, and proceeded to beat his mates four games in a row. The threesome drifted off to sleep laughing about how Ian had set them up to smell like pigs.

No one slept well at Camp Five that night. In the morning, Ian was willing to give up his turn and let someone else dive first. But no one else wanted it. So Ian was back in the bone-chilling water at noon.

Ian worked his way to where Steve had quit the day before, picked up the third reel, and dropped down over the boulder as Steve had correctly advised. There he found a passage about five meters wide. The visibility was still hazy, so he couldn't see the floor. He tied on a new reel, followed the ceiling, and at about twenty-five meters below the sump surface he discovered a huge borehole. There he spotted a segment of an old dive line going up at forty-five degrees. *That's got to be Stone's old line.* To avoid diving any deeper than he had to, he followed it up toward the surface, and found another small airbell, with a silt-plugged crawlway leading to it. But once again, his exploration of the airbell caused silt to rain down on the chamber below. Dropping back down, he found himself in the middle of another silt-out, so he set the line and returned to Camp Five.

"The way on looks to be straightforward," he told Noel on his return. "Follow the old dive line."

Steve helped Ian out of the gear, and prepared the rebreather for Noel. He was helping Noel kit up when he saw flashes of light up the tunnel leading from Camp Three. Soon they heard Kenny's wisecracking voice echoing down the catacomb. A few moments later, Kenny was climbing up to Camp Five bearing a load of munchies. Bill and Barbara showed up a few minutes later, with oxygen, lithium, and, inexplicably, yet another gallon of dried potatoes. The three of them had spent the day before hauling gear from the 620 Depot to Camp Three, and they were eager to hear how the diving was proceeding.

Noel tucked himself into the cooking alcove to make room on the tiny platform. Steve grabbed the newly arrived trail mix and slid up into his hammock. Ian regaled the visitors with a summary of the first four dives. He figured they'd pushed roughly 250 meters into the sump, and predicted that when it bottomed, the big borehole he'd found that morning would set a new depth record for Huautla. Barbara and Kenny congratulated the dive team, unloaded their packs, and headed back toward Camp Three.

Ian suggested to Bill that after the three of them cracked the sump, Bill and Kenny should move forward and scoop the booty beyond.

"No," Bill replied. "You three should push as far as you can go. You've earned it."

Undeterred, Ian tried to approach his point from another route. He suggested that to get back in time, they'd have to begin de-rigging by May 1. And for everyone to have a crack at the booty before then, they should begin rotating teams sooner, rather than later.

Bill couldn't believe his ears. It was only March 24. They hadn't even cracked the sump and they were already talking about going home. He had no idea how grating life at Camp Five had become, and couldn't understand what was going on. He tried to brush off Ian's point: "Oh, we could begin de-rigging on the 14th and still have plenty of time to make it back to the States by the 1st of June."

Ian scoffed: "I don't mean to be rude, but I don't think you're dealing with reality."

Bill still wasn't getting it. *What's happened down here?* he wondered. *Only a couple days before, they were vying for this challenge.* He looked to Noel for support. But his old friend stayed put in the alcove, his big blue eyes avoiding Bill's steely gaze.

"Oh, man, you're not going to pull the same game you pulled on me last year, are you?" Bill asked, referring to how Noel skipped out of the training exercise to go back to work at his hospital a few weeks earlier than planned. Bill could tell all three of them were afraid of something, but didn't understand what it was.

Noel said nothing. He just gazed at his bare feet, dangling above the sump.

"I'm in this for the long haul," Bill shouted, a bit louder than he needed to be heard above the waterfall. Louder still he added, "Do you guys want to win or don't you?"

Steve slunk back into his hammock. He was shocked to hear those words come out of Bill's mouth. He felt as though Bill was treating him and the other team members as pawns in some sort of a grand game, a race to the bottom of the world. He feared that like a pawn, he, too, might be expendable.

Bill looked at each of them. Not knowing what else to say, he added: "If this thing is still going come the 1st of May, I'm staying." Then he unloaded his pack, and began muttering through an inventory of what needed to be hauled down next. He was killing time, waiting for Noel to resume kitting up for the next dive, waiting for things to somehow return to something that felt like normal.

Ian played along, and began spooling new dive line onto one of the reels they'd emptied the day before.

Noel knew exactly what Bill was doing, and he understood better than the others that Bill's expeditions succeeded exactly because he could remain so hard-charging long after everyone else was exhausted. But Noel had been harboring a bad feeling about this dive all day. He'd been unable to pre-visualize the dive the way he usually did. He'd awakened to a disturbing dream the night before. And this conversation hadn't left him feeling any better.

"I'm somewhat spooked," Noel finally said, without leaving the alcove.

Ian looked at Noel and saw he wasn't kidding. He glared briefly at Bill, then walked over to where Noel was, and said, "Look mate, if you're not up for it, Steve can go. Or I'll go down again."

Bill was disappointed. Noel was right where they'd both fought for ten years to be—face-to-face with the cave, *mano a mano* with the beast—and he'd balked. But Bill knew he'd already said too much. He knew that the three of them had to sort this out among themselves. So he wished them "good luck" and left for Camp Three.

As soon as he left, Steve agreed to make the next dive. Noel chattered relentlessly as he prepped the rig. "Screw Bill," he said, still smarting from the "want to win" jab. "I have a contractual, binding responsibility to the medical corporation that will cost me not only money, but also seniority, extra calls, and loss of my shareholder status if I'm not physically in that hospital taking my thirty-six-hour shift on June 1." He apologized for shirking the dive. Then he apologized again—and again, and again. Between apologies he rambled on about the foreboding dream he'd had the night before, and about his long family history of premonitions.

Steve was scared enough as it was. He was able to tune Noel out for a few minutes. But the veteran caver's stream-of-consciousness fear-mongering quickly proved even more annoying than the damned waterfall.

"Look," Steve snapped. "If you don't want to dive—for whatever reason—that's fine by me. But I don't want to listen to all your negativity while I'm getting ready to make a dive. Okay?"

Noel's bulging blue eyes recoiled into their sockets. He knew at once that Steve was right. Screwing on a calm mental attitude was every bit as vital a part of the pre-dive routine as strapping on the rebreather. He apologized one last time, and sheepishly went back to prepping the rig.

Steve dropped into the water late that afternoon and followed the guideline through the tunnel, down the shaft, over the breakdown, and through the great bluish white haze in the borehole to the bend Ian had described. He tied a new line to the wall, and the thin white cord spun off his reel as he swam across the hazy canyon in search of the other side. The far wall popped into view after about six meters. He followed it forward through the haze.

After a short swim, he came across a fissure in the wall. A small tunnel sloped downward. He stopped and studied the narrow passage, probing its jagged features with his hand-held primary light. He thought it looked a little tight to squeeze through with the rebreather on his back. But it wasn't a long restriction—about one body length—and it looked like it would open up on the other side. He pressed his body into the crevasse.

The rebreather scraped against the limestone as he pulled himself into the restriction. Sound grows louder underwater. So does fear. In the narrow passage, each rock-on-fiberglass nudge felt like a full-fledged "CRUNCH." And each contact fueled his dread: What if he couldn't get back through? He tried backing up a bit, just to see. He got stuck immediately. Unable to back up, he moved forward, deeper into the narrow tunnel.

Soon Steve was past the tightest part. But it was obvious this would never be a trade route through which a team of divers would pass with packs on a daily basis. So he decided against exploring farther down the crevasse. By going out the way he'd come, he could take up the line, thereby eliminating any potential confusion on subsequent dives.

Passing out through the restriction proved to be more difficult than getting in. Hoses were getting caught on rock protrusions everywhere. He had to back up and reassess the aperture every couple of feet. He considered taking off the rebreather and pushing it through in front of him, holding on to the breathing hose by gripping the mouthpiece in his teeth. It was a classic Florida cave diving maneuver, something Wes Skiles had taught him how to do years ago, something the Moles did almost every weekend. But he'd never practiced the move with a bulky Mk-IV. Neither had anyone else on the expedition. As Steve struggled in the restriction, his fear led to flashes of anger. First at Bill; then at himself. He knew better than to dive in a place like this with equipment he wasn't fully comfortable using.

Fear returned. And for a few moments, he was unable to shake unpleasant thoughts about a teammate finding his lifeless corpse permanently wedged there. But he remembered the Moles' mantra—there's always slack somewhere—and he did finally manage to writhe his way out, one gentle twist at a time.

Back in the main chamber, he rested at the dive line. It took a couple minutes to calm his heart and slow his breathing rate. He checked the rebreather's onboard computers against his personal dive computer. Both showed he had plenty of dive time left. No harm done. He pressed on.

He followed Ian's line back to the old red guideline, left by Bill in 1981. He then followed Bill's line another twenty meters into a low, sand-floored tunnel. The ripples in the sand suggested that this was the way most of the water flowed. Having had his fill of adrenaline for the day, he followed Ian's line back to the breakdown, and started up the shaft.

As Steve began to rise up from the base of the deep shaft, he reached for the dump valve on his buoyancy control device. Like Noel, he found the valve difficult to use because it was positioned much lower than the top of the bladder where the gas wanted to rise. Making matters worse, he wasn't dumping air from the new drysuit. As he rose, the air in both the bladder and the drysuit expanded, and became more buoyant.

Unable to manage it all, he began to rocket up the shaft. Such uncontrolled ascents are the cause of many serious diving injuries, as air expands inside a diver's body. If one were to release a balloon filled with air at twenty meters depth, for example, the balloon would burst before reaching the surface. The same thing can happen to a person's blood vessels, or lungs.

Steve yanked at the dump valve again and again, but because he wasn't also dumping gas from the drysuit and the rebreather's counterlungs, it wasn't enough. He began clawing at the silt-covered limestone walls, desperately hoping to find some lip or ledge to hang on to. Soon he saw the mirrored surface of the airbell approaching rapidly. He exploded through the water's surface and into the dark little airbell. The velocity of his far too rapid ascent thrust his head well above the surface of the water, like a torpedo breaking the waves. He scrambled to get back beneath the surface, venting his buoyancy compensator, drysuit, and counterlungs as rapidly as he could, and pushing down off the muck. Breathing heavy, his heart racing, he finally made it down to the tunnel toward Camp Five.

He hugged the bottom of the inverted pear all the way back. He took his time returning; the extra decompression time would help make up for the uncontrolled ascent. He used the manual override to increase the oxygen concentration, allowing him to use pure oxygen to flush some of the helium out of his bloodstream. He surfaced at the dive platform eighty-four minutes after he'd left.

A few minutes after climbing out of the water, he noticed muscular pain in his left arm. *Just a strain from my struggle in the squeeze? Or a symptom of decompression sickness?* He feared what would happen if he were to get the bends at Camp Five: There was simply no quick evacuation possible. He lay in his hammock that night, wondering what strange bubbles were coursing through his body.

Noel awoke in a better mood. Having visualized a successful dive, he bustled about the platform performing his morning rituals and prepping his gear. His mood was so dramatically improved that Ian wondered whether he was feeling all right. Noel assured him he was, and entered the water shortly before noon.

The swim through the inverted pear seemed like a familiar commute. Rather than wasting the battery in his handheld primary light, Noel followed the line using only the smaller flashlight affixed to his helmet. The rebreather was working smoothly, he was warm enough in two layers of pile, and his buoyancy was fine.

He penciled survey notes on a white plastic slate as he worked his way in. By counting the knots in the dive line, he figured how far each section of tunnel stretched. Using a compass, he determined in which direction each section was headed. By referring to his diver's depth gauge, he was able to record the depth of each junction. Cavers don't consider a cave to have been explored until a survey is complete. Noel made a point of surveying all they'd seen up to that point, knowing with years of certainty it would be the first thing Stone would ask to see when they returned to Camp Three.

As he floated down the breakdown shaft, he switched on his primary light and searched the room for major details, which he also sketched on the slates. At the bottom of the shaft, he felt oddly short of breath. He settled on the break-down block and considered scrubbing the dive. He switched to open circuit for a couple of breaths, then back to the closed-circuit rebreather. After a minute, everything seemed fine. So he continued forward collecting survey data.

In the long, low tunnel Steve had found, Noel's primary light faded unexpectedly. *That's weird. This is only the second dive on this charge.* He switched on the helmet-mounted flashlight he'd been burning on the way in. Carrying three sources of light on every cave trip is the first rule of caving, and Noel had three with him. But with his primary dead, and the small electric on his helmet nearly spent, he was left with only one small flashlight in reserve. He had no choice but to turn around. Feeling short of breath again, he switched to open circuit briefly, then continued back to the shaft, up to the pear, and back to Camp Five.

Back at the dive platform, he described his breathing problems, and suggested they check the lithium hydroxide canister. But Ian, intent on making the next dive as soon as possible, argued that since the canisters had provided eight hours of dive time in Florida, and the unit they'd been using had less than six hours of dive time on it, the lithium couldn't be the problem. No one checked the canister. Ian entered the water with a new battery pack for the primary light, and made his way quickly to the twenty-meter break-down shaft. By the time he reached the bottom, he felt a headache coming on. When he reached the end of the line Noel had laid, he was short of breath. He switched to open circuit for a minute to clear the air in the breathing bag, but the difficulty returned only a few moments after he returned to closed circuit. He realized Noel had been right: The lithium hydroxide was exhausted. He scrubbed his dive, and made a slow exit. Steve and Noel were at the lower platform when he returned.

"Not a good day at the office," Ian complained. "Noel was right. The lithium is spent."

Ian's carbon dioxide headache stayed with him. And as

Noel and Steve helped him out of the water, the three embarked on a mutual bitching session.

"This damn drysuit is four sizes too big for me," Ian complained. "I'm always fiddling with the gas to maintain my buoyancy."

"Yeah," Steve chimed in, "but a loose drysuit is not a problem compared to a BC that won't dump gas!" The others moaned in agreement. After a bit more complaining, Noel raised the question already on each of their minds.

"Maybe we need a surface break?" he asked. "You guys wanna let Kenny, Bill, and Jim take a turn?"

The mood brightened.

"I wouldn't mind a couple days on the surface," Steve said. "Get away from this damned waterfall. Get away from that overflowing biohazard-bag we've been using as a head."

"Right, mates," Ian added. "We'll stroll up into Huautla and eat everything in sight. How many restaurants do you think that lively little burg might have?"

They repacked the rebreather, inventoried the gear needed, and left Camp Five by 6:30 in the evening. Ian packed out the spent diluent tanks. Steve carried the dead battery packs. And Noel shouldered the oxygen tanks.

Bill and Barbara were finishing dinner when the first dive team marched into Stonehenge. Bill had spent the day struggling to rig a small hydroelectric generator at the tweve-meter-high Li Nita waterfall just below Camp Three. The hydro station was intended as an alternative to carrying heavy replacement batteries for the primary dive lights. But the charging system couldn't accommodate the voltage fluctuations created by the uneven flow of water, and kept shutting itself down. Bill had noodled with it for hours, and was already frustrated by the time Ian, Steve, and Noel showed up.

Ian delivered the bad news: They'd made three more

dives, but failed to lay a single meter of new dive line. They were tired, hungry, and still angry over the discussion that had taken place at the sump between them and Bill two days ago. They needed a break from the waterfall. And they wanted a couple days at the surface.

"We're leaving for the surface tomorrow," Steve said, in a tone meant to discourage further discussion on the issue.

Feeling under attack, Bill slumped forward in the big stone chair. He stared at the ground and rubbed his face with both hands. He said nothing when Steve added details to the account of his troubled dive, nor even when Noel handed him the log notes from his survey dive. But his posture betrayed his silence: *So you guys are telling me that with the most powerful gear on earth, you still couldn't make it past my open-circuit dive of thirteen years ago?*

Miffed by Bill's reaction, the dive team shuffled off in silence to unpack their gear and change into pee-free fleece. After they left, Barbara sat next to Bill and started to rub his shoulders, but he shrugged her off. "Don't get so uptight about it," she said. "There's still plenty of time."

Bill ran his hands through his hair. Then he picked up Noel's survey notes. Within a half-hour he'd plotted Noel's numbers, and added what he could remember from the 1981 dive. The data showed what had gone wrong. By trying to follow his old line, they'd missed the way forward by taking a wrong turn in bad visibility. The way to overcome their malaise, he convinced himself, was to head back down and crack the thing quickly. After a few more minutes alone at the camp circle, he set out to find Kenny.

Having correctly interpreted the returning dive team's body language from a distance, and knowing Bill was in a dark mood, Kenny had studiously avoided the ugly scene at Stonehenge. Bill found him at his sleeping bag.

"Hey dude," Bill said, trying his best to sound casual. "You ready to go diving tomorrow?"

Kenny answered Bill with a look. His eyes said, "With you?" Over the past few days of hauling packs, he'd grown weary of Bill's zeal. He wanted to dive, but he wasn't psyched about spending several days alone with Bill at the thundering sump. "I'll go if Ian does," he said. "I'm not going to dive without him there to back me up."

Bill nodded. He'd seen how close the two had become. "All right, I understand that."

Once Bill was gone, Noel strolled up and asked Kenny what was going on. "I . . . I respect Bill," Kenny stammered. "But I can't deal with him. Not all by myself. Not while I'm trying to get focused for a dive."

Noel was surprised to discover animosity in Kenny, who was usually among the team's happiest campers. "What do you mean?" he asked.

"He has no freakin' leadership skills," Kenny blurted. "Everything upsets him. Even the kind of stuff that goes wrong on every big expedition. Like, he's all shocked that his high-tech hydro turbine is fitzing out under these conditions? Like, he's all rush-rush, hurry-hurry, everywhere we go. I know this expedition is important to him. I'm just tired of dealing with it."

Noel nodded. He'd heard this rap before. Bill's strength was the way he stayed goal-oriented in the face of any obstacle. That was also his weakness. These same sorts of complaints had led to a petit coup during the Peña Colorada expedition. "You told Bill all this?" Noel asked. "Just now?"

"Hell no," Kenny said. "I told him I won't dive without Ian. I mean, like, you and Steve are headed out, right? We can't count on Jim. And Barbara is as green as they come."

Noel nodded again. He was used to teammates telling him all the angry things they were afraid to tell Stone. He and Bill had been through a lot together, and their trust ran deep, even when they disagreed with each other. On previous expeditions, Noel had always found plenty of face time to tell Bill what was going on behind his back. But he wasn't getting much one-on-one time this year. Ian was managing the expedition. And Barbara was managing Bill's volatile emotions. So while Noel understood what Kenny was telling him, he wasn't sure what to do with it.

While Noel and Kenny continued chatting, Bill made his way out to the alcove where Jim Brown had pitched his private camp. Jim had told the others he was camping by himself as a courtesy, to shield them from his loud snoring; but in reality, the storm of fear and anger was still brewing within him. He'd only spent a couple nights at Camp Three by the time the first dive team returned, having taken every opportunity to head to the surface, where he maintained the dive gear and performed whatever other technical odd jobs were required. He wasn't prepared to leave the expedition, but he wasn't going to dive the sump either. His little camp in the rock had become a sort of purgatory, and he seemed to be expecting Bill's visit.

"Hey man," Bill said, after making certain Jim could see his lips. "You ready to push the sump?"

"Well, ya see, I'd love to," Jim lied. "But my ear's been botherin' me. I don't think I can dive."

"Okay," Bill said. "How about making a resupply run to the surface? You and Steve could head out in the morning."

"Yeah, okay, but my legs are still sore, ya know? I think I'd better wait another day."

"I see," Bill said. It wasn't until that moment that he realized what had already become obvious to the others: Jim had quit the expedition without actually leaving.

Bill told Jim he hoped he'd feel better soon, and headed back toward where the others had gathered at Stonehenge. Steve was giving Noel a speech similar to Kenny's: ". . . this was supposed to be ten-day camp. After that, he promised we'd get a break. Now he wants us to keep pushing. He's all push-push-push, with never a word of thanks. He's all . . ." His voice trailed off as Bill approached the circle.

Steve looked at Noel for support, then turned to Bill and stated, "I'm headed out tomorrow. No matter what. I need a break."

"All right," Bill said, catching Steve off guard. "Just let me give you a list of items we need brought back from the surface, will you?"

"Uh, sure," Steve stammered, still expecting a fight.

Steve's declaration left Noel torn. Noel wanted to spend a couple days on the surface, take a bath in the Río Iglesia, hike into Huautla, and phone home. But he was also reluctant to miss any of the action. He sensed they were close, and figured they'd break through after a few more good dives.

Bill told Noel to do whatever he felt he needed to do, and that small measure of respect was all Noel needed to feel good again. He returned to his sleeping area, and before falling asleep in the blissful silence, he wrote in his personal journal: *I am as happy down here as I am on the surface. I'm used to Bill's personality when he gets in situations like this . . . I'll sleep on it and we'll see what tomorrow holds.*

Bill wasn't feeling so blessed as he and Barbara settled in for the night.

"All three of them want a break," he whispered to Barbara. "I guess they need it, what with the noise and all. But the second dive team has totally fallen apart. Kenny doesn't want to dive without Ian, and Jim won't dive at all."

Bill slumped into his bag. Barb gave him a back rub, and he quickly fell asleep. She zipped into her sleeping bag, and lay awake in the darkness. She was sorry the others weren't getting along. But they were big boys. They'd take care of themselves. And maybe, after the fallout, she'd get a chance to dive.

CHAPTER SIX _____

In the morning, Ian paced. From his sleeping area just outside the camp center, he nervously circled the stone chairs, hiked down the hill to the Metro, doubled back through camp toward the rock latrine, and looped Stonehenge again. He had his cave pack in his hand, and was more or less filling it with gear, though he was doing so in a remarkably inefficient manner.

Kenny joined him for a second lap down to the Metro. Kenny was eager to dive, but wanted Ian there with him. Ian wanted to go to the surface, but didn't want to let Kenny down. Kenny prevailed, and Ian reluctantly agreed to return to Camp Five.

Noel joined them at Stonehenge for his morning syrup. As he poured coffee into his sugar, Noel talked about returning to the sump with them. He figured Ian's can-do spirit and Kenny's wisecracking would shake him out of his negative mood. But a few minutes later, he'd changed his mind again. He caught Ian alone, and tried to persuade him to leave the cave. He told Ian that he was still troubled by the vague sense of foreboding that had overcome him at the sump, and he felt that if they took a break for a few days, everything would be all right.

Ian snarled at the suggestion. "Somebody's got to keep the momentum going. If nobody else will do it, I bloody will."

"Two days topside won't make a difference," Noel pleaded. "A little sun. Something solid to eat. We'll come back and finish the job refreshed."

Ian shook his head. "I'm going back down," he said, cinching his pack closed. "I don't want to talk about it anymore." Noel nodded. He admired Ian's commitment. So much so that he changed his mind again, and returned to talking about accompanying the two of them to the sump. But when they marched out of Camp Three a few minutes later, he remained behind.

Kenny and Ian had grown remarkably close. They were the youngest members of the expedition, at twenty-seven and twenty-nine years of age respectively. Both were perfectionists who employed sarcasm as a defense mechanism. And after eleven stressful days underground, both had grown dependent on hourly hits of humor to make it through the day. By the time they reached Camp Five, both were having a great time.

While Ian began repacking the rebreather with oxygen and a new charge of lithium hydroxide, Kenny began suiting up for his first dive. Ian told him about the buoyancy problems the first dive team had experienced with the airtight urethane drysuit, and suggested he wear a simpler—but less warm—wetsuit instead.

"Nah, I'm gonna dive it naked," Kenny said. "It's not cold down there, is it? We big-shot Florida cave divers don't get in the water until it's, like, eighty degrees."

"No problem, mate," Ian replied. "We have the technology." Grinning wildly, he tossed up the wetsuit. Kenny jerked his head up at the lame Six Million Dollar Man riff. That was exactly how he had intended to finish the joke. Ian had not only learned Kenny's incessant shtick, but he'd begun to lob the corniest verbal shrapnel back at him.

In addition to finishing each other's jokes, the two were soon finishing each other's thoughts. They refined the complicated kitting up procedure to a smooth ritual in which Ian was silently offering Kenny his masks, reels, and other items in the same instant Kenny realized he needed them. At just the moment Kenny would mutter, "Ah . . . gosh . . . I need to find my pouch," Ian would hand it to him.

Kenny slipped into the sump and followed the guideline for 228 meters until he reached the confusing breakdown chamber that had confounded Noel and Ian on their last dives. There his years of slithering along with the Moles paid off. He stayed deep—as Bill had advised after reviewing Noel's survey notes—and drifted around the underwater maze, shining his handheld light up several possible routes, until his instincts led him through a narrow opening and into a large passageway. Once past the constriction, he lightly touched the velvety silt bottom with his fin tip, applying barely enough pressure to loosen a spoonful of sediment. He watched to see which way the small silt column drifted. A slight current carried the fine silt out the passageway he'd selected, confirming his hunch. He laid a line along the promising route.

By the time his reel ran out, he'd begun to shiver. The wetsuit was far less hassle than the drysuit, but because it merely kept the diver warm—but not dry—it also provided far less protection against the bone-chilling water. Kenny tied off the guideline and headed back to Camp Five. When he arrived, Ian had a pot of hot tea waiting for him.

The two friends enjoyed a freeze-dried dinner and traded tales. Kenny told Ian about the research for his doctoral dissertation, which involved studying the distribution patterns of crack cocaine in Jamaica. Ian shared stories from the RAF mountain rescue team, as well as glowing reports about his three children.

At bedtime, Kenny fashioned an amusing-looking defense against the merciless pounding of the nearby waterfall. The clothing manufacturer Patagonia had been one of the expedition's many sponsors, and had provided each team member with a polyester fleece balaclava. Kenny rolled his into a thick cloth donut and pulled it tight over his ears. Ian did the same, and the Kenny Broad headroll became part of the Camp Five lifestyle.

Late that night, Kenny got up to relieve himself. Afterward, he padded back across the wet platform. Sitting down in the darkness, he misjudged the exact position of the hammock when he sat down, flipped out the other side, and banged his head on the limestone wall. Writhing in pain from the blow to his head, he then slipped off the platform and began falling toward the sump below. He threw out an arm and somehow caught one of the ropes that secured the platform to the canyon. Hanging by one hand, he yelled as loud as he could. But the drone of the waterfall and the padding of the headroll prevented Ian from hearing him scream.

He felt like someone had hit him over the head with a baseball bat. He could feel himself becoming light-headed, and worried that he would not be able to hold on much longer. He used his weight to get himself swinging, and managed to grab another anchor line with his other hand. Then he shimmied himself up to the edge of the platform. He lay there for another ten minutes or more, still reeling in pain, before gingerly crawling back into bed.

At breakfast, Kenny related the terrifying episode to Ian. They both found it hilarious. Ian admitted that he'd come close to flipping out himself on his first night.

Noel continued waffling for an hour after Ian and Kenny headed to Camp Five. He didn't want to miss the action. After investing so many years in Huautla, the thought of being on the surface while someone else cracked the sump was unbearable. But Steve—who'd never been below ground so long—was antsy to return to the surface. And given Steve's relative lack of vertical experience, no one thought he should climb out without a partner. So Noel stifled the inner voices that were calling him back to the sump, and accompanied his friend Steve out of the cave.

They spent most of the rest of the day working their way up the Upper Gorge, frogging up the six long drops of the Bowl Hole series, climbing the twenty-three steps of the Stairway, inching their way up the Jungle Drop, and hiking up two steep cornfields to the village. Though it was long past dark by the time they arrived, they made their way straight to the cookhouse, where they feverishly ripped into family-sized tins of fruit and nuts. After slurping and snorting through anything that wasn't freeze-dried, they giggled their way across the narrow street and collapsed into bed.

Three British cavers joined them for breakfast in the morning. Mark Madden, Paul Whybro, and Rick Stanton had arrived to help ferry gear and tour the cave. Noel gave them instructions from Bill about what gear they should haul in, including Bill's diving masks, which were still at the surface.

After the three Brits headed out for the cave, Noel and Steve were soon driving along the ridge top road to Huautla in search of more food. As the Cave Lord filled the little green valley with a thick blanket of morning fog, Steve finally found the nerve to ask Noel what had freaked him out of his turn to dive the sump three days earlier.

"Well . . ." Noel replied, "this might sound strange, but the thing is, I get premonitions. And that morning I had this premonition that someone was gonna die."

He proceeded to explain his lifelong interest in the paranormal, which blossomed at the age of twelve when a summer camp witch gave him a human skull.

"My first real premonition was in 1992. It was the final day of the rebreather training exercise in Florida. I was sitting in front of my tent—soaking in the sunshine, ya know?—when Rolf Adams came up and asked me if he could borrow my dive gear.

"I had this immediate response," Noel said, leaning closer. "Immediate! Okay? Like if I were to say to you right here, 'Give me a thousand bucks? I need it now! My life depends on it!' You'd have some reaction, right? Maybe you think yes. Maybe no. Whatever. You have some instantaneous thought, some immediate reply. Right?"

Steve started to answer, but Noel wouldn't be interrupted.

"My immediate thought was: 'I'm not gonna lend my equipment to a dead man.'"

Noel returned his gaze to the winding road, and slowed the truck as he overtook a scraggly herd of goats. As they pulled up alongside the herdsman, they recognized him as Bernardo, the old man from the village. Noel and Steve waved enthusiastically and shouted greetings. Bernardo replied by slowly raising a small, stiff hand. Coming from a man dressed in the standard white work clothes of a *campesino*, the gentle gesture seemed like a blessing.

"I'm not gonna lend my equipment to a dead man," Noel repeated, once they'd passed Bernardo and the goats. "I didn't want to deal with my regulators after he drowned on them. That was my immediate thought."

"You said that to Adams?" Steve asked.

"No. I made up some lame excuse about having my gear all set up for a dive I was going to do that afternoon," Noel replied. "Rolf accepted that, and wandered off. He borrowed gear from someone else. And within five minutes he and Jim Smith were down at the Jon boat."

Noel slowed the truck again as they rolled through the dusty village of San Andrés Hidalgo, with its narrow row of stucco storefronts.

"When I heard them fire up the outboard, I realized I needed to say something," Noel said. "I realized I'd had a premonition. I leapt up and ran down to the river. But I couldn't catch them. They were too far down the river. So I just let it go."

Noel paused, and studied Steve's face for some clue as to whether his new friend was buying this.

"A couple hours later I could hear the boat coming back up the run," Noel continued. "I went over to Bill and said, 'Rolf's dead.' Bill just stood there looking at me blankly. He was, like, 'What?' But I knew Rolf was dead. I just knew it. And he was. He got lost in a silt-out, panicked, and damn near took Smith down with him."

The truck groaned as they rounded the final curve and headed up the hill into downtown Huautla. Noel wound up his story.

"Anyway, that's why I skipped my turn. I had a bad feeling, not unlike with Rolf, only it wasn't a specific thing, more an underlying feeling that something was going to happen. It was weird."

They drove along one of the canyon roads leading out of Huautla, and parked near a spectacular waterfall. After a swim, they basked in the sun on the warm boulders below the falls. On the way back, they stopped for a late lunch at a little restaurant on the cliff, overlooking a river.

After they ordered, a hippie-looking Mexican came in. He walked up to the two gringos and asked if they'd be interested in having him tell their fortune. The man produced a deck of Tarot cards from a canvas bag.

Noel shuffled the deck several times, and the stranger from Vera Cruz dealt the cards in the shape of a pyramid, facing Noel. The grimy Tarot cards had holes in them. He flicked them down on the simple wooden table with dirty, worn hands. The sun streamed into the dusty little cantina, lending a warm orange glow to the room. The fortune-teller explained that each card represented an aspect of Noel's life: one card for him, one for his family, and, finally, a card that suggested the fate of his friends . . .

It was the death card.

Though Ian had gone back to the sump intending only to support Kenny's dives, he got caught up in the excitement of the new passage Kenny had discovered, and agreed to make a dive the following morning. They joked through an early breakfast. Ever since the day, weeks before, when Bill had said "The Cavalry has arrived," the duo had sarcastically referred to Bill and his entourage as "the Cavalry," sometimes with mocking bugle noises. After days on a freeze-dried diet, Ian had developed a mild case of diarrhea, and had to hop up to the bio-bag several times before suiting up. More bugle noises. More laughter.

The joking gave way to their graceful, almost tai chi–like kitting up routine on the lower platform. Once Ian was in the water, Kenny prompted one of Ian's bits of shtick. Invoking a traditional exchange among Royal Air Force mechanics and their World War I fighter pilots, Kenny gave the mechanic's line: "Chocks away!"

"Back in time for tea and medals," came Ian's reply. Then he inserted his mouthpiece and slipped into the sump.

Ian carried a second bailout bottle into the water with him, and stashed it near the entrance to the new passage Kenny had located the day before. He then followed Kenny's line to the end, tied in a new reel, and laid another 120 meters of guideline.

The passage continued to head up. It was a true canyon, roughly seven meters wide. The walls were highly defined, solid, and scalloped. The river flowed smoothly through the oval-shaped gallery, and the bottom was filled with coarse sand and gravel. By the time his reel ran out of line, Ian was growing cold. He turned around and made his way back to Camp Five.

After a hot meal, Ian repacked the rebreather while Kenny suited up. Kenny's head still hurt from the night before, and the swelling was so large he had to let out the plastic headband in order to get his helmet on.

He tied a new reel into the end of Ian's line, then followed the right wall and ceiling. After less than forty meters, he saw a large mercurylike surface up ahead. The excitement of spotting the surface sent a shiver down his already shivering spine.

He floated as far forward as he could, then let his knees sink into the muddy sand. Rising to a kneel, he lifted his head and shoulders out of the water. After checking his gas levels and shutting down the rebreather, he removed the mouthpiece and breathed the warm, humid air above. The air tasted good.

"Woo-hoooooo!" he shouted. The sound was still echoing loudly as he switched on his handheld light.

The light barely reached the end of the vaultlike chamber. The hall was roughly 100 meters long and twelve across, with a high arched ceiling. The floor was covered with black water that oozed smoothly in all directions like oil. Two sand atolls lay across the center of the foreboding black pond, like silent islands in a secret sea.

Though he'd explored numerous underwater tunnels, Kenny had never surfaced anywhere so alien and remote. He could see the limestone with his eyes, and knew there were bounds to the chamber; but the echoes rolled about the hard rock room again and again, and his ears tried to convince him that the black sea continued in all directions. He knelt in awe for some time, intensely aware that no one—*no one*—had ever been to this place before. A shiver shook him back to the present, and he mumbled only one word: "Awesome."

He didn't feel ready to take the rebreather off, and it was too heavy for him to stand up with gracefully. So he took off his mask and fins, and crawled along the first sandbar on his hands and knees. The coarse sand was marked with ripples. He waded through the shallow water between the islands, crawled up the second sandbar, and waded into the water beyond.

He could see that there was a way forward underwater, another passage on the other side of the giant airbell much like the one he'd come through. He was less sure whether there was a dry route out. While he was confident of his instincts underwater, he felt Ian had a better sixth sense about finding dry cave. Worried about the battery power in the rebreather, he decided to head back and let Ian take a turn.

As he swam back, Kenny grew excited about telling Ian. They'd cracked the sump together, and he wanted to share the news. Nonetheless, he couldn't resist the chance to mess with Ian's head a bit, so he turned off all his lights as he approached Camp Five, and finished the dive by feeling his way along the dive line in the darkness. He reached the lower platform without Ian noticing, removed his mouthpiece, and let out a howl.

"Yeeeeaahhhhhh!" Kenny shouted.

Ian scrambled down from the upper platform, grinning in surprise. Kenny told him of the giant airbell. They hugged and howled.

"This is what it's all about, partner," Ian said.

After another hot meal, Kenny repacked the rebreather while Ian suited up. He had to hop in and out of the wetsuit a few times, as his case of diarrhea drew him back to the increasingly disgusting bag one last time.

Ian planned to surface in the airbell, and, if possible, remove the rig and explore on foot. If not, he'd start pushing the underwater passage Kenny noted on the far side of the airbell. The time he might spend in the airbell meant his trip could be much longer than the usual sixty to ninety minutes. He urged Kenny not to worry. "Don't call out the Cavalry unless I've been gone for six hours," he said.

"Righty-o, partner," Kenny said. "Chocks away."

"Back in time for tea and medals," Ian replied.

Kenny spent the first couple hours of Ian's dive tidying up the camp kitchen. When he was finished, he fired up the little butane stove and fixed some tea. The tea grew cold, so he fired up the stove and reheated it. A half-hour later he did it again. Like a nervous mother waiting for her son to come home, he reheated Ian's tea at least eight times over the next four hours. And each relighting of the little stove felt more ominous than the last.

At 10:00 P.M.—exactly six hours after Ian left—he refilled Ian's carbide lamp and left it on the lower platform. He took out a yellow-covered caving notebook, and scribbled out a note: "Ian: 10 P.M. I went for the Cavalry! Kenny."

Bill awoke to the familiar clanking of ascenders and cara-biners, a sound that meant someone wearing vertical gear was plodding up the flowstone slope to Camp Three. It was almost midnight.

"Where's Bill?" Kenny called out as he clanked into camp. "Is Bill here?"

"Over here," Bill replied. He and Barbara sat up quickly, figuring Kenny's quick return meant he and Ian had cracked the sump. "Good news?"

"Not exactly," Kenny said, crouching alongside Bill's sleeping bag. He stroked his scraggly red beard by placing the palm of his hand over his nose, and pulling down. He explained that he'd broken through to the airbell, that Ian had gone to check it out, and that after six hours Ian hadn't returned. Kenny wanted to organize a return dive immediately.

The rest of the camp gathered round while Kenny spoke. Jim Brown and Don Broussard arrived first, then the three visiting Brits: Mark Madden, Rick Stanton, and Paul Whybro. They'd arrived at Camp Three earlier that night, and spent the evening introducing themselves to the American team by telling—what else?—Ian Rolland stories.

Jim asked about the rig. He was still worried that the shakedown tests had been too hasty and the dive teams too unfamiliar with the complicated machines. But Kenny discounted the possibility that a diving-related problem would have trapped Ian beyond the sump. First because the rebreather had performed well over the course of ten challenging dives. "And besides," Kenny added, "Ian had a bailout bottle with him. Plus, there's one stashed eighty meters into the sump, and another one about 120 meters in. That's more than enough gas to make it back. Even a catastrophic rig failure would have been manageable."

They discussed the possibility that Ian could have somehow injured himself in dry passageway beyond the sump or perhaps miscalculated and run out of light. But no one considered that likely, especially not the Brits. Ian had proven himself a highly skilled and unusually cautious climber. All agreed the odds he panicked were even less likely.

Which left the question of a diabetes-related problem. Kenny worried that Ian might be in insulin shock beyond the sump. He noted that Ian had suffered from diarrhea on the morning before his dive. And he wondered if, caught up in the thrill of exploration, Ian might have forgotten to eat the two Power Bars stashed in his hip pouch. Don Broussard conceded that insulin shock was a real possibility if Ian hadn't eaten enough, or hadn't been able to retain enough of what he had eaten. But since he'd counseled Ian about this risk, Don felt sure that if Ian had experienced warning signs—such as light-headedness—he would have sat patiently on the far side of the sump and waited for someone to bring him food.

Kenny argued again for an immediate return to the sump. But the group was tired. After a long day ferrying gear down from the 620 Depot, most had slept less than two hours. They weighed the various scenarios, and on the basis of Don's opinion, concluded that if Ian were alive in dry passage, he could survive several more hours. They'd be able to mount a more effective—and safer—rescue effort after a few hours sleep. Bill made the decision final: "I don't want to lose a rescue diver doing this."

Kenny stood up and glared at Bill, who was still sitting on his sleeping bag. Only then did Bill realize Kenny hadn't cracked even so much as a hint of a joke since arriving in Camp Three more than half an hour earlier. The crow's-feet along Kenny's eyes—a side effect of his grin—were gone. Bill had never seen him so angry.

"I'm not comfortable leaving Ian over there," Kenny repeated. "We should go now."

"In a few hours," Bill promised.

Kenny was furious. Don stopped by his sleeping area to reassure him, but it was of little use. Though he'd been up since the previous morning, Kenny didn't sleep. He lay awake in anger, making lists in his head of what gear would be needed.

Bill didn't sleep either. He'd assured the group that Ian was alive and well beyond the sump. But privately, he was less confident. He kept thinking about what Kenny had said about Ian's diarrhea. After learning that he had diabetes in 1993, Ian fought to convince his family, the Royal Air Force, and ultimately Bill that he could continue with the expedition. Out of respect for Ian's drive, Bill had not stood in his way. But as he lay awake in the darkness, he wondered if he should have.

At 5:00 A.M., Bill led Jim Brown, Mark Madden, and Paul Whybro down to the sump. They arrived at Camp Five by seven, and spent the next three hours assembling a second rebreather. Once he'd rigged and tested every system, Bill turned the unit over to Jim for a complete and independent double check.

Kenny and Rick Stanton arrived about the same time. Stanton had left Camp Three early for a solo run up to the 620 Depot where he retrieved Noel's exhaustive medical bag. On Don's advice, they'd assembled a kit for Ian that included carbide, a space blanket, candy bars, and a glucose injection kit.

Camp Five was crowded to capacity with six large men

moving about. Kenny had a hard time finding a place to compose himself for the dive. He finally lay down underneath the hammocks on the upper deck. When he was ready, he climbed down to the lower platform, where Bill and Jim helped kit him up.

Just before Kenny slipped into the water, Jim shouted over the noise of the waterfall: "You'd better be prepared to find a corpse."

Kenny stared blankly, in disbelief. Bill was furious at Jim's lack of tact, especially as Kenny was trying to get psyched for a dive. Bill told Jim to go back to the upper platform, and wait with the Brits. Jim shrugged, and slunk back up the ladder.

Bill sat down on the lower platform and faced Kenny, who'd already slipped into the cold water. He leaned forward and spoke into Kenny's ear: "You okay to do this?"

Kenny nodded, though not convincingly. He slipped into the sump. After a ten-minute pre-breathe test of the new lithium hydroxide canister, and an in-water leak check of the newly assembled rig, he aimed his handheld light at Bill, still watching from the dive platform, and waved it in a slow circle—a diving version of the okay signal—and disappeared.

Kenny swam swiftly through the sump, wasting little time searching about underwater. He had little interest in recovering a body; in spite of Jim's realistic warning, he was still holding out hope for a rescue. His head popped through the looking glass and into the airbell twenty-eight minutes later. He spat out the mouthpiece, pulled himself to his knees, and cried out, "Ian!"

He waited motionless, but heard nothing other than the endless echo of his own voice. He switched off the oxygen, peeled off his helmet, mask, and hood, then cried out again.

"Ian! You here, mate?"

Kenny knelt silently in the sand, and with his ears

exposed this time, listened as intently as he could for any noise, hoping to hear even a distant reply or a feeble scratching. But there was nothing.

He switched on his powerful handheld dive light, and searched for a clue as to which way Ian had gone. It wasn't hard to find. There were footprints leading straight up over the sandbar.

Rather than following directly—which would have required either removing the rebreather or walking through sand while still wearing the heavy rig and backup gear—Kenny waded in the shallow water alongside the sandbar. In this fashion, he followed the footprints up across the first sandbar, back into shallow water, and over the second bar.

The far side of the second sandbar sloped gently down into crystal-clear water. From the surface, he noticed something on the bottom. He pulled his mask back on and swam about fifteen meters across the surface.

There, less than three meters below, Ian lay motionless on the bottom.

Kenny dove straight for him, hoping against all odds that somehow his friend was still alive. But as soon as he grabbed Ian's stiff shoulder, he knew he was dead.

As he floated silently in the still water, Kenny was startled by how relaxed Ian looked. Many drowning victims, as they gasp for air, flail about and rip off their masks. The sand around Ian's body showed no sight of such a struggle. He looked serene, as if he'd simply fallen asleep.

Kenny was overwhelmed by how at ease *he* felt, too. The silt storm of terror—a cloud of fear that had been steadily thickening in his soul during the more than twenty hours since Ian left Camp Five—cleared in a heartbeat.

"There," Kenny later wrote, "in the stillness of a space untouched by humans, with not a sign of struggle or pain, lay Ian, a reel of going line still in his hands, resting peacefully on the edge of beyond."

He dropped down alongside Ian for a closer look. Ian

was lying on his right side, facing the unexplored passage. All but one of his tanks were full. The rig was still delivering oxygen. The buddy light was on and Kenny could see the head-up display glowing in Ian's mask. All the gear was in place except the mouthpiece. He fished around for Ian's main computer display and found what he most wanted to see: the main oxygen sensor values. They were reading a breathable mixture.

So what happened? Because he didn't have a slate on which to record all the evidence that would be necessary to sort out the mystery, Kenny decided not to disturb Ian's body. Instead, he followed Ian's line, looking for clues. It ran along the east wall at shallow depth, into the virgin passage beyond, and then turned back to where Ian rested in open water.

Why'd you turn back? he asked. *You figured it out that this place was just an airbell. You ran a line along the wall, systematically probing for a route deeper into the cave. And then you found it. So why turn back?*

He hovered over Ian's body a moment longer. *You knew something was wrong, didn't you?* Kenny finally asked, gazing down at his silent friend. *Something serious. Something that with all your diving experience, you couldn't solve underwater. What?*

The sense of peace that had overwhelmed him upon finally knowing Ian's fate had passed. Now he was afraid of the rig again, afraid that whatever had happened to Ian could happen to him. He decided to head back before he lost his cool. He waded back over the sandbar again, repositioned his gear, and headed back to Camp Five.

It took all the concentration Kenny could muster to focus on the dive and not on thoughts of Ian as he swam back. He kept himself occupied with the tasks of diving. He rechecked both bailout bottles on the way out, and tested the regulators. He retied a couple of awkward spots in the guideline. And he stopped for two short decompression safety stops on the final ascent to Camp Five. Floating quietly in the dark passageway, with no busywork to occupy his thoughts, his mind drifted.

He remembered something Wes Skiles had asked him back at Ginnie Springs shortly before the team left Florida. Wes was videotaping short interviews with each of the team members, for use as part of the derailed documentary film. Wes asked Kenny if he'd thought about the possibility he might die on this expedition.

"Well, the highways are a dangerous place," Kenny had deadpanned, "and it's a long drive down there."

Wes growled, "That's a cliché, Kenny." Off-camera, Wes was growing frustrated after half an hour of struggling to persuade his wisecracking friend to answer a question—any question—seriously.

Kenny nodded, then said, "Driving with Bill Stone is extremely dangerous."

Hovering in the sump, he wondered if he should have given the question more thought. Ian was the best all-around man on the team. He was the best on rope, and he was among the best divers. If Ian could die out here, Kenny thought, anyone could.

Ian had been taped, too.

"So, um," interviewer Jeffery Haupt struggled to ask Ian, "I mean, that brings up to me, an obvious question, I mean, do you realize that you might *die* on this trip?"

Ian knew where Haupt was headed long before he got there. It showed on his face. When Haupt finally uttered the word *die*, Ian's eyes darted up and to his right as he formulated his response. He drew in a breath and started to answer, but stopped short, still thinking. He paused, drew in a bit more breath, and finally replied.

"Everybody, I think, has contemplated the possibility of death, for either themselves or somebody else." He swallowed and looked up again. "It's a subject Bill and I discussed at length at his house when I first arrived in Washington."

Ian returned his blue-eyed gaze to Haupt. "In high-altitude Himalayan climbing, which is probably the most dangerous sport in the world, I think something like one in ten die on expeditions to 8,000 meters. I forget the statistics, but it's like a constant trend through history. However, in caving and cave diving, the statistics are nowhere near that bad. But it's always a danger.

"And the discussion was: First . . . what should happen to the expedition. We both felt that if something happened to . . . to one of us, the expedition should continue, because it's something we all believe in.

"The second one was, if somebody died, what happens to the body? And again we all agreed that if it was safe to retrieve the body, we would. But if it was going to be a danger to our fellow team members, then it shouldn't be done, because there's no point in putting them all at risk." Ian paused briefly to wet his dry lips. "No point, just to bring out a dead body."

He completed this statement in level tones. He looked straight at Haupt.

Haupt plowed ahead: "So tell me about your personal justification for risking your life."

Ian was annoyed, and his faced showed it. He stifled a smirk, and let out a quick breath of exasperation.

"My personal justification for risking my life is perhaps a dramatic way of putting it," Ian gently countered. "I don't consider what I'm doing really that dangerous, 'cause I think about any risk I take and I've calculated . . . I mean, there's risk in everything you do, in life, and there's no exception; not even in the cave-diving world. But as long as you stick to the cardinal rules, you cut down on the possibility of an accident happening."

Paul Whybro saw the first flicker. He pointed it out to the others huddled vigilantly around a solitary carbide lamp at Camp Five. They watched as the flicker grew into an eerie blue-green glow gliding back through the sump.

Bill looked at his watch. Only ninety minutes had passed since Kenny left. After subtracting at least half an hour for the dive in and another half-hour for the dive out, that meant Kenny had spent less than a half-hour looking for Ian. "This isn't good," he said, to no one in particular.

Kenny swam up to the lower deck and started handing Jim his gear. Bill couldn't hear what they were saying over the roar of the waterfall. But he saw the unmistakable words, "Ian" and "drowned," form on Kenny's lips.

His heart plunged. "Not Ian," he blurted out. "Not Ian." He'd been steeling himself for this all day, but it still left him dizzy. His mind reeled. *How could it have gone down like this? And now what are we going to do about it?*

He snapped out of it and helped Kenny up onto the lower platform, crouching alongside him. He put his hand on Kenny's shoulder. Kenny grabbed it and held it tightly. The two of them stayed like that for a moment, without saying a word.

After Kenny got out of his gear and delivered the heartbreaking details, the Brits headed back to Camp Three. Bill, Kenny, and Jim stayed the night at Camp Five. Emotionally exhausted, they climbed into their hammocks early. Jim fell asleep. Kenny and Bill talked for what seemed hours. Both were numb. They reminisced about Ian, and spoke of the pain that lay in store for his wife, Erica, and their three children. And they began weighing the task ahead of them: recovering Ian's body and getting it out of the cave. For while Ian may have been comfortable remaining there forever, Bill knew from grim experience that the Mexican authorities would demand a body.

It was obvious to Bill that Kenny, who was still deep in shock, wasn't up to the job. With Noel and Steve on the surface, the job would fall to Bill, and Bill alone, with no one to come after him if he had a problem. The thought of all that had to be done intimidated him.

Before putting out the light, Bill and Kenny locked hands, and swore to each other that they'd leave the sump alive.

Bill lay awake for the second night in a row, drowning in waves of emotion. The cave walls were still trembling from the pounding water. *Camp Five*, he thought. *It may as well be called Camp Fear.* He swung in his hammock, engulfed by the thundering darkness. And privately, he mourned one more casualty. *After ten years of preparation, the expedition is effectively over. Failed. What will I do with my life?* After an hour of this, he fell asleep.

He awoke after what seemed like a few minutes, but was actually several hours. Unable to get back to sleep with the locomotive noise of the waterfall echoing through his head, he fired a carbide lamp and began preparing for the grim task that awaited him. Kenny, who was in the next hammock, woke immediately.

"Are you ready?" he asked.

"Yes," Bill said, though privately he wasn't so sure. "Let's do it."

Jim slept for another half-hour, waking only after Kenny shone a light in his face and said, "Get up!"

After breakfast, Kenny led Bill through the graceful kitting up procedure he and Ian had perfected. He set Bill's helmet up with new lights. He prepared a set of underwater slates with blanks that prompted Bill to gather all the essential data they'd need. And Kenny packed Bill a kit of essentials: a strap to haul Ian out, extra carabiners to suspend him, and spare straps to tie up his arms and legs, in the event rigor mortis had already set in.

"Use as much of Ian's gear as possible," Kenny advised. "Save your own gas for use if you have to abort."

Up until the moment he slipped into the sump, Bill had

forgotten how cold the water was. A chill shot up his body as he plunged into the sixty-four-degree water. Over the course of his long absence, he'd gradually, steadily, and intentionally numbed his mind to this place and its ever present danger. It all came flooding back as the cold, clear water surged into his wetsuit. It felt like fear.

He did a five-minute pre-breathe to check the rig, and was ready to go. Kenny grabbed his shoulder, and hoarsely choked out a line they both knew well: "Back in time for tea and medals, right mate?"

Bill nodded solemnly, and slipped into the San Agustín sump for the first time in thirteen years.

After weeks of living on rope, the rig felt cumbersome, and a bit intimidating. But five minutes into the dive, the old habits all came back. He soon relaxed. He could see about one body length through the blue-white calcite haze. He passed the heavy red guideline he'd laid in 1981, and continued on into new territory. He was impressed with the route pioneered by Ian and Kenny. Half an hour on, he saw the sandy floor rise, then spotted the mercury reflection that marked the surface of the airbell.

He knelt in the sand. He switched off the mouthpiece, and breathed deeply. It felt weird to be there. It should have felt great. But under the circumstances, it didn't.

Bill crawled around the right side of the airbell, where Kenny said the water was a bit deeper, and floated across the surface for another fifteen meters before spotting Ian. Like Kenny, he was struck by how serene Ian looked.

For the next two hours, Bill took an inventory of Ian's condition, and the status of his rig. With a soft pencil in his right hand, he recorded everything on a series of white plastic divers' slates. All of Ian's gas supplies—primary, secondary, and bailout—were full, save the primary diluent, which was still pumping a few tiny bubbles now and then out through Ian's mouthpiece when Bill arrived. Clearly,

Ian hadn't run out of gas. His oxygen partial pressure readings were in the normal range, so he hadn't suffered hypoxia.

When his survey was complete, Bill moved Ian to the nearby sandbar. Kenny had expected that the job might require two trips: one to survey the situation, and another to actually transport Ian's body. But Bill wanted to get the job over with. At the sandbar, he ditched Ian's weights, fins, the spent pink heliox bottle, and his trademark green Wellington boots. He then dragged Ian around both sandbars and into the passage leading back to Camp Five. The weight of two full rebreathers plus Ian was almost more than Bill could manage. His heart was pumping on overdrive, and he was sweating heavily.

Once he got Ian back into deeper water, Bill began experimenting with the bag of weights he'd brought along, attaching small amounts of lead to Ian's harness and feet until he was able to achieve something close to neutral buoyancy. Using three webbing slings and two carabiners, he secured Ian for transport back through what he'd begun to think of as Sump One.

After rechecking his own rebreather settings, he positioned Ian face up beneath his chest in the water. He deflated his own buoyancy compensator and, by adding or subtracting gas from Ian's, was able to control the buoyancy for both of them.

He took it slowly as he worked his way back through the sump. He kept one eye on the dive line and the other on their buoyancy. It was a tedious process.

Midway through the sump, he overcompensated for Ian's weight, adding too much gas. The two men rose rapidly—locked face-to-face in a mortal embrace—until the sump's ceiling abruptly halted them. The loud "CRUNCH" of rock against the fiberglass case of the rebreather was jolting. The rugged rig survived the collision, however, and another one just a few moments later.

Towing Ian through the sump was hard work. Bill stopped on one of the rocks in the large breakdown room to rest, and again at the first pothole. All together, it took forty minutes to make it through. Upon reaching Camp Five, he slid Ian under the dive deck and clipped him off to a gear line. Then he raised his head and yelled up to Kenny.

"Did you get the data?" Kenny asked as he scurried down from the upper deck.

"I got more than that," Bill replied, pointing to Ian's body, which floated just below the surface.

Kenny helped Bill out of the rig and fixed him a cup of hot lemonade. While they were resting, the British cavers Rick Stanton and Paul Whybro returned. They informed Bill and Kenny that Barbara, Don Broussard, and Mark Madden had left for the surface with plans to contact the British consulate and Mexican authorities.

The five of them inventoried all of Ian's gear, and reviewed each and every system aboard the rebreather in detail. Despite being underwater for nearly two days, the carbon dioxide absorbent canister was dry and the system fired up. Only one thing was odd: A switch that shut off the flow of oxygen was thrown.

"What does that mean?" Stanton asked.

"It means," Bill replied slowly, "that Ian intentionally cut off the flow from the automatic oxygen control system. He had a habit of doing that. He would throw the valve as soon as he hit the surface, to conserve every ounce of precious oxygen. But, for some reason, he never turned it back on."

"Does that mean he ran out of oxygen?" Whybro asked.

"No," Kenny said, "the oxygen level was fine when I got there. I could have picked up that mouthpiece and breathed from it."

As the discussion of the details wore on, Whybro concluded, "I guess there's no way of knowing what happened."

"Ah, not quite," Bill said. "One of the onboard computers records all the system parameters—you know, like a black box on an airplane. But we'll have to send it back to the States to be analyzed."

"Well, then we best get on with it," Stanton said. "What do you want us to do?"

"We need a way to move Ian out of here. But we don't have a litter," Bill said.

"Not a problem, mate, we do it every day," Stanton replied. "We're firemen, remember?" They packaged Ian for transport while Bill and Kenny rounded up Ian's personal effects, including the damp teddy bear. Jim headed out with the personal gear. The others carried Ian up through the Lower Gorge.

Stanton and Whybro went ahead on most of the pitches and rigged a two-to-one block-and-tackle system, while Bill and Kenny remained below to push Ian along. They all had a particularly hard time getting though the Washing Machine, and the Fissure Drop above. The crawls were the worst, because they had no leverage. It was all they could do to move Ian forward a meter at a time. It was grim business. As they twisted and pushed Ian's body through the winding crawlways, they became covered in the bloody fluid leaking out of their friend. Even when they could avoid the fluid, there was no avoiding the smell.

They finally reached the Sala Grande de la Sierra Mazateca about midnight. Noel and Steve had just arrived from the surface, having heard the news. Exhausted, Bill and Kenny hit the sack.

Refreshed after a couple days topside, Noel was the first one up the next morning. Fearing that the pop of a full-sized Petzl ceiling burner would wake the others, he tiptoed about to the dim glow of a small electric flashlight. Jim showed no such concern. By ten A.M., he'd disturbed everyone.

Noel confronted him: "Have you done anything here but eat and sleep and get in the way?"

"I twisted my knee," Jim tried to explain, unaware of what he'd done to offend Noel.

Noel shook his head and walked away. "Always some damn complaint," he muttered as he fired up a stove and started fixing breakfast.

Besides being the team doctor, Noel was also an instructor and the chief physician with the National Cave Rescue Commission. He'd assisted with a half-dozen body recoveries, and perhaps twice that many successful rescues over the years. As he served breakfast to Bill and the others, he wryly noted that they were completing what was surely the most remote body recovery ever conducted, anywhere. Kenny shot Noel a cold stare; he was still in no mood to joke about Ian. Noel changed the subject, but resolved quietly that he would take another swipe at gallows humor before the day was through. If his experience with the rescue commission had taught him anything, it was that the grim work of hauling a body out of a cave was a spiritual endeavor. It was a cathartic process that, for the men at this camp circle, would serve as memorial and wake rolled into one.

After a late breakfast, Noel and Steve hiked down to the dive depot and repackaged Ian. They wrapped him tightly in Bill's blue plastic camp tarp before lashing him into the orange rescue litter Noel had packed in the day before. The tarp cut the smell somewhat. Noel tied long hand lines to the sides of the litter.

Bill tied two of the litter's hand lines to his harness, and dragged it up through the Metro like a sled. The smooth plastic Sked litter slid easily over the slippery flowstone. Kenny and Noel swam Ian across the lake, and then all eight of them—Bill, Noel, Steve, and Kenny, along with the British crew of Mark Madden, Rick Stanton, Alex Wade, and Paul Whybro—began hauling him up the ropes of the Upper Gorge.

When they reached the Space Drop, Bill and Noel cannibalized the existing rigging to create a pulley system. The crew then took turns hauling from the top. Noel was taking a turn at the haul when the pungent litter finally rose within a whiff of the top. He sensed the chance he'd been waiting all day for, and he seized it.

"I can smell progress," Noel declared loudly.

This time, his weary teammates shook their heads and laughed. By 11:00 P.M., they had the stretcher up to the traverse line at the top of the drop. They then took turns rappelling back down the Space Drop and back to their beds at Camp Three.

Bill woke in pain the next morning. His arms and legs were numb from the exertion. His biceps ached. He had seven blisters on his left hand alone. He'd bought a large box of rubberized gloves before leaving Maryland, but the box had been misplaced somewhere along the way, and everyone was suffering. He rolled over and the muscle pain grew worse. *I don't remember it hurting this much. Maybe it's because I'm forty-one.* He rolled on his back and lifted his legs, raising his mummy-bag-covered feet directly above him. A large plastic bottle of pills dropped onto his stomach. Ibuprofen. He'd stashed it there for mornings just like this one. He twisted off the safety lid and gagged down three of the reddish caplets straight from the bottle. Kenny walked by as he flicked the bottle back down into the nether regions of his sleeping bag.

"Vitamin I," Kenny deadpanned. "Breakfast of champions."

Though there wasn't much passion behind the quip, it was nonetheless the first wisecrack Bill had heard Kenny attempt since Ian's death. He scooted out of his bag and followed him to the cook circle.

"I'm burned out, man," Kenny confided, once the stove was fired. "I haven't slept through the night since . . . since it happened. You . . . you've got plenty of hands down here. Those Brits are strong cavers. I'll . . . I'll just slow everybody down. So if it's all right, I'm going to bail for the surface today. Head out."

"That's fine," Bill said, pouring him a cup of the hot lemonade. "You've done more than your share." He knew how close Ian and Kenny had been, and he could see that Kenny was physically and emotionally exhausted. "You want somebody to head out with you?"

Bill sat in one of the stone chairs, but Kenny declined to sit with him.

"Nah. I want to be alone," Kenny replied. "Thanks." And with that, he left the cook circle, packed up his personal gear, and left Camp Three before most of the others had risen.

After breakfast, the rest of the crew slogged back up through the Upper Gorge, ascended the Space Drop, and continued ferrying Ian toward the surface. The sheer drops of the Bowl Hole Series each presented unique rigging challenges, as the team ripped apart the existing ropes and rebelays to jury-rig a series of pulley systems. The massive One-Ten posed the toughest challenge of all. Rick Stanton wanted to rig it one way; Noel Sloan another. Paul Whybro proposed a third alternative. Each stubbornly insisted his was the best. Tempers were growing short when Bill cut them off.

"Well, I'm sure Ian would have had something to say on this subject," he said.

After a few seconds of silence, everyone laughed.

"Oh, yeah man, he could be such a pain in the ass about rigging," Noel blurted. "Every time he came down through here, he tightened up the loops on the rebelays. He'd make 'em so small I couldn't get my leg up in 'em. Like this," Noel finished, reaching his arms around his raised leg to illustrate his point.

"That was Ian?" Bill asked. "I thought that was you and Steve."

"Hell no—" Noel began.

"They're supposed to be short like that," Stanton interrupted, grinning widely so that everyone knew he was ribbing. "You Yanks are far too sloppy about such things." That brought another good laugh.

By three in the morning they'd reached the Stairway to Hell. Everyone was burned out. After agreeing as a group to head to the surface for the night, Noel looked down at the orange stretcher and said, "We've got a bottleneck here. Some of us are going to end up waiting a long time while the others climb out."

"Not if you're the first one to reach the rope," Alex shot back with a grin. The others turned to look at him, and slowly took his meaning. "Ready?" he shouted. "One, two, three . . ." Before he'd finished counting, everyone dashed up the streamway in a pack. The next drop was only thirty meters away, but the amount of splashing and yelling that went on along the way made it seem a lot further. Gear clanked and shoulders collided. Alex leapt at the rope, and managed to snap on an ascender. He got three meters up, then stopped and asked Noel, "What, mate, are you waitin' on me?"

And the movable wake marched on.

CHAPTER SEVEN _____

It was drizzling as Bill dragged himself up the Jungle Drop. Cool water trickled down the vines that dangled into the sinkhole, and soothed his aching muscles as he hoisted himself out of the cleft. After sixteen days below ground, the incessant chatter of the jungle and the musky smells of the vegetation overwhelmed his senses. He crested the dirt balcony, stowed his muddy yellow Jumars, crawled through the rocky entrance tunnel, and stepped out into the adjacent field. Corn and black beans had sprouted in his absence. He felt conflicted as he sat down on a jagged boulder to wait for Noel: Life was much more comfortable here on the surface, but also far more complicated.

The dusty trail up to the village had turned to mud, and Bill's rubber-soled Bata boots provided no traction. He slipped and fell repeatedly. Picking himself up for the umpteenth time, he joked to Noel that he was beginning to understand what it was like to be a greased pig. Noel replied with an off-color joke about greased pigs. By the time they reached the cookhouse, they were both covered with mud.

Barbara heard them coming, and walked down from the bunkhouse. She fixed them a stew of military-style MREs (meals ready to eat) served over spaghetti, and tried not to wince as Noel slurped down two large bowls. As they ate, she filled them in about events on the surface. The Mexican authorities had been notified about Ian's death, as had the British embassy. Bill's longtime friend Sergio Zambrano was en route from Mexico City to help navigate the local bureaucracy, and a team of British cavers was on the way down from an expedition at Cuetzalan to assist in the evacuation. Rob Parker had broken the news to Ian's wife, Erica, and had made arrangements to return to Scotland with his body.

"There's something else you need to know, G," Barbara said. "Parker is here. And he's really, really upset. He thinks the rig killed Ian."

Bill looked up from his food to glare at her. She held up her hand to preempt his rebuttal.

"I know, I know," she replied. "I'm telling you what Parker thinks. He thinks the rig killed Ian. He believes that. And he's got most of the rest of the camp believing that, too."

Bill gulped down a mouthful of food and began to voice a question.

Barbara answered before he could get a word out: "Farr, for sure. Maybe Porter, hard to tell."

Bill took the news hard. He flopped his elbows onto the table, dropped his head into his hands, and said nothing. He hadn't slept a full night in almost a week. He had bags under his eyes, and bruises all over. On top of all that, the emotional defeat was crushing. Barbara gave him a hug, then washed the dishes.

Wes Skiles ambled into the cookhouse a few minutes later. He'd arrived earlier that evening, along with fellow Moles Tom Morris and Paul Smith. They'd driven straight through from Florida, three large men crammed into the cab of Tom's small Jeep; upon their bleary-eyed arrival in San Agustín Zaragoza, they were greeted with the news that

Ian was dead. Wes stood in the cookhouse doorway, took one look at Bill, and said: "You're trashed, partner. Go to bed." But another truck rumbled into the quiet village before Bill could excuse himself. It was the Brits from Cuetzalan. They'd been alerted by Parker that a recovery operation was on and that help was needed. Five of them—Dick Ballantine, Pete Hall, John Palmer, John Thorpe, and Pete Ward—had just returned from a thirty-hour caving trip, packed their bags, and hopped on the morning bus heading out to Puebla. It took them a full day to reach Huautla. Some were still in their jump suits. By midnight, the entire replacement crew was crowded around the perimeter of the small cookhouse. They took turns introducing themselves. Most added a few words about their friendships with Ian. Slouched at one end of the table, Bill reviewed all that had happened, and the group divvied up what still needed to be done. The crowd of newcomers listened somberly, with grim faces and folded arms.

While they were talking, the villager who'd rented them his home for use as a cookhouse staggered in. Lázaro was a moonshine runner. He loaded up his burros with two five-gallon containers of *aquardiente* at stills secreted in the jungle, and delivered the clear cane liquor to buyers throughout the region. On this particular night, he'd obviously tasted his supply. He stumbled into his own home and seemed surprised to find it packed full of gringos, as though he'd forgotten that his wife, Olivia, had rented the building to the cavers for the season. Like most Mazatec of his generation, Lázaro spoke only a few words of Spanish—and no English at all—but that didn't stop him from joining the circle. He stood alongside the Cheve and Cuetzalan cavers, folded his arms the way they did, and nodded knowingly whenever they did. When the room fell silent for a long moment, he stepped forward and delivered a brief but passionate speech in slurred Mazatec. No one understood him. But no one interrupted him, either.

When he'd finished, the cavers nodded respectfully, and resumed their discussion.

Bill and Noel slept late the next day. The Cuetzalan contingent rose early, and went into the cave to retrieve Ian. They were joined by Joe Ivy and Harry Burgess, a couple of strapping Texans from the Cheve expedition, as well as Karlin Meyers, who'd just returned from Cerro Rabón. Barbara rolled into the cookhouse shortly after they left. There she found Bill Farr, a caver from California who'd dropped off the dive team before the expedition began. Farr was regaling the visiting cavers with speculation about how Ian's rebreather had failed. She was irked by the way he portrayed himself as an insider even though he'd done less to assist the expedition than some of the visiting Cheve cavers, and she was furious at the way he attributed Ian's death to the rig.

"Excuse me," she interrupted, "but what in the hell are you talking about?" She threw down the pot she'd been scrubbing. "There's no evidence that problems with the rig caused Ian's death. There's *no* evidence for that."

"Well, but, we've had problems ever since Florida," Farr rebutted. "And Noel told me he almost went hypoxic on his last dive—"

"Who's *we*, kemo sabe? I don't recall seeing your smiling face at Ginnie Springs. The rigs were working fine. But you don't know that, because you weren't there, were you? As for Noel, he didn't run out of oxygen. He had hypercarbia because he forgot to change the damn lithium hydroxide canister because Noel— well, because he's Noel. That was an operator error, not a problem with the rig," she explained. "And Noel completed that dive without incident, didn't he? That's because all he had to do was switch to the offboard bailout system. If that had somehow failed—which it didn't—he could have grabbed one of the bailout bottles stashed in the sump. So there were lots of bailouts. Ian knew all about the bailouts. But you wouldn't know about those, would you? Because you didn't dive, did you?"

Farr looked stunned. He'd never seen Barbara so forceful. She looked a bit surprised herself.

"The fact is, we don't know what happened," she continued. "We'll review the data that Bill and Kenny collected, and we'll adjust our procedures, if necessary, so that every dive will be a safe dive—"

"There aren't going to be any more dives," Farr interrupted. "This expedition is over."

"You don't know that," Barbara shot back. "That's not your decision to make. We'll have a team meeting tomorrow or the next day. And the team—that means the people who actually do the work around here—the team will decide whether or not to continue with the expedition."

Farr shook his head condescendingly, and then attempted to pull rank. After mentioning a few of the expeditions he'd led and accidents he'd investigated, he asserted that unlike mountain climbing—where deaths were often caused by severe weather—most caving deaths resulted from equipment failure or misuse. "They terminated the Cheve expedition after Chris Yeager died. This project needs to be stopped, too."

Barbara glared back at him but didn't feel like arguing anymore. She made some excuse, and left the cookhouse. Finding Bill and Noel still asleep up at the bunkhouse, she tiptoed in to retrieve her journal, then stepped outside to find a quiet spot to sit in the sun and write. Mark Madden strolled by a few minutes later. He pointed his thumb back toward the cookhouse, where Farr was still carrying on, and observed, "Quite an immediately dislikable fellow, that one." Barbara laughed, and agreed.

Parker passed by a while later and told Barbara that he was soon to head into Huautla to confer with the local officials. She emphasized to him how important it was to not tell the authorities that the expedition was over.

"In reality, it might be," he replied.

She could see he was deeply troubled over Ian's death. "It's not Bill Farr's, Rob Parker's, or my decision as to the fate of the expedition," she said. "That's a decision the whole team has to make."

Sergio Zambrano arrived from Mexico City a few hours later. A caver as well as a diver, Zambrano had helped plan the expedition. With Zambrano's fluent translation, Parker learned that the Mexican officials wanted a police inspector to be present when the body was removed from the cave.

Barbara accompanied them into Huautla. The bank and post office were closed in observance of Good Friday, an event that had completely escaped the cavers' notice. She bought vegetables at the market while Parker lobbied Zambrano to halt the expedition. On the way back to San Agustín, they passed slowly by a detailed reenactment of the Last Supper, complete with elaborately costumed disciples and a Mazatec Jesus. After that, no one felt like talking.

The police inspectors showed up on Saturday morning, and watched from the surface as the team hauled Ian's body up the Jungle Drop. A surreal scene awaited their arrival. A dozen men and nearly a hundred women from the village stood in a loose half-circle around the cave's rocky entrance; each woman clutched a lone white calla lily. Scattered about the craggy limestone boulders that guarded the chasm's foyer, smoldering fistfuls of copal incense filled the air with a musky herbal scent.

The cavers set Ian down in the soft black soil at the edge of the cornfield and stood blinking in disbelief. As their eyes adjusted to the bright midday sun, their hearts soaked in the meaning of the somber greeting party. A Mazatec ended the soulful standoff. He nodded respectfully to Bill, placed a flower alongside one of the burning smudges, stepped forward to the orange plastic stretcher, and seized one of its built-in handles. The rest of the men—cavers and Mazatec alike—then scurried to the remaining holds. Together they began the hike up to the village. Within a few paces, the cavers discovered that the Mazatec had yet another gift for them: stairs. Using hoes and machetes, the villagers had carved an elaborate stairway into the steep hillside. The wide earthen risers led all the way from the cave entrance to the village, and tiny piles of incense smoked along the trail.

Noel was humbled by the hard work that had gone into building the kilometer-long stairway, and overwhelmed by the embracing sense of community. *These people, who have so little to give, have given so much,* he thought. *Most are merely nodding acquaintances. Some have been vocal opponents of our activities in their caves. Yet now they treat us like family. Would we do as much for them?* His thoughts were jerked back to the task at hand when the three Mazatec helping to carry the stretcher abruptly let go. The redistributed weight yanked painfully at his shoulder. He twisted his neck around as far as it would go to see what had happened.

One of the Mazatec had spied a snake alongside the path. Without hesitation, he let go of Ian and unsheathed his machete. He lifted the long blade high above his head, and then slashed violently downward, slicing the snake in two. Five others leapt to join the execution. A half-dozen gleaming blades whirled through the air. They assaulted the defenseless creature savagely, as though it were an arm of the Cave Lord himself, stretching up through the loose top-soil. And they continued to puree the snake long after it stopped twitching, as though driving *Chi Con Gui-Jao* back into the underworld. When there was nothing left to strike, one of them grabbed a bundle of burning incense and waved it ceremoniously over the bloody patch of dirt. The others holstered their machetes and returned to the stretcher.

As they crossed the upper cornfield and trudged up into the village, Bill could see that a large crowd had gathered in the road: dozens of women and men, grandparents and tod-dlers. Most were dressed in their Sunday best. All awaited

Ian's arrival. Seeing them, it finally dawned on Bill that the villagers hadn't come down to the cave entrance merely to lend a hand; rather, Ian had become the centerpiece of a full-fledged Mazatec Catholic funeral procession. And when they turned right at the main road, he realized that they weren't bound for the gear shed, where he'd planned on repacking Ian's body for the long drive to Oaxaca City, but to the white stucco church at the center of the village.

The pallbearers carried Ian across the village square, a small saddle of nearly flat land between two plunging *dolinas,* and through the church's hand-carved wooden doors. They laid him down on the cool turquoise blue tile of the center aisle, at the center of the cross-shaped sanctuary. Bowls of incense were placed alongside, and wisps of smoke wound their way up the dark red columns that supported the church's vaulted sky-blue ceiling. The rest of the team, along with the rest of the village, crowded in behind. They filled the small wooden pews as well as the side aisles, and squeezed into the standing room at the back. Another fifty or so villagers leaned against the outside of the church, and listened through the windows.

There was no priest in the village, so Jaime Escudero—son of Bernardo and father to Virgilio—led the assembled parish through a short memorial. Reading from a large book, Jaime offered blessings and sprinkled the muddy stretcher with Holy Water. The Mazatec regarded themselves as Catholics; they brought each of their children to be baptized, and stood in line to receive Holy Communion whenever the priest visited their village. They were a practical people, who survived Aztec, Mixtec, and Spanish invasions by abiding the alleged conquerors, and by selectively assimilating the new cultures. Ancient Earth Lords like El Rabón had long ago assumed thinly veiled identities alongside the Roman pantheon of saints and virgins, whom the Mazatec understood not as historical figures but as independent deities. By the end of the twentieth century, the Mazatec had grown quite fond of the

Catholic cast of lesser lords. This was primarily because, with the notable exception of Satan, the gods of the missionaries were far more benevolent than the capricious Earth Lords handed down by their ancestors.

But while officially Catholic, the practical Mazatec also hedged their spiritual bets by attending ancient rites, such as the annual public offerings to the mountain lord El Rabón, and by visiting local healers, called *curanderos*, who employed psychedelic mushrooms as diagnostic tools, then administered sacred herbs as cures. And on the day before Easter, no one in the village of San Agustín Zaragoza needed any more proof of the vengeance of *Chi Con Gui-Jao* than the sight of Ian's body on the blue tile floor. They had seen the lively Welshman with their own eyes, recognized him as a good-hearted man respected by his friends. If *Chi Con Gui-Jao* could take a man like Señor Rolland, they figured, he could take anyone.

Jaime concluded the short service by leading the villagers through several call-and-respond prayers in Mazatec. They were deep-throated incantations—almost like Gregorian chants—so penetrating they traveled halfway across the village and woke Barbara, who was in her bunk stricken with stomach flu. Unable to understand the words, the cavers in the church were left alone with their thoughts.

Steve stood at the back of the small sanctuary. He was numb with fear. And a bitter truth was gnawing within him: Ian's death mocked his own chivalrous notions about the thrill of adventure.

Kenny sat with his head in his hands, three rows from the altar. He was angry with Ian, though he didn't know why. Was he angry that he hadn't been more careful? Was he angry that maybe his friend hadn't monitored his blood sugar well enough? Was he simply angry that Ian had left? Or was he angry with himself? For talking Ian into going back to Camp Five, for luring his friend back to the sump that killed him.

Rob Parker sat next to Kenny. He'd known Ian for years. He was angry at Bill for having jeopardized Ian's life to conduct what Rob regarded as a research and development project for Bill's private high-tech firm. And he was furious at himself for having introduced Ian to Bill all those years ago at Wookey Hole.

Noel sat in the next row up, on the aisle, next to Ian. Noel was humbled by the villagers' spirit, and the power of their faith left him feeling as though he'd lost his own spiritual power somewhere along the way. He was angry with himself for not voicing his premonitions more forcibly. Hadn't he promised himself, after his premonition about Rolf, that if he ever felt like that again, he'd take action?

And Bill sat next to Noel, as filled with self-doubt as he'd ever been in his life. Was there something wrong with the rebreather that he hadn't been able to identify? Was the rig just too complicated, loading the operator with too many tasks? Should he have bumped Ian from the expedition because of his diabetes? Why Ian? And how many more friends could he bear to lose?

After the service, the crowd followed Ian's body out of the church and back through the village center. The stretcher was carried into the gear room, where Jim Brown had cleared off a plywood worktable. Bill thanked the village for their assistance and compassion, and asked for some privacy. Few understood his Spanish, so Jaime translated into Mazatec. After leaving their flowers and incense at a makeshift altar outside the fieldstone building, the villagers drifted off to their homes.

Bill stepped inside to find the two police officers indicating to Sergio Zambrano that an autopsy had to be performed because no one had witnessed the death. They had a small fishing tackle box with them, which contained an X-Acto knife, a test tube, a couple of syringes, some cotton swabs, and a pair of red rubber gloves. They handed the gray plastic box to Noel, because he was the team doctor, and instructed him to begin.

Noel's large blue eyes bulged beyond normal. "Ah . . . you want . . . what?" he asked.

"He's dead serious," Zambrano explained. He pointed to a piece of paper the police inspector was holding. "He said he must witness the operation, and then you must sign that form."

Noel gasped. "Ian . . ." he pleaded, "he's been dead for a week, man. Sealed up inside that wetsuit. Decaying in his own juices. Even if we had a forensic pathologist here—and a real medical center—I doubt we'd learn much if anything about his oxygen or insulin levels at the time of death. And under these circumstances . . ." He turned to Bill and added, "Maaaan, I thought stuff this absurd only happened in the movies."

Zambrano took up Noel's case with the police inspector. An advertising executive by trade, Zambrano embellished Noel's plea. He flattered the police officer for his preparedness, then appealed to his sense of compassion by suggesting that without a proper autopsy, Ian's life insurance company might never pay, and that Ian's wife and children would starve. Zambrano said he could tell the inspector was a compassionate man, having chosen to become a public servant and so forth. After several minutes of this, the inspector agreed to merely inspect the body, and leave the question of an autopsy to his superiors in Oaxaca. Zambrano then explained the deal to Noel, who sighed in relief.

When the inspector was ready, Noel provided a pair of surgical scissors and cut away the first tarp, then the second, then the wetsuit, then the two layers of polypropylene pile underwear. A small flood of body fluids ran down the table and poured onto the floor, prompting the police officers to step back suddenly. And a horrendous stench filled the room, causing Bill to throw open the door and the wooden shutters that covered the open windows. Everyone gagged and held their nose, except for Noel, who patiently displayed each side of the body to the inspector, then rewrapped Ian and gently placed him into a simple wooden coffin.

The stench penetrated the gear room's simple wooden ceiling, and quickly overpowered the upstairs bunkroom. While Zambrano had been pleading with the police inspector, Rob Parker was upstairs packing. The church service had lit his fuse, and he walked out even angrier than he'd walked in. He ranted in incomplete sentences as he threw his gear into a large duffel bag. He was ready to leave San Agustín for good.

"The bloody thing is, Ian himself said 'Somebody's going to die on this machine,'" he muttered.

"Why?" asked Joe Ivy, one of the Cheve crew who'd helped carry Ian out of the cave.

"Because it's too damn complicated," Parker said. "You're too task-loaded. The thing is so complicated that when you get underwater and fire it up, your IQ is cut in half." Parker whirled around and all but yelled in Ivy's face. "You know who said that? Ian said that. 'Your IQ is cut in half.' That's what he said . . ."

The smell chased them both out of the bunkhouse. Outside they found Ian's coffin loaded into an ambulance bound for Oaxaca. The fog rolled in and it had begun to rain. Zambrano and the officials were already in the vehicle. Parker threw his gear in and left without saying goodbye to anyone.

Bill stood in the rain and watched the ambulance bounce down the lane. When it was completely out of sight, he stepped back into the gear shed and closed the door. He moved what was left of the putrid wetsuit outside, and washed down the worktable. The smell was still pretty overwhelming, but he didn't care. He figured it was the one place in the village he'd be left alone. He was wrong.

The door creaked open a few minutes later, and Wes walked in with a couple of bottles of beer in one hand. He'd dragged thirty bodies out of underwater caves. He'd been Sheck Exley's apprentice at the time Sheck grew weary of body recovery work, so Sheck taught Wes how to do it, and handed over the thankless job to a fellow North Florida boy. He'd been in San Agustín for only twenty-four hours, but in that short time had already served as camp counselor to Noel, a friend with whom he served on the National Cave Rescue Commission, and to Kenny, a former student and part of the Mole family. So Wes had a pretty good idea how Bill felt, and he took it upon himself to do what he believed Bill would have done for him had the tables been turned.

Bill thanked Wes for the beer, took a sip, and set it down on the same plywood table where Ian had lain only an hour before. He'd opened up one of the rebreathers, and was dissecting it under the dingy glow of a bare light bulb hanging from the dark ceiling. Wes stacked a couple of plastic tote boxes to make a seat for himself, and settled in to wait.

"I don't understand," Bill finally said, several minutes after Wes arrived. "I don't understand why this happened. I . . . I . . . don't understand how this happened or why it happened." Wes could see the pain in his face as he looked up and added, "And I don't understand what I could have done about it."

Wes let Bill stammer on for a while amid the stench. Then he went to work on his grief-stricken friend.

"You don't go—you don't attempt to go—into the deepest system in the Western Hemisphere, and get to the bottom and put on advanced experimental diving equipment, and go exploring, without there being risk of death," Wes said. "I don't think there's a soul on the planet who'd say, 'No, Bill, there's no chance of anybody getting hurt.' Nobody thinks that. So when it does happen, is it really a surprise?"

He paused to draw a sip of his beer. Bill continued picking at the rebreather.

"No. It's not a surprise," Wes continued. "It's no surprise that something went wrong. And it's no surprise that, when something goes wrong in a situation like this, people die. What's surprising, as far as I'm concerned, is that more things don't go wrong."

Bill held up a printed circuit card he'd extracted from the rig. He gazed at it for a moment, and then looked up at Wes. "But I still don't know what went wrong. How can I let anyone else go down there until I know for certain what happened to Ian?"

"It was Ian's choice to face those risks," Wes replied. "He fully assumed the risks for both the condition that he had, and, ya know, the risk of diving the rebreather."

Bill set down the circuit card, which contained the rig's core computer memory. "I don't know," he muttered. "I just don't know."

"Ya gotta . . ." Wes began, his native Florida drawl creeping back as he scrambled for words, "ya gotta keep going." He paused, debating for a moment whether to say the next thing. "Ya know, we interviewed Ian about this back at my place. He said that if anything were to go wrong, he wouldn't want his death to stop the expedition. He was very clear about that."

"Yeah?" Bill asked.

"Yah," Wes confirmed.

Bill took another sip, half-smiled at Wes, and asked, "You didn't happen to bring that tape with you, did ya?" Wes guffawed and shook his head. Bill continued, " 'Cause even if you sold me, I don't know if we can sell the others."

Wes smiled back. "Well, aah got me an idea about that."

Wes hadn't driven all the way to Huautla just to buck up an old friend. He was there on assignment for *National Geographic* magazine. The editors told him to bring back a dozen underground images as good as Nick Nichols's legendary Lechuguilla photos. It was a plum gig. But it was over if the expedition ended before he could start shooting. So he reminded Bill of the subterranean showboating that tends to happen whenever a big-time magazine photographer drops in on an expedition. And then he suggested that he and Bill ask the rest of the team to stick around just long enough to make a few pictures for *National Geographic.* "My bet," he concluded, "is that after they get back in the cave and have some fun, they'll remember why they came. And then they'll want to keep going."

Bill grinned at Wes, and held up his beer for a toast.

Steve rose early the next morning and started making breakfast for the group: French toast and Hungarian bacon. Bill joined him, and served everyone at the long plywood table Ian had built in the cookhouse. For the first time in a week, the team seemed in good spirits. It was one of the few times they'd eaten together since leaving the States. After everyone had gobbled up several servings, Bill stood up at the end of the table. He leaned far forward and put his large, blistered hands on the back of a small wooden chair; then, rethinking the body language such a posture communicated, he stood up straight, bumping his head against the rafters of the low tin roof.

"We're arguably at the low point on this project," he began. "We've all gone through a hellacious amount of stress. We all—and probably myself more than anybody— started off on this thing with some grandiose ideas about what was possible. And we all received a rather humbling slap on the wrist here about just how difficult the job is, about the risks that are involved.

"The things that happened early on, they were kind of like warning shots, in my mind. One was that we had people from Cheve use some shoddy rigging that had been there for fifteen years. A hanger broke, and a guy fell and broke a rib. The second was the rebelays, and the incident with Angel. The third incident involved Barbara; she got her hair stuck in her rack." Bill swallowed. "And the final thing is the issue with Ian."

He reviewed what he'd found when he recovered Ian's body, in an attempt to set the record straight. "The rig was working properly," he stressed. "We went through a complete diagnosis of the whole thing. There was nothing wrong with it." He discussed the possibility that Ian might have made an error in judgment—or even have blacked out—as a result of his diabetes. And he explained that like the so-called black box on an airplane, the rebreather's central computer contained details about the rig's operation that could be retrieved once they returned to the States.

"The history of exploration is rife with failed expeditions," Bill went on. "Even the ones that were successful, three or four hundred years ago, on ships, would often lose 30 percent of their crew in the course of a voyage. The difference between us and them is that our society now places so much importance on life. A lot of us have put a great deal of our life's effort into making it possible to do something—not simply a number on a depth chart—but something inspirational to the human race. This is the frontier in 1994. There is no place more remote on this world. There just is not. When you're talking about remoteness, this is it. You all felt it. Everyone who was at that sump felt it. That feeling meant you were there."

He surveyed their faces, making eye contact with each and every one before continuing.

"Really what we must decide at this point is: Can we all stay together as a team?" He paused again. "I know each one of you personally. I could tell you anecdotes about everyone at this table. I feel like you're my family. We've just gone through a family tragedy. The question is: Do we now pick up and try to pull a rabbit out of the hat in the next two months? Or, do we fall apart? I vote for the former."

Bill concluded his St. Crispin's Day speech with the suggestion that the team take a break. "Take the time you need. Leave this place if you wish. Go take a hike somewhere. Do whatever you feel is necessary, to relax your minds and get away from what we've been doing as our daily job for the last month." And then he turned the floor over to Wes.

Wes's native Florida drawl was as different from Bill's measured tenor as a human voice could be, but their tune was in perfect harmony:

"Ya'll have reached a pinnacle of great achievement. Even though it has a tragic footnote, it is a great achievement," Wes began. "Whether you go further into the cave or not, recognize right now that ya'll have made one of the greatest exploration accomplishments of all time. This is a mission that is successful. You took those rebreathers *beyond* beyond. You proved it could be done.

"My belief," Wes continued, "and I think it's shared by ya'll, is that exploration without documentation is like scoopin' booty without a survey. It is for naught. Ya'll are without the kind of documentation that will allow this project to stand for many years in a photographic sense. If you want to pay off the debt of sponsorship—and if you want to give something back to Ian—then photographic documentation is of the utmost importance." He shuffled his stance for his conclusion, as he proved that being a *National Geographic* photographer is as much about making things happen as it is about making pictures. "But I can't even begin to take these photographs without a team effort. I'm going to need people who'll be the makers of the photographs, and I'm going to need people to be *in* the photographs. If we can stay together as a team, you'll be rewarded, all of you will be rewarded."

He stepped back.

"Comments?" Bill invited.

Noel went first. "I agree with Wes in two big areas. Without documentation we have nothing to show for the effort. And number two, being involved at the level I was in gaining sponsorship, we've got to have something to give them. I think the big demoralizing factor through so much of this was the lack of manpower. I'm in favor of continuing to expend the equipment we have down there already for exploration. Beyond that, requiring any more gear to be hauled into the cave, I think that would be very tough . . . But that's a decision to be made in the future."

Steve went next. "Well, I'm in agreement with what's already been said. I believe we ought to get the documentation. I was not in favor of continued exploration. I think there's a possibility I'd continue exploration, but I'm not decided on that right now." And he added, "I'd be in favor of taking a short break here."

Kenny was less surefooted. "I'm in favor of, uh . . . personally, I can see myself supporting the still photos and getting done what we have to get done . . . not screw the sponsors and what-not."

His quick wit lost in a fog of mourning, Kenny stumbled onward. "A lot of it, for me, is not bailing out on each other. A lot of times I just get a feeling that I want to get the hell out of here. You know, since Ian's . . . uh . . . what happened to Ian . . . I mean . . . I mean we were, like, I was feeling that it was hard enough when we had everyone. We were still pushing hard and it was tough. And we've lost a very productive . . ."

Noel leapt to finish the sentence for him: "One of the most productive team members."

"Yeah," Kenny said, nodding, "team member. Right now the way I'm feeling is, I'm willing to do what I think the team needs to do: the photos and the documentation." He looked up at Bill. "I'm undecided about pushing the sump further."

Noel cut in again, "I don't think that decision has to be made now."

"I know that," Kenny said. "But I'm telling you . . . I feel in my head that after we finish the photos . . . I'm not sure . . ."

Unable to put words to his own feelings, he concluded by fulfilling a promise he'd made to Parker. "And . . . this is

Rob Parker talking now . . . what he asked me to get across: He felt, out of respect to Ian, that at this point the exploration should be stopped. I'm . . . I don't necessarily agree that's our reason for not pushing it, or for pushing it."

Bill could see at once that while Parker wanted the expedition halted, the rest of the divers were merely looking for a gracious way to quit. And he realized that *his* task was to help them find an equally gracious way to stay on.

Barbara was the last of the core team to speak. After agreeing with the photo plan, she moved on to the lingering central question. "Other than taking a break—which I think is a real good idea—is anything gained by Rob's notion that out of respect for Ian, we should stop exploration? That just doesn't make any sense. That isn't respect for Ian. It was Ian's goal to crack that sump, and to tie into the resurgence. I think we should keep that as our goal. We may not be able to complete that goal, but I don't think stopping is the answer. I don't think it does anything for Ian, at all."

Bill saw that she'd given him an opportunity, and he seized it.

"I agree with Barbara. Ian would be appalled if we quit at this moment. There wasn't a single fiber in his body that was not driven to explore. The man was the essence of an explorer. I've met a lot of people. That man had it. To give up in Ian's name? He would be shocked."

The team agreed to take a week off, to help Wes make pictures for another week or so, and then to reconvene. The meeting ended about noon. As Bill hiked up the sunny hillside toward his truck, he tallied his remaining dive team: Steve was scared of the rig, Kenny was grieving, and Jim had checked out mentally. That left him and Noel as the only divers with experience exploring underwater caves; and Barbara, who was willing to dive once a line had been laid. Then there was Wes. The Main Mole. He and Tom Morris were perhaps the only two divers on the planet who could walk off the street and pick up where Ian and Kenny had left off.

As Bill watched them walk down the dirt road together, he realized that if he could persuade the Moles to take up exploration after they'd made their pictures, he'd have a second dive team again. Bill knew better than to twist Wes's arm. Wes was as bullheaded as they come. Besides, he figured, he didn't have to tempt Wes; the sump itself would do a fine job of that. What he had to do was lure Tom, and let him work on Wes. So when Bill ran into Tom while readying to drive into Huautla that afternoon, he subtly started recruiting.

"It's just like Florida," he said. "You cook through there. I was through that sucker in twenty minutes. And it's not that deep. Seventy-eight feet, max."

"You mentioned there was sand up there?" Tom asked.

"Yeah, you come up in a huge sand pile."

"So you were in rock at the start of the sump, then a big sand pile at the end?"

"At the downstream side of the sump," Bill confirmed. "And it's not dirty sand. It's clean washed gravel. So I know we're near moving water."

Tom agreed. "That's what you'd expect. In Florida, wherever we find sand dunes, we generally find a big bell up over the top. Yeah. Sounds real promising."

Tom wandered off. Bill started his truck. He looked at Barbara and said: "Now all we have to do is keep these guys from freaking out between here and the sump." Then they drove into Huautla to make phone calls.

Most of the rest of the team celebrated the first afternoon of their break by heading down to the Río Iglesia for a party. Just south of San Agustín, the Río Iglesia was one of several rivers that swirl around the ridge top village, each flowing in a different direction. From the nearby village of San Andrés across the valley, the water flowed southeast before falling into the Sótano de San Agustín. Beyond San

Andrés, the water flowed west. And south of the village, the Río Iglesia flowed northeast, drifting down the fertile little valley before plunging into the Sótano del Río Iglesia, a 535-meter-deep cave first explored in 1967. Somewhere deep underground, this crazy quilt of surface streams all converged into what expedition leader John Fish dubbed the Main Drain in 1968. But thus far, no one had figured out the plumbing.

In the dry springtime, the Río Iglesia is just a small stream. There is a natural dam created by some large boulders, which forms a pool upstream that's just deep enough to stand up in. The group hiked down the steep valley to the pool, and waded, bathed, and then sunned themselves on the boulders, and on a hump of grass along the riverbank.

Though in great physical shape after their daily workouts of the past couple months, the group all had pasty-white skin like mushrooms. They relished the time in the sun, and all sunburned quickly. Noel spiked a liter of Crystal Light and passed it around. Someone brought a boom box and played tapes of Mexican songs. Tom Morris passed around cheap cigars, though he himself preferred chewing on them to smoking them, to preserve his lungs for diving.

Bill was the main topic of conversation. As the liquor flowed, most of those gathered told "crazy Bill" stories, each a bit wilder than the last. It fell to Noel to try and explain how Bill could be so admirable—and so grating—at the same time.

"Bill's biggest failing is that he is absolutely committed to the project," Noel said. "Absolutely committed. That can wear on folks. And it's very difficult for him to understand that other people might not be that way."

Steve shifted the target to Barbara. He complained about her relative lack of dive experience, and worried she wasn't ready to push this sump. "Let's be honest," he concluded. "She wouldn't even be here if she weren't Bill's girlfriend."

"So what?" Tom asked. "She's like some dream Amazon. Some tall, blond, geologist caver, who dives his rebreathers. Good for friggin' Bill."

The sun was dipping farther down toward the horizon when Barbara and Bill finally arrived at the river to wash their clothes after having driven in to Huautla to make phone calls. Shortly thereafter the party broke up and all but one of the first group hiked up the steep Río Iglesia sinkhole. The remaining partier was one of the visitors, an Irishman named Tony who'd become too drunk to walk back up the steep hillside. Barb carried both packs up the side of the *dolina* while Bill hoisted Tony over his shoulder and carried him back to the village.

The next morning, most of the crew left town. The Brits went back to Cuetzalan. Don Broussard caught a bus to Texas. And Noel and Steve caught a bus to a beach town called Zipolite, on the southern coast. Scattered along a two-mile-long crescent-shaped beach, Zipolite became a hippie hangout in the 1960s, and remained a place filled with people going far out of their way to be hip. There were thatch-roofed shelters along the shore that rented hammocks for $5 a day. The beach faced south, so Noel and Steve were able to see both the sunset and the sunrise without stirring from their hammocks. They laughed about how much more comfortable these hammocks were than the ones at Camp Five, and soon the game was to lie about in the morning and debate who'd break and get out of bed first, if at all. They spent days snorkeling, eating fresh fish, and sun-ripening their bodies. Nights at discos, drinking *cervezas* and mingling with a lot of pierced and tattooed folks. One night an exotic-looking Mexican woman with long black hair was screaming and running topless around the hut where they rented their hammocks. She ran into the open-walled hut, held up a stick with a snake wrapped around it, and started chanting over Steve. Then she started whipping him with the snake.

CHAPTER EIGHT _____

B ill and Barbara had the base camp more or less to themselves with Noel and Steve at the beach, and Kenny off fooling around with his old friends Wes and Tom.

Barbara rose early the next morning and hiked into Huautla to shop. She'd done quite a bit of sewing as a teenager, and though she rarely found time to indulge in needlework anymore, she enjoyed examining all the elaborate embroidery at the local market. She chatted with the women there, and bought a dress and serving cloths.

Bill spent most of the morning alone at the big table in the little cookhouse. He snacked on canned fruit—a luxury after so many freeze-dried meals—and played the guitar. Noodling around on guitar was the closest thing he had to a hobby, and one of the few things he did that wasn't part of some larger goal. He didn't play whole songs, but instead picked out five or six bars of a classical composition, then strummed a few riffs of a pop tune, then jumped to something else. He found it meditative.

Between noshing and noodling, he began drawing up a list of gear he'd need if—just a "what if" exercise, he told himself—if he were to head back down and attempt a push on the sump while the others were away. He penciled "mask and dive gear" in his Bob & Bob waterproof notebook, then strummed an Alice Cooper riff. He wrote "new computer module," swallowed a big spoonful of peaches, then picked a few bars of some medieval tune. He wrote "dive reel," then lost his train of thought.

With the guitar still on his lap, he leaned back against the cookhouse's sheet metal wall and gazed out the open doorway. Ian had been clutching a dive reel when he died. Its aluminum handle lay just inches from his fingers when Bill found him. Ian had started into the second sump, and made two tie-offs before mysteriously turning back. When Bill arrived, the thin white line led from the reel's large red plastic drum and curved loosely off into the going chamber. Remembering all this in the cookhouse, it suddenly felt as though Ian had been speaking to him. The hand, the reel, the line; it all seemed to say, *This way, mate! This way!*

Bill slipped the notebook into the pocket of his dirty white painter's pants, hung up the guitar, and strolled up to the gear shed. There he located another Dive Rite Expedition Reel, identical to the one Ian had been using. It was empty, so he dug out a spool of new parachute cord and began winding it on the reel. As he slowly turned the plastic handle, his fate reeled into view. There was unfinished business down there at the sump. He'd waited thirteen years to cross through that abyss. Ian had pointed the way. All that remained was for him to complete the job.

He finished loading the reel, and tied if off. It was clear to him now. Not only was this his last chance to crack the San Agustín sump; cracking the sump was most likely his *only* chance at bringing the expedition back together. "Hey guys," Bill said quietly, imagining the speech he'd give were he able to crack the second sump. "I've been over there. Guess what? No more sumps! It's wide-open borehole! Easy booty! It goes."

He then pulled down one of the spare rebreathers, and

began to disassemble it. While he was working he noticed that Bernardo, the old man of the village, and his grandson Virgilio were sitting together on a hillside across the little valley, watching him. Bernardo's shock of white hair reminded him of Jim Bowden, and Bill lost himself in another remembrance. The white-haired Bowden and the diminutive Sheck Exley had huddled together on the hillside above Jackson Blue Springs while Bill's team put the rebreathers through their paces during the 1993 training exercise. What Bill hadn't known at the time was that Bowden and Exley were preparing an assault on the 1,000-foot mark at a place called Zacaton. While Bill and his crew had been carrying Ian out of the cave, Bowden and Exley had been staging their gear. They hung two dive lines, about ten meters apart. Each line was marked in twenty-five-foot increments, so they would know how deep they were even if their gauges imploded from the pressure. And on each line they hung more than a dozen large bottles of breathing gas. Their dive plans were fairly simple: drop straight down for twelve minutes, tag the 1,000-foot mark, then spend the next twelve hours slowly ascending through an elaborate series of mixed-gas decompression stops.

As he tore apart the rebreather, Bill speculated about the elaborate gas staging that Bowden and Exley were surely engaged in at their secret hole. At 1,000 feet below the surface, an average scuba tank—those ubiquitous eighty-cubic-foot aluminum cylinders that recreational divers routinely breathe from for forty-five minutes or more—would last for a minute or two at most. The rebreather, Bill chuckled to himself, would still provide breathable gas for at least six hours, regardless of depth. He retrieved the core module, packaged it carefully in a dry box, and set the box alongside the reel. To the pile he added some backup dive lights and 400 meters of seven-millimeter climbing rope. He intended to use this to rig a strong line through the sump to the first airbell. Unlike the parachute cord, the seven-millimeter line could be pulled on underwater without fear of breaking. He'd done something similar during the 1984 Peña Colorada expedition and had found that a diver could halve his transit time through a sump by pulling himself along the heavier line.

Barb returned shortly, and Bill shared his plan to push the sump. She'd assumed he'd do so sooner or later, and readily agreed to support his dive. They spent the rest of the evening and most of the next morning packing, and entered the cave the following afternoon. But by the time they reached the bottom of the Jungle Drop, Bill was beginning to have second thoughts. They both were suffering from mild stomach cramps.

"You want to go on?" he asked. "We could take another gonk day, wait until our stomachs are stronger."

"No," she replied. "No, let's go down today."

"I'm serious," he pressed. "It's okay if you want to abort. We'll ditch our packs here, go back to the house, maybe try again tomorrow."

"Well, I'm just not having fun," she replied. "Caving used to be, well, you know . . . fun?"

He looked confused. It had been a long time since he'd thought of this as fun, or even as caving.

"Let's do it," she said. "Let's take our time. Let's make this trip fun, for a change."

"Okay," he said. "Let's have a good time. You set the pace. I'll follow. No hurry." They took their time and reached Camp Three in a little more than six hours.

While Bill and Barbara worked their way back into the cave, Wes and Kenny drove into Huautla. They planned to have lunch, make a few phone calls, then return to San Agustín in time for Kenny to lead Wes on a short acclimatization day trip into the upper reaches of the cave.

Wes was his usual upbeat self on the way into town, and tried to buck up Kenny's spirits by reminding him how fortunate it was that he and the other Moles had arrived when they did. "Maybe we got here just at the right time," Wes suggested. "We're like fresh blood to the expedition. This thing is going to have a whole new life to it. You'll see."

By the time Bill and Barbara decided to "just have fun," Wes was talking to his wife, Terri, on the phone at the register of the Bellas Rosas restaurant. He told her about Ian. She gave him even worse news.

"Oohhhh, Wes," she told him. "Sheck . . . he's dead."

"What?" Wes asked.

"Sheck's *dead*," she repeated.

"Naaah. No way. You sure?"

"Yeah," she said. "He died this morning. They haven't been able to get his body out. He's still down there."

Wes collapsed. His body slumped to the cement floor below the pay phone. The proprietor eyed him suspiciously. Wes was barely able to hang on to the black plastic receiver.

"R . . . really? You're sure?"

She explained how a mutual friend had called looking for Wes because they needed help with the body recovery, and what few other details she knew. Wes was in shock. He managed to hang up the phone when they were done, but remained hunched on the floor. The hotel proprietor looked at the crumpled American with concern, as Wes simply mumbled over and over again, "What happened?"

Wes would have loved Zacaton that morning, had he been there. A steady wind whipped patches of clouds over the round rim of the sinkhole, some seventy feet above the water level. Bowden and Exley swam across the surface, did their pre-dive checks, then took a few minutes to meditate. They visualized the dive and slowed their rate of breathing down to four or five deep breaths per minute, half the rate of a normal person at rest. When they were ready, they nodded to each other and slipped into the warm, clear water.

Bowden descended at the rate of about 100 feet per minute. The line markers shot past quickly as he slipped down past a ledge at 250 feet and into the darkness below. After three minutes, he switched from breathing air to his travel mix; after six, to his bottom gas. At 800 feet, Bowden slowed his descent in order to watch himself closely for muscle twitching or buglike vision problems that might suggest an onset of HPNS. When he glanced at his pressure gauge, he began to suspect that either he'd miscalculated his gas supply or he'd been breathing too heavily. By the time he reached 900 feet, he knew he didn't have enough gas to make it down to 1,000.

He hit the inflator valve on his buoyancy control vest. Nothing happened; he continued to descend. He hit it again, hard. At that depth, it took a lot of gas to generate enough buoyancy to reverse his downward momentum. He felt the urge to kick his legs and propel himself upward, but fought the instinct. At those depths, any vigorous exertion would overload his bloodstream with carbon dioxide, which could increase his susceptibility to nitrogen narcosis, oxygen toxicity, and decompression sickness.

"Ooooh," he thought, releasing the syllable slowly, refusing even to think in sudden movement. "Oooh . . . God . . . do hurry. Please hurry."

When he finally felt his body begin rising, he watched the 925-foot mark slip through his gloved hand, poised loosely about the line. Slowly at first, then faster, he rose, venting the expanding gas from his vest as he ascended. When he reached his first stage bottle, its regulator failed. Instead of letting out sips of the precious gas, it shot out a freely flowing stream of bubbles. He accommodated the problem by turning the knurled plastic knob off after every breath, and by making his way expeditiously to the next stage bottle. His ascent continued without another incident. His dive partner, Ann Kristovich, came down to check on him after about forty-five minutes, as planned, and found him doing fine.

After cresting the ledge at 250 feet, Bowden was back within daylight's reach. There he saw for the first time that Exley's stage bottles were still hanging on his line. He figured Sheck had made it all the way down to 1,000 feet and was simply a step or two behind on the decompression ladder. But as Bowden climbed through his 210- and 180-foot stops without seeing Exley—or the telltale clouds of bubbles that would signify his presence below—he grew worried. At each subsequent stop, Bowden scanned the water for some sign of Sheck; at each stop, all he saw were unused stage bottles, their regulators dangling like dead octopi. His girlfriend, Karen Hoehle, dove down to check on him at 110 feet. She brought a slate with her. On it she'd written: "We lost Sheck."

Jim was dumbfounded. For the next eight hours, as he decompressed his way slowly toward the surface, his disbelief grew. Exley had written the book on safe cave diving, a safety manual entitled *Basic Cave Diving: A Blueprint for Survival*. The blue-paged booklet was divided into ten chapters, each of which stressed a fundamental: lights, the guideline, avoiding silt, air supply planning, and so forth. And each chapter opened with a cautionary tale about a fatal accident at which he'd recovered the missing diver's body. Having safely returned from some 2,000 cave dives, Sheck Exley had become nothing less than the Earth Lord of the Floridan Aquifer. *How could such a god be dead?*

As long shadows cast by the high canyon walls plunged Zacaton into near darkness, Bowden recalled the title of the third chapter of Sheck's unassuming little book—"Too Deep"—in which Exley advised cave divers never to voyage below the 130-foot depth limit observed by recreational divers. The chapter concluded, "The foolhardy who insist on diving to deeper depths anyway should contact experienced cave divers first for guidance." Bowden had done just that: He'd contacted Sheck. So had Bill Stone, Wes Skiles, and just about every other expeditionary caver who took up diving. As he clung to his line in the swirling gloom, Jim Bowden felt suddenly and terrifyingly alone.

Still slumped beneath the pay phone, Wes felt abandoned, too. During the years he'd served as Sheck's apprentice, he'd attended three of the body recoveries described in Sheck's book. Florida cave-diving fatalities had declined steadily in the years since *Blueprint* was published. So for Wes, the Moles, and a host of fellow divers, the very premise that it was possible to venture into underwater caves and come back alive was based in large part on Exley's experience. Now Sheck was gone, and so was the core of Wes's belief. He dragged himself up, paid the proprietor for the use of the phone, and stepped out into Huautla's dusty main street. He broke the news to Kenny with three short words: "God is dead."

Back in San Agustín, they suited up and headed down to the sinkhole. Kenny led the way through the entrance crawl and onto the lip atop the Jungle Drop. Wes threaded his rappel rack, and started to shuffle his feet backward toward the lip, then stopped. He stared down the gaping abyss, plunging more than a football field directly beneath his feet. Then looked up at Kenny. There were tears in his eyes.

"I ain't goin'," Wes stammered. "I'm done." Then he began to sob.

Kenny gently pulled Wes from the edge, and led him to a place he could sit.

"I'm . . . I'm through," Wes said, no longer trying to choke back the tears. "I don't want to have anything more to do with this." He unthreaded his rack, stowed his vertical gear, and left. He was halfway across the lower cornfield, on his way back to the village, by the time Kenny caught up with him.

"I . . . I'm sorry, man. I've just had enough, ya know?" Wes told Kenny on the hike back up to the village. "I want to go home."

Kenny nodded.

"No, that's not right. I don't want to *go* home. I want to *be* home. Ya know what I mean?" Wes said. "I'm gonna see about catching a plane out of Oaxaca."

Wes marched back up to the bunkhouse where he'd been staying and packed up all his stuff. While he was packing, Jaime Escudero stopped by. Jaime had heard grumbling about the rats, which were attracted by the corn stowed in the rafters. Unaware of Wes's troubles, Jaime dropped by to tell Wes, in simple Spanish, that he'd arranged for another house nearby, without rats.

Wes didn't want to hear about it. But he didn't want to offend Jaime either, since the Escudero family was the team's host in the village. So he went with Jaime to see the other house. It was nice. There was a large open space, and two worktables where Wes could spread out his photo gear.

"You may stay here if you like," Jaime said.

Wes felt touched by the gesture. And he suddenly realized he was very, very tired. So he resigned himself to staying one more night, and went to sleep.

Bill and Barbara made their way down to Camp Five early the next morning. Bill was kitted up and in the water by 9:30 A.M. But before he reached the first bailout bottle, he heard a gurgling noise. On the rebreather, such a noise is a potential sign of trouble. So he returned to the dive base within twenty-five minutes of leaving. He and Barbara spent the next hour checking the rig for leaks. The hoses all checked fine; the breathing circuit and buoyancy control vest, too. None of the regulators were leaking either. Whatever it was, it didn't seem to be a serious subsystem failure. Bill struck off once again into the sump. But just a little ways past where he'd turned back the first time—past the oxygen stage bottle but not as far as the breakdown chamber—he heard the same "glug-glug-glug" sound he'd heard before.

Damn, he thought. *No choice but to turn back.*

This time he and Barbara hoisted the rig to the larger, upper platform and tore it completely apart. Finding nothing wrong, Bill concluded the problem had to be the buoyancy control bladder. He took the bladder off the rebreather, filled it with air, and held it underwater. Sure enough, a small stream of bubbles emerged. He tested the bladders from the other rig, and found those were leaking, too.

"No wonder those guys were having problems with their buoyancy," Barbara noted.

Bill figured he'd have to head all the way back to the surface to fetch another buoyancy control setup.

"Wait a minute," Barbara said. "There might be a patch kit around here somewhere." Within a few minutes, she found one. The kit contained some urethane patching material and a tube of Aquaseal, but no tube of chemical accelerator to dry the glue. Barb cut little circular patches about the size of a quarter, and together they applied them. Bill then held the patched material over one of the cookstoves, hoping to speed up the curing process. They continued for almost three hours. When the bladder finally seemed dry, Bill filled it with air and thrust it into the sump.

"No bubbles!" he cheered. "I think we're back in business."

Barbara repacked the rebreather while Bill suited up again. He was back in the water by mid-afternoon.

"If I make it through, I'm going to get out and hike around a bit," he reminded her before departing. "So don't get worried for at least five or six hours, maybe a little longer. Okay?"

She smiled. "You just scoop some booty, G," she said. "I'll take care of things over here."

After he left, she cleaned up the camp and snuggled into one of the hammocks. She picked up a book of Oscar Wilde stories someone had left behind, and tried to read, but was bored by Wilde's chatty characters who spoke in endless similes. So she napped.

Neeld Messler showed up about an hour later. A tough young caver, Messler had come to San Agustín to assist Wes's photo team. After hearing the bad news about both Ian and Sheck, he persuaded Jim Brown to lead a hauling trip into the cave. While the others rested at Camp Three, Messler pushed on to Camp Five. Barbara was surprised to learn that'd he'd come all the way down by himself, and was shocked at the news he'd come to deliver.

Sheck? Dead? She couldn't believe it, and quibbled with his version of the facts.

"He died near Ciudad Mante," he explained.

"No he didn't," she said. "He wasn't at Mante. He's got a new cave somewhere. He and Bowden were working it."

Messler persisted: "I heard he died at the Mante."

She started to correct him again, then bit her tongue. Maybe the rest of his information was wrong, too, she thought. Maybe it was Bowden, not Exley; or two other cavers. They fixed some hot food. As the two of them sat waiting for Bill, she wondered what it must have been like waiting for Sheck to return.

She would have found it much like her own nervous vigil. Sheck's longtime partner, Mary Ellen Eckhoff, had reluctantly agreed to support his bid for the 1,000-foot record. Though she held her own share of diving records—in caves and open water—Sheck had asked her to hang back at Zacaton. So she watched the two descend from atop the cliff above the sinkhole, then walked around to the staging area and kitted up to go check on his decompression. By the time she got back to the sinkhole, it was obvious that something was wrong: There was only one set of bubbles breaking the sinkhole's blue-green surface, and those were clustered around Bowden's line.

Mary Ellen dove to the ledge 250 feet down, hoping to

find that Sheck's bubbles were simply being somehow trapped or diverted by the large underwater shelf. She lay there on the ledge for a moment, peering into the darkness below, but saw nothing.

Ann Kristovich spotted Mary Ellen on her way back up. Ann, who was the team doctor, was making a decompression stop after having checked on Bowden. She was surprised to see Mary Ellen swimming erratically, jerking about in the water. Ann reached out and grabbed Mary Ellen's arm, to prevent her from ascending any further. Mary Ellen was convulsing, her body almost collapsing with every breath. Ann checked Mary Ellen's dive computer, and figured she'd blown right past at least one decompression stop, but was still puzzled by the convulsions. Then she looked at Mary Ellen's face mask. It was flooded with tears.

Ann held on to Mary Ellen's arm, and helped her clear her face mask. It flooded again quickly. Mary Ellen continued to sob. Ann hung on tightly. The two remained in grief's painful embrace until it was safe to proceed upward through the afternoon gloom. Mary Ellen was still distraught when she finally reached the surface some time later. "Sheck always comes back," she said, sobbing. "Always. He always comes back. Why didn't he come back . . . ?"

Messler waited with Barbara for a couple hours, then left for Camp Three. Barbara tried to nap again, but couldn't. Waiting for Bill hadn't been that bad before she found out about Sheck. But now she couldn't relax.

The sketchy facts kept trickling through her head like water through the cave: *Sheck is dead. If Sheck can die in a cave, then anyone can die in a cave. Bill is in the cave. He's in the same place Ian died. Bill's going to die* . . . She tried again and again to stop obsessing, but it was like trying to stop the waterfall.

She couldn't eat, sleep, or read. She refused to look at her watch, because that seemed too close to marking the min-

Skiles: overleaf, left, above, and below right

team spent the early weeks of the expedition rigging a "nylon
way" of rope to the sump. Noel Sloan (overleaf) rappels down
Jungle Drop, while Barbara am Ende and Bill Stone descend
One-Ten (at left) - a plunging 110-meter abyss at the heart of
Fools' Day Extension - with their packs tethered below them for
roved balance. After one team member died beyond the sump,
survivors were surprised to find the entire village of San Agustín
agoza waiting for them at the cave entrance. The villagers led
cavers on a procession to their tiny Catholic church (at right)
re villager Jaime Escudero led a service in Mazatec (above).

Wes Skiles (above, below, and opposite)

Bill Stone (below right)

In mid-April, an early tropical storm deluged the surface and severely flooded the underground river passages 800 meters below. Steve Porter, Noel Sloan, and Kenny Broad (above) were among those trapped below. The dangerous high water remained days, and blocked all attempts to exit the ca such as those by Noel Sloan (at left) and Kenny Broad (below). The trapped photo te waited out the flood at Camp Three (facing page), pitched in a vast underground void nearly 60 meters above the river level. Cam Three's cook circle was known as Stonehenge.

Camp Five (facing page) was a set of four small fabric platforms suspended above the San Agustín sump; the divers slept in hammocks slung between the narrow canyon's hard limestone walls. Barbara am Ende (left) pushes slowly through the sump, following a thin white dive line through the bluish silt. Camp Six was a spartan bivouac where she and Bill Stone (below) used their wetsuits for sleeping pads and subsisted on nothing but pulverized freeze-dried food for a week. From that remote base, the couple explored nearly three kilometers of new passageways in the heart of the Huautla Plateau and discovered the dramatic Río Falls (overleaf).

Stone (above and opposite)

Bill Stone (above and overleaf)

utes until it would be her turn to call out the Cavalry. So she
just lay in her hammock, alone in the thundering darkness,
and wondered: *Will Bill come back this time?*

After two false starts, Bill took it easy on this third venture into the sump. He swam slowly and listened intently
for leaks. For while bubbles were signs of life for an open-
circuit diver, they signaled trouble on a rebreather. He
checked the oxygen and heliox stage bottles—their rubber
handles had already grown slick from silt—and every 100
feet he clipped numbered white plastic marker arrows onto
the dive line. He dropped down the breakdown shaft,
finned through the hole at seventy-eight feet, and reached
what he'd come to think of as the Rolland Airbell within
thirty minutes.

He waded slowly around the right-hand side of the airbell, breathing heavily as he sloshed along with 140 pounds
of rig on his back. His breathing echoed repeatedly across
the silent airbell, until it sounded ominous, as if some other
mouth-breathing creature were in the chamber with him.

Atop the final sandbar he spied Ian's Wellingtons,
standing right where he'd left them, like green and tan
guard dogs, waiting to lead him through the second sump.
They taunted him. After decades underground, Bill had
developed a strong opinion about every piece of gear his
team took into the cave. He considered the popular British
mud boots a poor choice for cave work. They lacked the
steel shank required for technical climbing. But as strong as
his opinions were about the boots, his opinions about Ian
had been stronger. He'd tolerated the Welshman's choice of
boots for the same reason he'd accepted his decision to continue diving in spite of his diabetes—out of respect for his
uncommon skill and drive. And now he could feel that presence again.

He restarted the rebreather, and coasted out from shore
for twenty meters or so until he spied Ian's plastic-and-

aluminum reel lying on the clean sand bottom. He picked it up and continued forward into Sump Two, bearing left into a gaping underwater tunnel. As he stopped to tie off the line, he saw another tunnel even farther back to his left. This, he realized, must be the primary passage. The Rolland Airbell was like an oxbow—an abandoned bend in the underground river—with little flow through it.

He swam gently forward into the main route, which opened up quickly. Though he could not see the bottom through the silt, he feared the large passage could go very deep. He hugged the ceiling, which to his great relief leveled off at only eight and a half meters deep.

Ian's reel ran out of line after about eighty-five meters. He spliced on a second spool, and continued on a southward direction. The tunnel began heading up, and about halfway through the next reel, he realized he was going to surface. He spotted the familiar mirrored surface about 170 meters beyond the Rolland Airbell.

He crawled up on a wide gravel beach measuring a good twenty meters across. He pulled his wetsuit hood open and listened: There was the distinct sound of a waterfall in the distance, which indicated this was no mere airbell, but open passageway.

"Oh, jeeez," he huffed to himself, still straining from the weight of the rebreather on his back. "Finally, we did it."

He rolled over on the gravel bank like a turtle, then began unhooking the rig. When he was free of it, he stood up and probed the expansive chamber with his electric light.

"Finally," he said. "Finally," he shouted. "Finally," he screamed, as the word echoed back to him. "We finally cracked this mother!"

He pulled out a small carbide lamp, fired it up, and started hiking up the gravel bank. He stopped himself after ten or fifteen meters, however, when he realized that in his excitement, he was still wearing his wetsuit socks. He ran back to the rebreather, put his boots on, stuffed the bottle

of carbide and a spare electric light into the day pack, and
started out again.

The boulders on the top of the hill were huge and
scoured. No mud whatsoever. Both were clear signs that a
hell of a lot of water flowed through here during the rainy
season. The large passage split in two up ahead. Bill took the
left-hand tunnel, but ran into another sump after only 100
meters. He tracked his way back to the right-side entrance,
and soon realized it led to the same sumping streamway.

"No," he said. "Noooo. Don't do this to me. I can't go
back and tell them I found another sump."

He traced his way back to the beach, and back up the
slope, to see if he'd missed anything. Sure enough, at the
point where he'd taken the right turn down to the sump,
there was a big breakdown slope heading up.

What the heck? he thought.

He scrambled over the breakdown for forty meters or so,
until it broke into a new chamber. Standing twelve meters
high at the low end—and arching up into the blackness—
this was no small room. He hiked down what seemed like
the center of the hall for another 100 meters or so, until it
opened into an even larger chamber. It was evident that he
had found a dry bypass around Sump Three.

"Hoooooeeeeeeey!" he shouted, as he began jogging
down the open passageway. Still wearing a complete wetsuit
and hood, he began to overheat. The light from his carbide
cap lamp reflected back off all the steam he was creating,
leaving him in a fog of his own making.

Despite the poor visibility, he worked his way over to a
canyon, and followed the river until it flowed into a sump
so large it looked like an underground lake. He spotted a
passageway above the lake, and climbed up to it. There he
found a clean-scoured tube, three meters across, which he
followed for about 100 meters, until he reached a steep pothole, about six meters deep. He began to climb down, then
stopped himself.

If it were anyone else, I'd tell them not to continue without vertical gear and a belay, he thought. *Maybe, just once, I should heed my own advice.*

He turned around and headed back to the rig, eager to share what he'd found with Barb and the others. He was hopeful his discovery was fantastic enough to entice them to continue the expedition—hopeful, but not certain. Just in case, he stopped and did something he normally wouldn't have done, something strictly forbidden by modern caving ethics: Using the carbide flame as a smudge, he wrote on the wall, "Bill Stone, April 8, 1994."

It took him an hour to prepare for the dive back, and another to make his way back through both sumps. He surveyed the second sump on the way back, and stopped just short of Camp Five to do a little decompression on pure oxygen. Hovering there in the darkness, he could barely contain his desire to shout up to Barbara and tell her about all he'd seen.

Barbara was half asleep when Bill shouted to her from the sump. She leapt out of her hammock, almost tipping over in the process. As she raced down the ladder to the lower platform, she yelled, "Yippeee!"

She helped him out of the rig and secured it to one of the platform lines. He was still dripping wet, but she gave him a big hug anyway. He excitedly began telling her about all that he had found, shouting so he could be heard over the roar of the waterfall. He was as happy as she could remember seeing him. He rambled on so enthusiastically about each passage he'd discovered that he couldn't manage to finish one thought before launching into the next.

She wanted desperately not to tell him about Sheck. She wrestled with her dilemma while he prattled on. The waterfall made it easy for her to tune him out. She recalled how she'd felt when her parents hid from her the news that her favorite grandmother had passed away until after she'd completed her final exams, but she concluded that was a very different case.

"Have Wes and his crew been down?" he asked.

She looked him in the eyes. She wondered how she'd explain Wes's absence without spilling the grim news. There was no way, she concluded. There was no way to keep this from him.

"No, they didn't make it," she yelled back. "Neeld stopped down this afternoon."

Still in his tattered black wetsuit, Bill followed her to the upper platform. She started heating up some water on the stove.

"Where are—" he started to ask.

"Well, there's some bad news," she cut him off.

"Really?"

"Sheck died."

"What?"

She turned toward him, so there wouldn't be any misunderstanding.

"Sheck. He died," she shouted.

"Not a chance."

"It's true. Neeld told me. He heard from Wes."

"No way."

"He died at Ciudad Mante a couple days ago."

Bill leaned back against the jagged limestone wall, and shook his head from side to side. "Uh-uh," he insisted. "Messler got it wrong. Sheck wasn't at the Mante. He and Bowden were headed to their new secret hole. Maybe something happened to Bowden; he's older and less experienced. Maybe . . ."

He let go of his denial, and hung his head. He was stunned. Fifteen years after his first venture into this sump, he'd reached the pinnacle of his exploring career. And he'd come back to word that the unthinkable had happened. He felt like he was on a roller coaster that had just come crashing down.

They'd intended to spend another night at Camp Five, then head for the surface in the morning. But now Bill just wanted to get away from the noise, and from the sump itself. He and Barbara secured the rebreathers at the lower platform, tidied up the upper platform, and started the long climb up to Camp Three. He packed out the computer module he'd removed from Ian's rig, the buoyancy bladders that still needed patching, and a bunch of trash. Barbara carried out the dry bag that the team had been using as a latrine. The biohazard-bag itself was waterproof, and most of its contents were deposited within individual Zip-loc bags, but every time the bag squished against a rock—something that happened often in the tight crawlways of the Lower Gorge—its pungent odor was expelled.

"Hey, G," she huffed atop a drop where they'd stopped to catch their breath. "You know how Steve was hassling you about how I'm only here because I'm your girlfriend?" she asked.

"Ye . . . yeah?" Bill said slowly, fearful of where the conversation was heading.

She plopped down next to him, and leaned back firmly against the biohazard-bag so he could get a good whiff.

"Well, next time he brings it up, you just tell him this," she said, smiling. "You tell him that I don't carry a man's crap for him when I'm on a date."

Bill burst out laughing. He was touched once again by Barbara's ongoing effort to maintain a good attitude. Figuring that one good scatological joke deserved another, he replied in kind.

"You think that smells bad? Get a whiff of this," he said, tugging the neoprene skin of the wetsuit he'd been wearing all day away from his sweat- and urine-soaked fleece.

"That's okay, sweetie," she said, scooting away like a sand crab. "I take your point."

The pungent pair spent that night at Camp Three, and

made it to the surface by nightfall of the next day. Barbara was dead tired, having not slept well for two nights. She bathed and went straight to bed. Bill found Wes in the cookhouse, slumped at the mess table. His usual strut and swagger were gone. One look at his crumpled countenance vaporized all of Bill's lingering hope that the news about Sheck was in error. Bill sat down next to him, and the two drank and swapped Sheck stories for the rest of the night.

Wes had learned a few more details about the dives. He explained to Bill how Exley and Bowden had been using two lines, and how Sheck had simply never returned. On the third day after the dive, while the team was de-rigging the sinkhole, his body popped to the surface. Bowden and Kristovich were working in the water at the time, and heard the splash. They turned around in shock, and saw Sheck. His tissues had ruptured as a result of the ascent, and they could see his bones in places. He fizzed, due to the nitrogen still seeping out of his muscles; and smelled, after three days in ninety-degree water.

"The dive line was wrapped around his arm three times," Wes continued. "Now, you and I know Sheck was waaay too methodical to do something like that by accident. They way I figure it, he knew something was wrong. He secured himself to the line to hold his position so he could get his head together or solve whatever problem he was having."

Wes paused, lifted his head from his hands, and thrust his finger at Bill: "Either that, or he knew he was screwed, and didn't want any of the rest of us to risk our lives trying to find his body."

"How deep was he?" Bill asked, offering the hooch.

"They said his gauge read 906," Wes replied, knocking back the bottle. "Bowden turned around at 925 feet. Suffered the usual aches and pains in his joints the next day, but other than that he's all right. Other than that and having the bad luck to be diving alongside Sheck on the wrong day."

"Yeah," Bill said, nodding. "I'll never understand why he

was so damned focused on hitting that number. But he was. Remember when he hit 780 in Mante? What was that, back in '88? I ran into him later that year. He comes up to me and tells me he wants me to check out his new dive computer. Which I'm thinkin' is kinda weird, since he'd never been much of a tekkie. So I'm lookin' at it, you know, toggling through the menus, and I come across the depth of the last dive. It reads '780.' I looked down at him and he was just standing there, grinning."

"Hmmm. Yeah. That's him," Wes agreed. "He didn't say much. He just did stuff."

Bill offered the bottle again. Both men drank.

"Eighteen," Wes said. "There's eighteen people I've known who have died in underwater caves. Eighteen I've known personally. A lot of them were pretty close friends. But none like this. I feel like . . . like Sheck took part of the sport with him. This thing we do, it'll never be the same.

"He could've, ya know, gone out in a car wreck or something like that," Wes continued. "It wouldn't have had the . . . I mean, we'd still feel a deep sorrow and loss but . . . when you lose someone when they're doing, ya know . . ."

"He died doing what he loved to do," Bill said, offering the cliché he guessed Wes was groping for.

"Yeah," Wes said. "And everybody will say, 'Who could ask for a better way to go?'"

He stared straight at Bill.

"Well, ya know what? I could. *I could* . . . and I do."

The wake stretched on for hours. As it did, Bill quit trying to buck up Wes, and settled in to ponder the emotional roller-coaster ride this expedition had become.

What the hell is going on? he asked, again and again, as the liquor slowly melted his brain. *Why is all of this happening?*

One answer came the following evening. The team drove into Huautla to give a pair of public presentations. The first was on the public square. The second, for local dignitaries, was at the Bellas Rosas restaurant, in the Hotel Rinconcito.

Noel and Steve returned to town just in time to join the team at a head table, and watch Bill show more slides. He described the project in his Texas Spanish, and made many comparisons to space exploration. Afterward, a few locals stood up and gave speeches. The last speech was by the opposition *presidente*.

"He who goes into space—the astronaut, as you call him—he will see heaven," the middle-aged man began, speaking in simple Spanish for Bill's benefit. "He who goes beneath the stone, he will wind up in a very different place." He shuffled over toward Bill in his dusty flip-flops, and continued.

"You say you don't know why you're having difficulties. You say that—despite all your medical science—you don't know why your friend died."

There was a hush in the audience. Bill craned his head and looked inquisitively toward Renato, who just shrugged.

Seeing that he'd acquired the attention he was seeking, the *presidente* continued. "I will tell you why this good man died. This happened because you did not seek permission of *Chi Con Gui-Jao*. You have been arrogant. And for this you must pay the price."

CHAPTER NINE _____

W es agreed to stick around for another week to fulfill his commitment to *National Geographic*. With Noel and Steve back from Zipolite, Bill led the group on a three-day side trip down into the Santo Domingo canyon, where all the rivers that carved their way through the dark heart of Huautla emerged. They pitched tents on a sandy beach, swam in the warm green water, and enjoyed campfires in the early evenings.

The divers made a few exploratory dives into the resurgence. Jim Smith had proved these were the same rivers that ran through Huautla in 1988 when he placed ten kilograms of colored dye in the San Agustín sump, and later recovered traces of it on charcoal sensors in the river canyon. All that remained was for a caver to follow the route through, and Sistema Huautla would be the deepest cave in the world.

The river taunted Bill. He waded in it as he helped the divers kit up. He bathed in it during the hot afternoons. He carried water from it for cooking. And every time he felt its cool water on his skin—the very same water he'd shivered in beyond the sumps—the river stirred his desire to organize one more push before packing up the expedition.

On the last afternoon of the short visit to the resurgence, as Wes took pictures of the others diving, Bill found Noel in his hammock convalescing from a mild case of dysentery. He seized the moment alone to lobby his old friend.

"Okay hombre," Bill said. "We need to talk about the endgame."

"Yeah, yeah, I know." Noel knew Bill well and had anticipated the conversation. "What do you want to do?"

Bill looked at the ground and rubbed his beard. Then he looked straight into Noel's big eyes. "I think you and I should go for a one-week push to the other side. And I think we should consider taking Barb. She's ready, and we could survey much more efficiently with a three-person team."

Noel nodded, and sighed. "I want to be there. But I don't see how we can manage a team of three. How are ya gonna get another rebreather down there?"

"I'll carry one down for her," Bill replied.

"And who's gonna haul it back out?"

Bill shrugged, holding out his upturned hands to concede the point. They both knew the job would fall to them. And they knew that without reinforcements there was a very real possibility they would have to leave some of the gear underground.

"Yeah, you're right about the de-rig," Bill replied. But he hadn't yet given up hope for a final push. "Look, we've been through a lot together. Can I count on you for this?"

"Yeah," Noel said without conviction. "Of course."

The group returned to San Agustín Zaragoza on the night of April 14. Kenny led Wes and Neeld Messler into the cave the following morning for a couple days of underground shooting. Wes planned on making some shallow dives into Sump One to photograph the rebreather. Over the years, he'd suffered so frequently from decompression illness—the bends—that he'd been forced to develop his own diving routines, with exaggerated safety margins. So before heading in, Wes left a note on the cookhouse message board that stated, "I cannot use Heliox 86/14 for shallow diving," and asked Bill to bring him in a scuba tank filled with air.

Noel and Steve followed a few hours later. They griped to each other most of the way down. Though it was meant as nothing more than a personal requirement, they took Wes's note to be a jab at Bill. The divers all knew that Heliox 86/14 was intended for deep diving: By substituting helium for nitrogen, it eliminates exposure to nitrogen narcosis; and by lowering the amount of oxygen from 21 to 14 percent, it reduces the risk of oxygen toxicity at depth. At a maximum depth of only seventy-eight feet, Sump One proved to be far shallower than Bill had expected, and the heliox proved unnecessary. Noel and Steve had become suspicious that the low-oxygen mixed gas might have been responsible for part of the problems they'd had during the first push, an unlikely theory that was encouraged by Bill Farr. The hitch was that the heliox was already down there. To switch to air would require hauling more tanks down to Camp Five, a task no one relished.

Tom Morris and Paul Smith, the Moles who'd come down to work as photo assistants for Wes, were the last of the photo team to enter the cave. Jim agreed to lead the divers through the rope work, but once underground he teased them. They'd get off rope and see Jim for a second or two before he deftly rappelled over the next drop, disappearing like the White Rabbit. They got to Camp Three late, and took the only camp spots left. Tom inherited Ian's old place, where up to that point no one had felt like sleeping.

For a variety of reasons, no one was very cheery at Camp Three that night. Paul became violently ill, and woke up most of the rest of the camp with his groaning and vomiting, which echoed through the chamber. He stayed at

Camp Three the next day while Wes took the team out to make photos. Surrounded by friends, Kenny started easing back to his old personality, poking fun at the dry cavers by expressing his contempt for their "holes in the ground," which were "too dry" for his taste.

Kenny woke up on the morning of the 17th, and thought the cave sounded different. "Hey, Noel," he whispered, "listen to the rocks. The waters sounds louder."

"Nah," Noel said sleepily, "that's just your imagination. Go back to sleep."

Wes woke to the same conclusion. As he was shuffling around in his bag, getting dressed, he bellowed, "Hey! It's louder down here." He and Kenny threw on their clothes and trotted down to the Metro to investigate. When they got there, the water was foaming, brown and flowing with torrential force.

"Holy Cow!" Wes shouted. "That mother's up five feet!"

The Upper Gorge carries water from the La Grieta, Nita Nanta, and Agua de Carrizo drainage areas, and is prone to flooding. A few inches of rain on the surface can render the gorge impassable for several days. Wes was thrilled. The extra water would make great pictures. He rousted his troops and marched them up the Metro to see how far they could make it, taking pictures all the way. He shot dramatic photos, alternating Steve and Kenny as subjects, with Neeld, Tom, and Noel holding strobes and gear.

The photo crew sloshed back to camp and discovered that Paul Smith had been playing Goldilocks in their absence, shifting around from bed to bed until he found one to his liking.

"Who's been reading my book," Tom asked as they settled back into camp.

"Who's been eating my food," Jim added, not long after.

"And what the hell is your wet ass doing in my sleeping bag?" Wes growled.

Over a dinner of freeze-dried potatoes and high-protein MREs, someone raised the specter of rationing food until the water levels dropped a bit. A quick inventory revealed they were stocked for between four and six days, so there was no immediate problem. But the very mention of the idea had a curious side effect: Everyone ate massive helpings at dinner.

Noel, who'd been trapped below ground before, found the tenderfoots' fear hilarious, and took to taunting them for fun.

"What if this is a cataclysmic flood?" he asked, pressing his bulging eyes up to the face of whomever he was tormenting at the moment. "What if a cave wall ruptures, and releases water from an adjacent part of the system? What if that torrent of new water roars down one of the big breakdown slopes, washing boulders down the Upper Gorge like sand through an hourglass, and traps us here forever!"

Wes was not amused. He'd experienced just such a freak event, on an expedition in Australia's Nullabor in 1988. He and the others were camping in a large airbell when the hair started standing up on Wes's arm, a result of ionization caused by water crowding into an enclosed area at high speeds. He asked whether it might flood, but the Aussies laughed at the idea and reminded him he was in a desert. Within minutes a wall of mud and rock came pouring over the ledge above them, and they were all running down the chamber ahead of the flow. They were trapped. After twenty-nine hours, he and a British cave diver named Rob Palmer found a new route out.

Steve whipped up a box of instant chocolate mousse, and passed it around the cook circle. Everyone had seconds. Paul Smith had thirds. "If we run out of food," Wes growled at Paul, "we're gonna eat *you* first."

Neeld Messler rose early the next morning, and headed up the Metro alone to check on the water levels. He returned shortly after ten to report that while the water was lower, it was still nowhere near low enough for anyone to pass the Grand Cascade. Wes then rounded up the team for a trek down to Camp Five, but after one look at the water level below the Li Nita waterfall, he turned back, too. The crew wound up spending the rest of April 18 making photos of Camp Three. A competition developed for the best Stonehenge chairs.

Camp Three was unusually hot and muggy. All the excess floodwater rushed in from the surface at a warmer temperature than the normal slow trickle. The warm turbulent water threw extra humidity into the cooler cave air, which condensed into a warm, heavy mist.

Over a big dinner of freeze-dried chicken stew and powdered potatoes, the group swapped caving yarns and speculated on whether or not Camp Five was still there, or whether all their gear had been torn off the walls and swept into the sump by the flood.

Kenny confided that he was thinking about leaving the team. "I've been on some really screwed-up expeditions in my life but none have been as bad as this." He listed his reasons, though he didn't need to: shortage of manpower, plunging morale, unproven technology, Ian's death, and the approaching rainy season. In spite of all this, he was loath to leave. "I hate quitters," he said. "I don't want to be a quitter. I don't want to quit on you guys."

Steve was looking for a graceful way out, too. "I only made it halfway through the sump. I want to see the rest. Or else . . . I'm afraid I'll spend the rest of my life merely imagining what it would have been like. And I want to see the place where"—he groped for the right words—"you know, Ian's final point of exploration." After a moment, he added: "I guess I'm trying to weigh the fear of what might go wrong against the high of going where no one has been before."

And he repeated his resentment toward Barbara, still rooted in her having been invited to join the expedition without having to jump through all the hoops. "If she feels pressured into making a dive that exceeds her experience, and there is another accident, Bill might find himself facing charges of criminal negligence," Steve suggested, "if not manslaughter."

"Or even murder," someone added.

"Aahhh. Say what you want about Bill," Wes said, "I've known him a long time. And as long as we're stuck down here, I'm glad he's up there. That's the next best thing to having Sheck around. Maybe better, 'cause no one can rescue your ass if you screw up on a cave dive. But if you're trapped in a dry cave and you get to pick your rescuer, I'd put Bill at the top of my list. There will be no stopping him from coming to get us, if that's what it comes to."

After two days of heavy rain on the surface, Bill had a pretty good idea what was happening below. He'd been trapped at Camp Three himself back in 1981, when a similar mid-April storm dumped nearly eight inches of rain on the plateau. The water level in the Metro rose by a meter, and he and his teammates spent two long days playing cards while waiting for the water to fall.

Up in San Agustín, he and Barbara weathered the storm by making preparations for a final push. Bill called San Antonio to see whether Bill Steele could round up the equipment needed to charge the Acurex tanks to 5,500 psi so that Noel, Steve, Wes, or Tom would have the option of tackling the sump on open-circuit scuba gear. Bill calculated that the work required to haul down a few of the lightweight fiberglass tanks was roughly equal to what would be required to carry down a third rebreather. It irked him that those tanks would have to be hauled out again after only one use, but since this was the endgame for this expedition, it hardly mattered. Meanwhile, Barbara conducted a bizarre experiment to prove that the helium-oxygen mixture already in place at the sump was safe. She threw a tank of

Heliox 86/14 in her knapsack, strapped on a mask and regulator, and completed a strenuous half-hour hike around the village. Because her brisk jog was more physically taxing than most dives, and because the elevation at San Agustín was significantly higher than at the sump, she figured that if 14 percent oxygen was good enough atop the high Huautla Plateau, it would surely be sufficient below. The villagers found the sight of her huffing through the village hilarious; Bill regarded her test as further proof that while she wasn't as experienced as the other divers, she had a much better attitude.

On Monday the 18th, the couple headed back to the cave to check on the photo team. They carried an Acurex bottle of air for Wes, along with plenty of food and carbide for the troops. The Dust Devil was unusually quiet. As Barb racked into the top of the seventy-seven-meter Space Drop, she yelled back to Bill, "I think the Gorge is louder than usual." He dropped down to take a look.

The Upper Gorge was wall-to-wall whitewater. He hung in his harness, his toes dangling inches above the froth. The large rocks where they normally landed were gone, lost beneath more than a meter of fast-moving water. Bill swung back and forth on the line until he was able to pendulum his way over to a large boulder that wasn't completely underwater. He looked downstream. For as far as he could see, the small boulders they normally walked across were buried beneath white, frothing waves. The river had reclaimed its cave.

"No doubt about it," he finally yelled back. "We're not going any further today. And if the others are at Camp Three—damn, I sure hope they're at Camp Three—well, wherever they are, they're there for the night."

They climbed back up to the 620 Depot, and inventoried the cache. They found two sleeping bags and two wetsuits. They decided to bivouac there for one uncomfortable night, using the wetsuits as sleeping pads. There was no stove on which to heat up any of the abundant freeze-dried food, but Barbara had packed a Nalgene of goodies for the photo team, so they shared a dinner of trail mix and jerky.

"I wonder what Camp Five looks like?" Bill asked, poking through the trail mix. He and Barbara cited hydrologic formulae to each other, to reassure themselves there was no way the sump could be as rough as the Upper Gorge. But privately, Bill worried. They'd left the rebreathers hanging at the lower platform, inches above the water. He wondered if they were still there.

They dallied about their makeshift camp in the morning—there was no rush, given the situation—and Bill rappelled back down to the Gorge about noon. The water level was unchanged. They left the supplies, including Wes's tank of air, along with a note at the depot, and headed for the surface.

As his long arms and legs pulled his thinning body up the long vertical shafts, Bill sketched out a rescue plan in his head. If the flood continued much longer, he figured, he'd return to the secret Depot Hole and get more rope. Then he'd begin rigging down an obscure 1979 route that bypassed the Upper Gorge. By the time he reached the top of the Stairway to Hell, he'd calculated how much rope would be needed.

Bill continued to fiddle with the rigging all the way out. Coming to the Dirt Slope, he pulled up the mud-encrusted handline they'd been using, and rerigged it along the left-hand wall. The new route swept down the moss-covered wall of the canyon and intersected the traditional route halfway up the Slip-n-Slide, sparing fifteen meters of rappelling and another fifteen meters of ascending on each trip in or out of the cave.

"You wouldn't happen to have a pencil and paper, would you?" he asked when he'd finished rigging the shortcut. He wanted to leave some sort of note alerting the others to the new route. She had neither. He figured they'd find the new route anyway.

They reached the cookhouse by dark. It was Barbara's fastest ascent yet, and Bill was once again impressed with what a trouper she'd become. Waiting for them were photographers Carl Ganter and Brita Lombardi, as well as Cis-Lunar programmer Mike Stevens. After washing up, they enjoyed a large meal of salad and spaghetti while joking about hunger at Camp Three.

"At least they've got plenty of water to drink," Barbara said.

"Hungry? Those boys are probably too tired to even think about being hungry," Bill chimed in, between licks on the guitar. "Wes is quite a slave driver, you know. He's probably got 'em marching neck-deep through the worst parts of the Metro, just so he can make it look as rough as possible for *National Geographic.*"

The oatmeal had run dry that morning. Breakfast at Camp Three consisted of meager globs of freeze-dried slop. The Nalgene read "Stroganoff," but no one believed it. No one felt like carrying more water up to the camp they all hoped to leave, so there wasn't much Crystal Light to go around that morning, either. A few still had candy bars tucked away in their personal gear; they ate furtively, in the darkness at the edge of the camp.

Besides being hungry and dehydrated, no one had slept well, either. The lack of circulating air made the potent aroma of human waste and spent carbide much more noticeable throughout the camp. And several team members acquired Paul's gut-wrenching case of diarrhea. They spent most of the night parading to and from the latrine. On one such run, someone hadn't quite made it all the way to the designated disposal site. No one confessed to the crime, though several had stepped in it by morning.

Wes marshaled the grumbling troops back to the Upper

Gorge in an attempt to exit the cave. The water level was only down a bit, but Wes was eager to exit the cave, so he pressed ahead. The loosely looped ropes that had been rigged as chest-high hand lines back in March were now underwater. Wes tiptoed along the knee-deep low spots, then clipped in his ascenders to climb up the last few meters of each line.

The largest of these had been a sloping hand line before the flood, but was now a true vertical drop. A powerful waterfall poured down precisely the same route where the line hung. Wes reached into the cascade and pulled out the base of the rope, then ascended it by leaning all of his weight awkwardly toward the left wall. Though the wall was too smooth and slick to actually hold on to, he was able to use his weight and a finger's touch to more or less make contact with the wall, barely holding himself out of the pounding water's path. Noel made the maneuver look easy, and Kenny, who was third in line, copied Noel's technique.

The next drop looked even worse. Noel and Wes huddled. It was too dangerous to continue. Reluctantly, they decided to turn the group around once again. Before they'd finished conferring, they heard a shout from below the noisy waterfall.

"Steve . . ." someone yelled over the roaring water, followed by an unmistakable cry, "NEEDS HELP!"

Steve hadn't seen the others ascend the waterfall drop. Instead of leaning to one side, he chose to straddle the column of water by placing his feet against the wall, one on each side of the flow. When one foot slipped, he swung forward into the brunt of the cascade and began gasping for air. His lower ascender was fastened directly to his climbing harness, and made it impossible for him to separate himself from the rope. He pushed against the wall with all his strength, but there was no way he could generate anywhere near enough sideways force to overcome the weight of the meter-wide column of water pressing down against him.

Making matters worse, he'd started the ascent with his half-empty pack still on his back, rather than tethered below him, as is standard practice for cavers on rope. The large urethane pack quickly filled with water, effectively doubling his weight. He was pinned.

Tom Morris was next in line, and watched in horror as Steve gasped for air. *Oh, man. Oh God,* he thought, *I gotta get up there.* But Tom was halfway across a submerged traverse line. There was no way he could reach Steve in time. And even if he could, he wasn't sure there was anything he could do to help from below. So he yelled as loud as he could: "Noel! Steve needs help! Steve . . . he's drowning! Noel! Steve! HELP! HELP! HELP!"

Trapped within the thundering column of water, Steve just barely heard Tom's cries for help. The words triggered a distant memory. Years before, he'd been free diving beneath an old stone dam. Finding himself trapped behind a solid rock wall—and running out of breath—he surfaced into a small air pocket inside the dam. Feeling a bit chagrined, he nonchalantly called out to his buddy Larry, who was taking pictures nearby. After helping Steve out, Larry admonished him for being so Minnesotan about his predicament. "When you're in a jam like that," he said, "you yell 'HELP!' And you keep on yelling until help arrives." Steve remembered all of this upon hearing Tom's unflinching voice. And he realized that yelling was what he should have done, too—ten or twenty seconds back, when he still had the breath.

Noel spun around and raced back to the drop as soon as he heard Tom's voice. He instantly recognized what was happening, and flew into action. With one hand, he clipped his Cow's Tail into a traverse line, providing himself a measure of security. With the other, he leaned out over the cliff as far as he could reach, and clipped his ascender to the rope on which Steve was drowning. Noel then braced his legs and, using his ascender as a handle, leaned back and tugged the rope aside, freeing Steve from the center of the waterfall.

Steve coughed out a mouthful of water, and gasped for air. Noel waited for him to catch a couple breaths, then shouted: "Ditch the pack, Steve! Drop your pack!"

Steve either didn't hear, or didn't understand. He tried to continue ascending, but managed to pull himself and his heavy pack up only a few inches. He felt weak, as though all his strength were drained from him.

Still holding the heavy line, Noel shouted again: "Your pack is filled with water. Dump it! Now!"

Physically and mentally exhausted, Steve finally grasped what was wrong. He reached around and freed one strap, then reached back and upended the bag, spilling most of the water. Without all the extra weight, he was able to frog his way up to Noel.

"You okay?" Noel shouted, once Steve was finally atop the ledge.

"Yeah. I think I am," Steve stammered. "Thanks, man. Thank you. Really . . ."

Noel looked him over. No evidence of broken bones. He seemed to be breathing all right. "The next drop is even worse," Noel interrupted. "We're not going to make it out today. We're turning around. Back to camp."

Music to Steve's ears. He was still clutching the rope in his hands, so he began threading it through his rappel rack.

"What the hell are you doing?" Noel asked.

"Rappelling," Steve snapped. He was anxious to get back to camp.

"I wouldn't do that if I were you," Noel shouted back. "Or, if I did, I certainly wouldn't use more than three bars. This used to be a hand line, remember? The bottom is tied off . . ."

But before Noel could finish, Steve rappelled back down the waterfall. Just as Noel had feared, his rack kept him tied to the rope, which was rigged not as a rappel line—loose hanging with a knot on the end—but as a hand line, running from one high bolt, down through the formerly dry pothole, and back up the other side. Noel watched in horror as Steve rappelled straight into the churning plunge pool below the roaring cascade. He stepped to the edge just in time to see Steve disappear beneath the swirling foam.

Steve paddled frantically toward the surface, but made no progress. He turned to see what was restraining him, but the water was too dark. He groped about the frigid water and discovered that his rack was still attached to the rope, and that the rope was under far too much tension to allow him to rise to the surface. *Oh*, he thought, *so this is what Noel was trying to warn me about.*

"Oh God," Noel muttered from atop the drop. "He's completely submerged." He reattached his upside-down ascender, and jerked on the line, but Steve was too deep for the motion to make a difference. The doctor began counting the seconds his friend was surviving without oxygen: *One one-thousand. Two one-thousand. Three one-thousand.*

Beneath the churning falls, Steve started to unthread his rack as quickly as his shivering fingers could manage—

"Not again!" Wes screamed from above.

Steve bent forward to create some slack in the line, and quit thrashing about to focus on the problem. With the line loosened, he swung one aluminum bar free. He twisted the rack around, and pushed the thick nylon line through from the other side. That loosened the next bar . . .

Thirteen one-thousand. Fourteen one-thousand. Fifteen one-thousand . . . Noel could see that Steve had stopped struggling. From where he stood, it appeared as though Steve had quit breathing, and relaxed into a slump.

"Dammit!" Noel shouted. "He's dead. That's two. Two friends who've died in this friggin' cave!"

Watching from the same vantage point, Wes reached the

same conclusion. "This can't be happening again," he mumbled.

With less tension on his rack, Steve somehow managed to pull himself to the surface. He sucked in another deep breath, released the rack completely, then swam downstream to where Tom was still frozen in terror.

Noel collapsed in relief, stumbling backward when he let go of the rope. Sitting awkwardly against the wet limestone, he gazed right through Wes and Kenny.

Noel repeated himself, absentmindedly. "That's two."

Camp Three turned serious that night. The high-spirited jokes and caving tales were replaced by a sober debate of exit strategies. Noel wanted to stay a few more days, wait for the water to recede, and lead the photo team down the Lower Gorge to Camp Five. But Neeld had a plane to catch. Steve and Kenny had had enough. And the Moles wanted out.

"You just need to realize it, Noel, this project is over," Wes said. "It's time for everyone to pack up and go home."

"I'm worried about Bill," Noel confided. "It's not like him to be overdue. It's easier coming down through the water than going up. So if he's not here, it's either 'cause we're really trapped, or he might be trapped somewhere else in the cave."

Wes reasserted his belief that Bill would be down as soon as he could, and guessed that he might be rigging one of the alternate routes that had been used prior to Minton and Steele's discovery of the Fools' Day Extension. But Wes was clearly weary of bungeeing back to Camp Three every night. Before going to bed, he suggested, "If anybody has any beliefs in God, or some faith in a higher power, ya'll say a prayer for lower water levels tomorrow."

Noel burned some copal incense and made a little offering of garlic and tobacco to the cave.

In the morning, the water appeared to have dropped

enough that an escape finally seemed reasonable. The photo team was so frantic to get out they were abandoning gear to lighten their packs. They were leaving behind expensive Nikonos cameras and custom-rigged flash units. Noel ribbed them into taking more gear out. "Ah, a new Nikonos," he said, picking up one of the dozens of expensive items Wes had jettisoned. "I could use one of these."

The plan was to shoot photos throughout the exit, hoping the water was down enough to allow them that final exit at the top of the gorge. Wes took photos through the Grand Cascade. After that he was whipped. "No more pictures," he said, his chest heaving during a rest break. "I just hope I can get myself out of this cave alive."

Noel had problems at the same waterfall that had nearly claimed Steve the day before. The traverse line stretched, and Noel got caught under the water. He was able to free himself quickly, but lost both contact lenses in the deluge, leaving him somewhat blind for the rest of the trip out.

"Porter Falls," he grumbled as he made his way to the next drop. "We'll call that one Porter Falls."

When Messler and Steve reached the top of the Fools' Day Extension they couldn't find the hand line that had run down the Dirt Slope. They stared over the lip. Messler was shocked to see Steve lowering his duffel over the edge.

"What are you doing?" Messler asked.

"Getting the hell out of here," Steve said.

"There's no rope."

"I don't give a rip," Steve shot back. "You can sit here if you want. I'm leaving." And with that, he began free climbing down the steep Dirt Slope, lowering his duffel ahead of him. A slip would have sent him tumbling fifteen meters to the hard rock below. It was a crazy move. Yet when Messler saw that it was working, he shrugged and followed.

Noel and Kenny found the new traverse line—the one Bill had moved a few days earlier—and used it as intended.

The four of them found Bill and Barbara up in the cook-shed.

Barbara greeted Noel with a mock interrogation. As a joke, she thrust the microphone from a portable tape recorder in his face and asked, "So, Dr. Sloan, what do you have to say about the survivability of breathing Heliox 86/14 on the surface?" She then told him and Steve about her heliox hike. Exhausted by his long trip out of the cave, and emotionally wrung out by the flood, Noel didn't find Barbara's experiment relevant or her mock interrogation funny. Without saying a word, he brushed her aside and headed up the hill to change his clothes. She shrugged and went to bed; Bill followed shortly.

After changing, Steve rolled back down to the cook-house and fixed a big dinner, figuring the Moles would be along soon. He and Noel sat up for nearly three hours, eating and waiting. At about 1:30 in the morning, Noel jogged up to the bunkhouse to fetch his caving gear and take a look.

"What's going on?" Bill asked, sleepily. He'd been suffering from the intestinal pains that had been going around, and wasn't sleeping well.

"I'm worried about Wes and Tom and Paul," Noel whispered. "They haven't shown up yet." He explained how Steve and Messler had missed the new route around the Dirt Slope, and climbed down without a rope. He feared the Moles had missed it, too.

"What are you? A bunch of lemmings?" Bill asked. "You don't go down a drop like the Dirt Slope without a rope."

Noel and Steve hiked down to the *sótano* and sure enough, the Moles were camped out on the balcony just above the Dirt Slope. They'd decided to wait until daylight, figuring that someone would come for them.

Noel yelled down the yawning sinkhole. "Rope . . . to . . . your . . . left." Tom and Paul, who were quite cold, found the new traverse line and made their way out. Wes, however, had a sleeping bag with him. He was exhausted. He just stayed there by himself, sleeping peacefully until morning.

The flood washed away Bill's last hope of rallying the team. Neeld Messler left the next day. Kenny followed a day later.

Jim wanted to leave but couldn't, because the Step Van—which served as the expedition pantry—had been registered in his name to bring it across the border, and couldn't go back without him. So he dropped out without actually leaving. He started sleeping in the little alcove above the van's cab, and spending a good portion of his days holed up in the van, too. The village kids would come and beat on the outside of the van until he'd open the rear door and hand out fistfuls of hard candy. Of course, the bribe only encouraged their return. Jim wound up doling out the expedition's stash of Fireballs and Jolly Ranchers to the Mazatec children. They called him He Who Knows the White Truck.

Wes loaned Bill a camera and some strobes, and spent an afternoon giving him a crash course in how to make pictures *Geographic* would like. He wanted to stay, but his desire to be home won out. The Moles squeezed back into Tom's pickup and rolled out of town that afternoon.

Steve desperately wanted to ride with them, but there wasn't enough room for him and his gear in Tom's little truck. Dejected, he sought out Bill and told him he'd help haul loads from Camp Three, but wouldn't dive. Bill thanked him for what he'd done, and thought they'd agreed to part on a positive note. But when word later got back to Steve that Bill had nominated Barbara as a replacement diver, Steve became angry and sullen.

Barbara crossed paths with him not long after the Moles rolled out of town. He was sitting on the front porch of the fieldstone bunkhouse, cleaning his boots. As she passed, he said calmly: "There's a black cloud hanging over this expedition."

"What?"

"A black cloud," Steve repeated. "Following this whole expedition. You know what I mean."

"Well, no, actually, I have no idea what you're talking about." She looked at him to see if he was going to offer a clue. He put his head down and went back to scrubbing his boots. "One thing I learned doing my dissertation," she said. "Everything is harder than you expect, everything takes longer than you expect, and things always go wrong."

Steve looked up and glared. "You wouldn't even be here if you weren't Bill's girlfriend, would you?"

"Well, I guess that's true," she said. "If I hadn't met Bill, I wouldn't have found out about this expedition, and if I hadn't found out about it, I couldn't very well join—"

"No. No. That's not what I mean," he interrupted. "I mean you wouldn't be here *now.*"

She'd known Steve resented her role in the expedition; clearly, he resented even more the possibility it might expand.

"Look," she cut him off. "Noel is in line to dive with Bill. And I think he should. But if he doesn't, *I'm* going to. And that's basically all there is to it."

"If you dive, I'm leaving."

She shrugged and walked away.

Noel was still vacillating. Before the flood, he'd planned on diving the final push. But Steve's close calls and all the talk about *Chi Con Gui-Jao* had rattled him. He'd heard the name before, back when he'd first visited Huautla. On this trip, though, he'd been warned about the vengeful Cave Lord over and over. Like the man at the slide show who'd accused Bill of being arrogant, many Mazatec had suggested that Ian died because the cavers hadn't sought permission from *Chi Con Gui-Jao*.

Hanging out with Steve had changed his perspective, too. Unlike Bill, Steve was just as interested in the cultural experience as he was in the cave. On their days off, Noel and

Steve had often gone asking after *curanderos*. And as *Chi Con Gui-Jao* would have it, the son of the man whose house Noel was bunking in had an uncle who was a *curandero* in a nearby village. An appointment was made—the *curanderos* insisted it be on a full moon—and while the Moles were rolling out of town, Noel slipped off with Blanca and Marcos Escudero, their landlord's daughter and son. He drove his Toyota pickup down through Tenango Gap, down the valley toward Río Santiago. They parked at edge of the town and walked through its dusty streets at dusk to a one-room adobe house with a dirt floor.

Inside, Noel was ushered to a small log bench. At the center of the room was one of those large wooden spools that industrial electrical cable comes on, used as a table. Copal was burning in a small tin can. A few small candles illuminated the table. On the other side stood a small white-haired man with hunched shoulders, who looked to be in his seventies. To the Mazatec, such men were more than priests. For while priests spoke of their faith, *curanderos* spoke of experience. After years of training with all sorts of hallucinogenic plants, the *curandero* had seen the Earth Lords and Catholic gods with his own eyes, heard them with his own ears, and was here to share the wisdom.

The man laid out a folded towel on the spool table. Inside was a handful of corn kernels wrapped in neatly folded paper. He laid the corn out on the towel in several rows of two or three kernels each. Then he spoke in Mazatec for some time, singing and chanting and waving incense over the neat rows of corn. He scrutinized the pattern of the incense over the corn, and carefully selected six kernels to set aside.

He then cut and folded two small pieces of paper into packets. He pulled out a couple leaves of the Herb of San Pedro, green leaves about as long as a man's palm and half as wide, and ground them to a powder. He sprinkled the powder into the packets he'd prepared. And prayed over them.

Speaking in Mazatec, he told his visitors that both the relevant Earth Lords—He Who Knows the Mountain, as well as *Chi Con Gui-Jao*—had given the journey their blessings. He told Noel not to be afraid, for fear would make him sick. And that if he became afraid, he should eat the sand he finds inside the cave entrance, for that doing so would bring him courage and valor. He gave Noel the packets of Herb of San Pedro. He told Noel to bury one at the entrance, and to carry the other into the cave with him. He also suggested that everyone entering the cave should carry a clove of garlic to ward off miscellaneous other evil spirits, such as those who appear as snakes.

As a benediction, he took a mint-scented leaf and walked around the room, touching it to various holy objects. Next he wiped Noel, Marcos, and Blanca from head to toe with the leaves.

Back in San Agustín, Marcos translated what the *curandero* had said, as well as the premonition: "Five people will enter the cave. You will find seven tunnels underwater. They all lead to the Río Santo Domingo."

Bill and Barbara suited up for their final, all-out push on the morning of Tuesday, April 26. They shared a big breakfast in the low-slung cookhouse—even after all these months, Bill still bumped his head on the corrugated tin ceiling almost every time he worked in there—and, on Noel's advice, they each stuffed a little bit of garlic into their packs. They donned their harnesses, helmets, and bulging orange duffels, then began hiking down the cornfield.

Along the trail to the *sótano* they met Bernardo and Virgilio Escudero, the white-haired grandfather and curious grandson who'd spent so much of the last three months quietly observing the team from afar. As his goats scurried off the path and into the dense underbrush, the old man said something in Mazatec and politely offered his weathered hand.

Bill extended his blistered hand in exchange. Their hands met along the flat, inside surface of their fingers, pressed together softly, and then withdrew. Bill had long been intrigued by the genteel, no-palm greeting common among the Mazatec; it provided respectful contact, while avoiding the macho gripping duel one might expect among U.S. businessmen.

Bernardo spoke gently to Virgilio in Mazatec. Though the old man could understand basic Spanish, he preferred to use his native tongue and let his young grandson—a star pupil in the village school—serve as translator.

"Grandfather," Virgilio began in halting Spanish, "he ask . . . he say that your doctor went to see our doctor." The boy was still a bit intimidated by Bill.

Bill was confused. He looked at Barb. She shrugged.

"*Curandero*," Bernardo whispered.

"*Sí*," Virgilio repeated. "He say the man with the big eyes went with Marcos to see the *curandero*."

Bill nodded to Bernardo, realizing just how small a village San Agustín Zaragoza really was. There were no secrets here.

"What do you think of that?" Bill asked in Spanish.

The old man spoke softly in Mazatec.

"Grandfather, he say this man your doctor go to see is a good *curandero*."

Bill looked puzzled again. "Are there bad *curanderos*?"

"Yes, yes," the boy replied, without prompting. "*Brujos*. These ones, they cause bad things to happen."

Bernardo whispered something else.

"*Brujos*, they are like warlocks," the boy continued. "But the man in Río Santiago, he is a good *curandero*. He is well known in the *sierra*."

"Do you believe in these spirits?" Bill asked the boy.

"Does your grandfather?" He didn't mention the garlic in his pack.

Bernardo spoke for several moments in Mazatec. Virgilio translated his story.

"He say that one time his father was walking down the trail to the Santo Domingo river. There he became ill. This sickness was caused because he was afraid of the gods down there. He was afraid of the river god, *Chi Con Nanda*. He had a fever, and spells. My grandfather, he say this man, this same *curandero*, he cured his father."

"Well, then," Bill stammered, unsure of what to say. "I guess we'll be okay, then, won't we?"

"*Sí*," Virgilio said, nodding. "You will be well."

Bernardo smiled, and nudged the boy up the trail. He nodded first to Barbara, then to Bill, then continued up the trail himself. Over his shoulder he cast a Mazatec farewell.

The cave was back to its usual dry season ambience. Bill and Barb had no problems on the way down. Camp Three, however, was a disaster zone. Bits and pieces of photo gear were strewn all over the place, and everything was coated with fungus. They spent the entire next day cleaning up the mess, and ferrying additional supplies of food and carbide down from the 620 Depot.

After a restful night—he always slept well in the peaceful silence of Camp Three—Bill woke early on Thursday, and lay in bed thinking. Noel was overdue, but Bill figured that was more likely a result of his old friend's newfound hesitation than any mishap. *If Noel doesn't show up by tomorrow, what would be the harm in going ahead with Barbara?* he asked himself.

She has the skills to dive the rig, and at this point, she's more mentally solid than Noel. Her pace is faster and she carries thirty-five pounds of cargo every day without complaint. The passage to Camp Six wouldn't be an exploration dive. There's a dive line running all the way—unless the flood took that, too—and we could do it as a buddy dive . . .

That was the flaw in the plan: They weren't equal buddies. Though Barbara trusted Bill completely, he hadn't yet reached the point where he trusted her with his life underwater. Every time he dived with her, a substantial percentage of his psyche was preoccupied with figuring out how he'd rescue her if something went wrong. *She knows her limits*, he thought, *but that doesn't help me. Because there are always things that can go wrong, that do go wrong.* The team had unanimously decided to explore the sump in a series of solo dives, rather than buddy pairs, because in the limited visibility a partner is just one more thing to get fouled in the line, and because in the extremis of panic, troubled divers were just as likely to kill their buddies as they were to be rescued by them. This sad but true fact was driven home during their training exercises when Jim Smith nearly died trying to rescue Rolf Adams. Rolf had slipped into nitrogen narcosis. When Smith came to help, Rolf panicked and grabbed the regulator out of Smith's mouth. Unaware that he still had plenty of air himself, Rolf sucked through Smith's in a few short minutes, all the while grasping hold of his buddy with both fists. Smith would have died then and there were it not for the fact that Adams broke the number one rule of diving and held his breath on the way up. The air within his chest expanded, his lungs burst, and his grip relaxed. As he fell away into the swirling murk below, Smith rocketed to the ceiling. The experience so unnerved Smith that he gave up diving.

"Sometimes ya just gotta back off and let the other guy die," Sheck had consoled Jim and Bill afterward, "because otherwise it's gonna be both of you."

Lying in the solemn soundlessness of Camp Three with Barbara asleep at his side, Bill realized he'd never be able to back off and let her die, no matter how severe the situation. *So the question really isn't about whether she's ready,* he concluded. *The question is: Am I willing to bet my life on her?*

After breakfast, they stuffed their packs with supplies for the rebreathers—three pink tanks of heliox and two bottles of lithium hydroxide—and headed down through the Lower Gorge. The violent flood had left its mark throughout the gnarly passage. On nearly every drop, Bill stopped to repair and rerig ropes that had become severely frayed. Barbara reached the dive base first.

"I see two rebreathers!" she shouted, to their mutual relief. But as they studied the damage, they quickly realized that Bill's wetsuit—which he'd left lying atop the lower deck to dry—was missing.

"Damn," Bill cursed. "I guess I've got to make another run back to the surface."

"Wait, G." Barbara picked up one of the high-intensity dive lights and shone it along the water's surface, slowly probing each nook and cranny of the canyon. Within a couple of minutes, she spotted the wetsuit floating downstream. While Bill inventoried supplies at Camp Five, she made a series of swims and collected a half-dozen more items that had been washed to the end of the canyon. After they'd located everything essential and prepped the two rebreathers, they trudged back up to Camp Three to spend the night.

Noel was waiting there. Much to their surprise, so were Jim and Steve; Noel had persuaded them to help haul gear out of the cave for a few more days. No one was in a good mood. Steve was upset because Noel had told him that instead of divvying up the expensive drysuits and other sponsor-provided gear at the end of the expedition—as Steve had expected—the expedition would likely have to sell most of the gear to pay down its debt. And Noel was still wringing his hands over whether or not to join Bill on a final push.

"After all these years, we're finally within striking distance of the promised land," Bill told Noel over dinner at Stone-henge. "I'm going for it. I'm going to do this. And I'd sure like you to be there with me."

As they finished a big dinner of freeze-dried chicken and potatoes, Bill realized he'd made up his mind about Barbara, too. If Noel wouldn't come with him, then he'd take her, despite the risk. The power of his resolve thrilled him. After she headed off to bed, he confided to Noel.

"Look, brother, I've shot my wad," Bill whispered. "I've lost my wife, my house, my money, all for this project. This is it. This is my chance, maybe my only chance." He leaned forward and slowly stroked his stubbly chin. "I'm gonna do this thing, even if it comes down to me, and me alone. I'm going to push this cave to the bitter end. No matter what."

Noel was terrified by the confession. Unaware of Bill's cold assessment of what he might face in a worst-case scenario accident with Barbara, Noel feared his old friend was contemplating martyrdom. He fumbled for the words to change Bill's mind.

"I . . . I don't know, man—"

"Just sleep on it," Bill interrupted. "See how you feel in the morning." And with that, he headed for bed. Noel remained alone in the carbide glow at Stonehenge, more conflicted than ever.

Steve crept up a few minutes later and knelt beside Noel. He'd overheard part of Bill's speech, and it had clinched his decision. "I'll help carry gear down to the sump tomorrow, and after that I'll haul a few more loads from here to the 620," he told Noel, in a tone every bit as conspiratorial as Bill's had been. "After that I'm leaving the cave. And then I'm leaving Mexico. And once I leave, I'm gone; do not count on me for backup. Because . . . because I, for one, am *not* willing to die for this freakin' cave."

Noel was once again at a loss for words. He just put his hand on Steve's shoulder and nodded. Steve hugged him awkwardly.

Noel tossed and turned all night. He ached to see what

lay beyond the sump. He yearned to scoop virgin booty in the heart of Huautla. He deserved the payback, after all the years he'd spent training for this mission. But he wasn't willing to die trying. And he didn't want to be trapped on the far side with an old friend who was clearly willing to try something slightly insane to fulfill his dream.

On top of all that, there was the total lack of backup. As an anesthesiologist, Noel's job was to look into the future, to see what life-threatening things might go wrong, then to prevent them from occurring. Cave diving was no different. But he could figure no good way to prepare for possible problems with this push. If he went through with Bill, the only person who could come after them was Barbara. To do so, she'd have to go to the surface and haul in everything required to build another rebreather—that would take at least three trips—then assemble it by herself at Camp Five. She'd have to kit up by herself, and dive through both sumps for the first time, also by herself. The odds of something going wrong over the course of all those firsts were just too high.

Wide awake in the enveloping darkness, Noel envisioned himself treating Bill for a fall beyond the sumps, then returning for help only to find Barbara's lifeless body floating somewhere along the way. As the sleepless hours stretched on, he began to wonder whether *Chi Con Gui-Jao* was laughing at his predicament.

There is no good decision, is there? Noel finally asked the Cave Lord, early in the morning. *But if I remove from the equation my own selfish desire to scoop booty, then my duty becomes clear. I'm better prepared than Barbara to be the backup. That's what I've got to do.*

Shortly after breakfast, Noel caught Barbara on the trail to the latrine. They stood alongside the path, shining flashlights at the gray dirt beneath their feet.

"If I don't go, how do you feel about this?" he asked her, concerned she might need some time to weigh her own decision before he told Bill. "Because here's the thing: I don't want to go without some backup."

Barbara was thrilled, but stifled her desire to cheer out of respect for Noel. In addition to being a more experienced diver, he had seniority, having been involved in the project since the 1984 Peña Colorada expedition.

"You don't have to decide until we get to the sump," she said.

"I've made my decision."

"Well, if you're sure . . ." she said.

"I am," he replied, his eyes glistening in her flashlight's faint glow. "Are you?"

She nodded. Noel realized she was concealing her excitement, and felt relieved by her enthusiasm. He smiled back. "Okay. Let me tell Bill."

"Right," she said.

Noel found Bill at the cook circle. He jiggled his flashlight to capture Bill's attention, and the two met away from Stonehenge, beyond Steve's earshot.

"Man, I've lost my edge," Noel began. "I'm under a lot of stress. I haven't slept in nights. I'm . . . hell, I went to see a *curandero*, that should speak for itself." He paused a moment, and decided not to fully explain his thinking about the lack of backup. As long as Bill and Barbara were going to do this thing anyway, he thought, why burden them with his worries. "Okay. It comes down to this: I shouldn't be diving."

Bill could see that Noel was in a different place emotionally. He didn't completely buy Noel's argument, but he could see that his old friend had finally made up his mind. So he didn't try to talk him out of it. After a moment, he asked, "Will you support Barb and me?"

"All the way."

The five of them threaded their way back through the Lower Gorge and down to Camp Five. They spent a couple hours taking pictures of the hanging camp as a favor to Wes—who'd been unable to make it down during the flood—then Steve and Jim departed. Bill, Barbara, and Noel turned in early, though all had the usual problems sleeping amid Camp Five's enduring thunder.

Bill and Barb were in the water by noon the next day, but one of the regulators on Barbara's rig had sprung a leak. Bill disassembled it and found a hole in the diaphragm. There was no spare at the sump. They debated diving to the oxygen stage bottle and stealing that regulator, but decided it was too risky to proceed without the option of that critical bailout.

Noel floated the idea of calling the whole thing quits. "All this stuff is like, just like a bad sign, man," he said. "Suppose another regulator blows?"

Bill snapped back. "Noel, I've put one quarter of my life into this project. I told you already, there is no friggin' way I'm giving up at this point. If I have to make a solo run to the surface, I'll do it."

Noel backed off, but didn't change his mind.

Barbara broke the stalemate. "I think there's another regulator at the head of the Upper Gorge." Bill and Noel each looked at her blankly. "The one we brought in for Wes."

"Hey!" Bill said. "You're right. All that effort of dragging the Acurex down for Wes wasn't wasted after all!"

Bill slipped into his vertical gear. Pumped with adrenaline and free of a pack, he shot up through the cave in record time, reaching the 620 Depot in only an hour. He tied the octopuslike hoses of the regulator around his neck, and sped back down, reaching Camp Five a mere two hours after he'd left. Noel and Barbara were amazed.

By late afternoon, Barb's rig was back together, but her depth sensor read zero no matter how deep she went. Bill examined it and soon realized that when he'd swapped the computer on that rig—to retrieve the black box record of Ian's last dive—he'd neglected to recalibrate the depth sensor. He then started to recalibrate it, but, racing through the job in the darkness, mistakenly connected a high-pressure hose to the sensor and destroyed the low-pressure sensor. Now *that* had to be replaced, too.

Bill stood up and pounded the upper deck with his fist.

"Can I get you something?" Barb asked sympathetically.

"Yeah," he said, "a stick of dynamite so I can blow this damn thing up."

Noel leapt right in. "I agree with that. These things are just too complicated to be reliable. Maybe we should just write this off now and let's de-rig."

Bill froze him with a stare, then let it pass.

To everyone's astonishment, a spare depth sensor was located at Camp Five. Ian had included it among a well-stocked kit of spare parts.

"It's like his ghost is here with us," Bill said as he installed the spare, working much more cautiously this time. "It's like he's saying, 'Another chance, mates. Chocks away!' "

By the time the rig was finally back together, it was too late to dive. Bill and Barbara removed their sleeping bags from the large orange duffel they'd packed for the trip through the sump. One of the Nalgenes had leaked, and Barb's sleeping bag was soaked. So Bill fired up one of the cookstoves, and he and Noel spent the next hour holding the bag above a flame. One held the bag upright, while the other insured that the bottom opening didn't directly contact the flame. Barbara thought it looked like a weird hot air balloon. The carbide cap lamp sputtered out, and the three of them ended the evening huddled around the primal blue glow of the stove.

CHAPTER TEN

Bill woke in the darkness. The walls of the cave were trembling. Mist drifted over his unshaven face. The sound of the waterfall careened into the hard limestone and echoed off the water below until it became a never-ending explosion that shook the narrow canyon's shiny rock walls. He knew at once where he was: Camp Fear. He'd caught a few hours shut-eye, but getting back to sleep was like trying to nap alongside a diesel locomotive at full throttle.

Engulfed by the thundering darkness, he swung lazily in his hammock. His sea green balaclava was rolled and pulled tight over his ears, Kenny-style. Bill longed for those early, eager days of the expedition. They seemed so far away now. He could almost hear Ian rustling out of the next hammock, firing the stove for a pot of tea, and chiding him over the roar of the waterfall: "Come on, mate! Chocks away! Back in time for tea and medals."

"Dammit!" Bill mumbled. *Why did it have to turn out this way?* Ian's death had unraveled his grand plans: Supplies were dwindling, gear was disorganized, the team had disintegrated to just the three of them, and the rainy season was fast approaching. And yet Ian's life was forcing him onward. *Even now*, Bill sighed, *you taunt us.*

A voice reached across the blackness.

"You awake, G?" Barbara called out from the next hammock.

"Yeah," he replied. "I'm ready to get up."

Bill slid out of his warm sleeping bag and plopped his feet into the cold puddle on the platform. He fired one of the ceiling burners, and turned toward Barbara.

"How do you feel?" he asked.

"I'm not as enthusiastic as yesterday," she said. She hadn't slept well either. The penetrating chill of Camp Five had worn her down.

"Look," he replied, "if you don't feel good about it, let's abort now."

She could tell from his tone of voice that something was wrong, though she didn't know what. She assumed he doubted her resolve. That annoyed her. After months of proving herself to him and everyone else, she wasn't about to let him take this away from her. Not now.

"Don't give me that crap," she shot back. Her defiance caught him off guard. "Let's do it," she continued. "Let's put smiles on our faces, and let's feel good about this."

He laughed. It was exactly what he needed to hear. Her humor pierced the darkness. And her determination touched his heart. In the faint glow of the carbide lamp, he reached out and took her hand.

"Okay. Let's give it one last try," he said. "If we get in the water and things aren't working completely right, then we can bail out."

Noel woke shortly thereafter, and Camp Five was soon abuzz with activity. Noel readied the two rebreathers, while Bill and Barbara repacked the giant orange duffel bag with everything they'd need to establish a new camp on the far

side of Sump Two: three cap lamps and six liters of carbide
to fuel them; harnesses, racks, ascenders, and a rock-bolting
kit; survey and photo gear; four liters of freeze-dried food,
a liter of potato dust, and a liter of gorp; two cups, two
spoons, a pot, a stove, and three isobutane fuel cans; two
rolls of toilet paper, four trash bags, and two sleeping bags.
To stay dry, everything was stuffed into Nalgene bottles. To
make the bag neutrally buoyant for the dive, Bill added
twenty-five pounds of lead weight to offset the trapped air.
Two ropes—eighty meters of nine-millimeter and 100
meters of seven-millimeter—were lashed to the outside. The
whole thing weighed 150 pounds, and looked like a pregnant orange golf bag.

Bill lowered it into the water, where it bobbed just below
the surface. He watched it for a moment and worried about
what would happen if water leaked into the Nalgene bottles
containing the carbide: If the resulting acetylene gas were
under pressure greater than two atmospheres—they'd reach
three atmospheres at the bottom of the central pothole—
the acetylene would self-detonate. He looked at Noel and
said, "Well, let's just hope nothing leaks."

Noel turned his attention to the rebreather checklist.
When he was through, that familiar goofy grin crept across
his face. He stuck his nose four inches from Bill's—as he
always did when he had something important to say—
eyeball-to-protruding-eyeball. Bill usually reacted to such a
blatant invasion of private space by backing up, but this time
it seemed strangely reassuring.

"Locked and loaded," Noel said.

Bill laughed. He was relieved to see that his old friend
had begun to recover from the pessimism that had infected
him for so many weeks. Having made his decision not to
dive, Noel had thrown himself into his support role. And in
the event of another flood or some other difficulty, he was
the one man in the world Bill wanted on the entrance side
of the sump.

"If something happens, you'll come after us, won't you?"
Bill asked.

The question startled Noel. He nodded. "Yeah . . . yeah.
Of course."

Bill smiled. "Give me a week—till the morning of May 8,
then call out the Cavalry."

Seven days. Noel nodded again.

Barbara kitted up first. Noel strapped her into the
rebreather and began clipping the half-dozen hose fittings
into place, each sounding a reassuring "pop" as the connection locked. He fitted her arm with the backup oxygen display, a depth gauge, watch, and dive knife. He clipped the
computer console to one of the stainless steel D-rings on
her harness, and the regulator for the open-circuit bailout
system to another. Backup dive lights and a spare mask went
into zippered pouches on her waist belt. Then he passed
Barbara her pink-rimmed mask; it was the only thing even
remotely feminine about the rig. With her helmet in place,
he reached behind her and pulled over the rebreather
mouthpiece. The reflections of the four LED lights from
the head-up display glowed green in her mask lens.

"You're all set, Barb," Noel said, patting her on the
shoulder. She touched her thumb and index finger to form
an "okay" symbol, then slipped into the cold water. She
swam slow laps around the end of the sump, adjusting to
and rechecking the rig. She was the first to dive it since Ian
had, and she wanted to be sure everything was running
smoothly. Her krypton headlight darted about the dark
water, painting circles around the dive platform.

Bill watched his steamy breath roll across the sump's surface while Noel kitted him up. When he slid in, the cold
water surged through worn spots in his tattered black wetsuit. Noel passed him the giant duffel, and he clipped it to
D-rings at his chest and waist. The two friends took
measure of each other. Bill stuck his opened hand out of the
water and Noel grasped it.

"See you in a few days, brother," Bill said. Then he inserted his mouthpiece.

Noel nodded slowly, then added: "Come back alive."

Barbara swam cautiously through the calcium carbonate haze. She kept her knees bent and made small kicks with her feet, to avoid stirring up a silt storm. She followed the tiny white nylon guideline tied to the ceiling of the canyon. The white plastic distance markers Bill had tied onto the line were ticking by like mileposts on an Interstate.

Bill finned a body length behind her, with the giant orange duffel bag suspended below him like a dirigible gondola hung from a parade balloon. The bag's inertia was awkward: He had to kick hard to get moving, but once underway he glided forward with surprising momentum. Barbara slipped in and out of view in the haze. Each time he caught a glimpse of her, he riveted his eyes to the instrument display on the back of her rig. The eerie glow of the green LEDs told him the oxygen levels in her rebreather were okay.

Stay green, baby, he thought. *Stay green.*

The white triangles ticked by slowly, and the narrow canyon widened into a blue-white void after 140 meters. The pair dropped slowly down the deep shaft to the breakdown maze that had confounded the first dive team. They followed the guideline all the way down, for while the shaft's walls were only thirty meters apart, they may as well have been nonexistent in the silty haze. The water pressed against their bodies as they gently drifted deeper and deeper into the sump. By the time they reached the breakdown pile, the pressure had compressed their wetsuits to half their surface insulation value.

They squeezed through the opening in the breakdown, and entered the large scalloped corridor with the gravel floor. With less silt to worry about, they were able to pull themselves along through this section of the sump by grabbing hold of small rock outcroppings in the floor and walls. They picked up speed. The guideline began rising. The pressure eased.

As the corridor narrowed toward the end, one of Barbara's fins grazed the fuzzy limestone. The noise startled Bill. All of a sudden, he realized how quiet it had been. The thunder of Camp Five was well behind them. And his rebreathers were functioning flawlessly: No sound meant no bubbles.

A half-hour after they'd left, Barbara's head broke the silvery surface. She'd been following the guideline so carefully that she hadn't even realized she'd reached the Rolland Airbell until she was in it. Bill's head came out next. The flashlights on their helmets darted about the dark cave above.

"Everything going okay?" he asked. His words echoed across the chamber. It was very quiet here, so quiet that the sound of water lapping at the silt-covered rock walls seemed much louder than it was.

"Extremely well," she replied. "Oxygen level was right on the money. The display was green the entire way."

"That's good. Just keep an eye on that."

"Where to now?" she asked.

"Over on the other side of that sandbar," he said, pointing with the beam of light from his helmet-mounted flashlight. "Best way to do it is just crawl."

The water along the sandbar was only a meter deep. They splashed along awkwardly, doing the best they could to stay low to let the water carry the weight of the heavy rigs and the pregnant duffel. In this fashion, they slogged nearly the distance of a football field. Bill halted as soon as they were into the slightly deeper water on the far side of the second sandbar.

"All right," he said. "You know the routine." His voiced boomed like a drill sergeant's in the echo chamber. "Manually bring up your PO_2, then start the program and let the software reset your oxygen set-point to one atmosphere."

"Okay. Got it," she replied. "Want me to lead again?"

He nodded, and pointed to the next guideline. "And watch those rock flutes on the roof. They're razor sharp."

Barbara descended and continued southward into Sump Two. The chamber dropped rapidly, at around forty-five degrees, and the ceiling was covered with slivers of rock. Bill studied the thin white guideline carefully, examining each of its tie-offs to be sure they were not too tight. He was afraid that if either of them were to tug on the guideline too hard, it would chafe against one of these rock flutes and slice itself free, leaving no guideline to follow on the way back.

The ceiling soon became smooth again and Sump Two unfolded below them as a broadly arched roof of black rock, partially painted with a thin film of ocher sediment. The floor drifted out of sight into the void below, but it might as well not have existed. Their lights—and their concentration—remained focused on the white parachute cord that ran along the roof of the cave.

Piece of cake now, Bill thought. He slowly moved his head around in a tight circle. The laserlike beams from the small flashlight banded to his helmet etched an O in the haze— the cave diver's "okay" signal. Without turning around, Barbara replied with the same gesture.

Bill spotted Ian's empty reel halfway through the 180-meter tunnel, still lodged on the pitted limestone shelf where he had placed it nearly a month before. He reached to pick it up, then stopped. He hovered and gazed at the red drum. *We'll just leave this here for Ian,* he chuckled. *Just in case that Black Dog needs Ian's help finding his way.*

The sump floor began rising. With less maneuvering room, Barbara began kicking up silt. Little ocher mushroom clouds burst forth with every fin thrust. Visibility dropped to zero. No longer able to follow the guideline with his eyes, Bill reached out for it with his fingers.

The line was gone.

He groped about for a moment, but the line was nowhere to be found. *No problem,* he thought. The floor was rising. He had surely reached the end of the sump. *There must be air overhead by now.* So he let himself rise, figuring he would surface just a bit farther from shore than planned. But he wasn't where he thought he was. Instead of surfacing, he floated up into an alcove of some sort, or possibly an unexplored shaft. After continuing to rise for a moment more, the realization hit: He was lost.

The lights on his head were useless. The silt was too thick to see anything, not even his hand in front of his mask. He was sure the guideline was just a few meters below. *But in which direction?* He reached for his gap reel, the small safety reel carried by all cave divers for use in just this situation. Standard procedure was to tie off and then sweep across the tunnel with the gap line, which would eventually cross—and thereby provide a route back to—the main guideline. Sheck had taught him to do this with his mask off, to simulate being lost in a silt-out. But when he reached for his gap reel, it wasn't there.

His long fingers crept swiftly up and down his harness. He groped each of the stainless steel D-rings, searching blindly for the gap reel's familiar brass clip. But it wasn't there. Somehow, in the confusion at Camp Five, he'd left it behind. He cursed. He knew that caving accidents—and especially cave diving accidents—typically resulted from a series of such seemingly minor mistakes. Those cautionary tales at the beginning of each chapter of Sheck's survival guide described how otherwise minor mistakes compounded to become fatal errors. Bill already had two such strikes against him: He'd lost contact with the guideline and he'd left his gap reel behind.

He cursed again. His breathing rate skyrocketed. The primal urge to panic forced more adrenaline into his system. Had he been diving conventional scuba gear, he would have sucked through his remaining gas at a frightening rate, compounding his predicament. His panicked breathing would have been his third, and fatal, strike.

But he wasn't breathing off an open-circuit scuba system. Rather than frittering away the gas he was too rapidly exhaling, the rebreather just kept on recycling it. The realization calmed him. It was as if his invention was talking to him. *Panic all you want,* the rig seemed to say. *You've got another six hours to sort this out.* He hovered in the ocher haze, waiting for his mind and body to relax.

After a moment's reflection, he decided to try a skydive. First he released some air from his buoyancy control vest. Then, as be began to descend, he thrust out his long arms and legs as far as they would reach. He floated slowly downward, like a flying X. It worked. His fin caught the guideline. And within minutes he was once again on his way forward through the sump.

Noel stayed on the lower platform after Bill and Barbara left. He'd blown out his carbide lamp and watched their lights disappear into the sump's inky depth. When they were gone, he sat alone in the darkness, pondering their fate, and his own. He'd been left behind, by his own choice. After agonizing for weeks, his decision to forgo the final push was now irrevocable. Bill and Barb were gone. For a week if things went well. Forever if they didn't.

Bill's startlingly earnest request kept replaying in his mind: *If something happens, you'll come after us, won't you? Give me a week—till the morning of May 8, then call out the Cavalry.* Noel stirred the cold water with his toe.

"What freakin' Cavalry?" he shouted angrily into the darkness. Kenny had left with Wes and Tom. Steve wasn't going to dive again. And Jim was basically just waiting for a ride home. Noel was the only diver left to go after Bill and Barbara. He shuddered at the prospect.

He lit his carbide lamp, climbed back up to the upper deck, and crawled into his hammock. He figured he'd hang around a couple more hours just in case they aborted the dive. As he scrunched into his soggy sleeping bag, he noticed a gap reel hanging from Bill's hammock. He reached over and twisted the drum. The name "Stone" was scribbled on the side.

"Oh my God!" Noel exclaimed. Had he kitted Bill up with someone else's gap reel? Or had he sent his old friend into the sump without one? He envisioned Bill lost in a silt storm, unable to relocate the guideline. Then he envisioned himself, shining a handheld dive light into one side passage after another, unable to locate Bill's body. He shuddered again. He pulled his sleeping bag up over his head, but couldn't sleep.

When his watch ticked past 3:00 P.M., he packed a duffel bag with spent equipment and began the long climb up the Lower Gorge. He made his way slowly, taking extra caution at every slippery step, aware that even something as simple as a twisted ankle could become life-threatening now that there was no one to help him out of this thundering hole.

Camp Three was empty as well. Noel walked straight to the center of Stonehenge and stood there, alone. He turned a slow circle, staring out into the gaping blackness. It was like being marooned on the dark side of some alien moon. He sat down in the best stone chair—the one Tom had hogged throughout most of those muggy late-night bull sessions during the flood—and longed for someone to talk to. He was King of Camp Three, and Chief Inmate at the same time.

He put on some water a few hours later. While he was fixing dinner, he heard the unmistakable clanking of vertical gear. Steve hiked up the flowstone crest and into Camp Three.

"Hey Steve!" Noel said, leaping over to shake his hand. "Man, am I glad to see you."

"Yeah, well, it won't be for long," Steve grumbled. "Jim and I are leaving tomorrow."

Noel's head drooped. He'd hoped for their company, at least, if not for their dive support.

Steve could see his friend was crushed. "Broussard's not far behind us," he added. "Looks like he's ready to settle in for a while, so you won't be alone."

Jim trundled into camp a moment later. He was relaxed and cheery. He told Noel, "This is the first day I've had any enjoyment in this cave."

Noel pleaded with the two remaining divers to stick around for a week, just in case he had to go through the sump to help Bill and Barbara. He also asked them to help him de-rig the camps, and begin the arduous job of ferrying all the gear back out of the cave. But Steve and Jim were convinced that the water in the Upper Gorge was slowly rising, and that it was only a matter of time before anyone still at Camp Three would be trapped for good. Noel had been watching the water levels, too, and hadn't noticed any rise whatsoever. He figured that Steve's daily encounters with the pothole in which he nearly drowned had no doubt influenced his opinion. Also, the two of them had been lugging pack after heavy pack from Camp Three up to the 620 Depot for the past several days, and figured they'd done their share of the de-rig.

Don Broussard clanked into camp a few minutes later. He'd caught a bus out of Huautla a couple days after the team meeting on Easter Sunday, and rode home to Austin to attend to his business. He'd left his baby blue pickup—the Big Dog—parked alongside the gear shed, its rusty bed still crammed with expedition gear. A Huautla veteran, Don knew Bill would need help with the de-rig. While in Austin, he stopped by a meeting of the local caving club. After delivering an impromptu report about Ian's death and the status of the expedition, Don asked whether anyone was willing to return to San Agustín and help with the unglamorous job of de-rigging the cave and cleaning up. Two young cavers volunteered: a carpenter named Chris Sobin, and his nineteen-year-old girlfriend, Bev Shade. But Sobin hurt his back on his first trip into the cave, and Shade stayed topside until she could join another group on its way down. So despite his valiant effort to round up recruits, Don arrived at Camp Three alone.

As he settled into a chair at Stonehenge, Don soothed Noel's concerns by suggesting that his young porters might still be of use after they'd had a few days to recover. And he delivered the news that Bill Steele had arrived with some fresh volunteers. The veteran caver—at whose San Antonio home the group had crawled through a storm drain—had brought four novices to help with the de-rig: Michael Cicheski, Ted Lee, Don Morley, and Carleton Spears. Don expected Steele's gang of Texans would head down the next day.

Noel was thrilled. Though neither Broussard nor Steele nor their ragtag team of novice cavers would be of any help should he have to go after Bill and Barbara—none were cave divers—the prospect of having a six-pack of live bodies to help haul a ton of gear back up to the surface was a tremendous relief. "Oh man, that's fantastic," Noel said. "Finally, we've got some help."

"Well, I wouldn't get too excited," Don replied. "Those fellows Steele has with him are going to have a struggle on their hands just getting down here. I wouldn't count on them carrying much of anything out besides themselves."

Bill completed his trip through Sump Two without incident, and surfaced to find Barbara already seated on the wide gravel beach. He crawled up next to her, and rolled on his back. After stepping out of his rebreather, he unpacked one of the small brass carbide lamps, and struck up a flame. The faint glow of the carbide flame warmed their wet faces.

He took her hand. Without a word about his own near-catastrophe, he said, "Very nicely done."

The gravel beach led into a field of polished breakdown. The streamway continued along the west wall from Sump Two to what appeared to be the beginning of Sump Three. Since the river itself had carved this cave, there was little doubt that diving directly into Sump Three would likely yield the most direct route toward the Santo Domingo resurgence. But the two Cis-Lunar rebreathers were their only means of getting back to Camp Five, and each additional dive increased the odds of something going wrong. And unlike the Rolland Airbell—from which the only route forward was submerged—several dry passageways proceeded beyond the gravel beach. After a short discussion, he and Barb agreed they'd dive no further. They powered down the precious rebreathers and stowed them on the highest ledge they could find. The rains would return any day now, and these low passages would flood quickly. If the next flood were to damage the rigs, there'd be no way out.

They unpacked the massive orange duffel and established Camp Six some 100 meters beyond the sump, atop a tiny island of almost flat gravel surrounded by a sea of jagged limestone. Camp Six was even more spartan than Camp Five. Their wetsuits went into clear plastic trash bags to create ground pads for sleeping. A chest-high ledge served as a kitchen where they set up the spindly "scorpion" stove and cook pot. Three Nalgene bottles held their food: freeze-dried Stroganoff, oatmeal, and potatoes. A gallon of carbide held a week's worth of light.

Barbara opened a one-liter bottle of trail mix—their entire supply of munchies. She poured out a capful, handed it to Bill, and said, "We're going to have to ration this stuff, you know."

"Yeah," he mused. He fingered a small date chunk, then sucked on it for some time before giving in to the urge to chew. He became suddenly wistful. He turned and smiled at her.

"I can't believe we're finally here," he said, "in the heart of Huautla."

She smiled and peered down the gaping arched corridor leading south into the blackness. "Yeah, and were gonna scoop some booty."

Sump Three to Sump Six
Side View

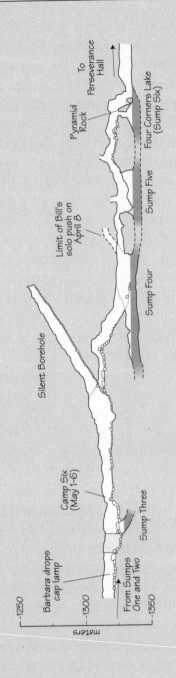

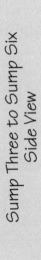

Barbara drops cap lamp

From Sumps One and Two

Camp Six (May 1–6)

Sump Three

Silent Borehole

Limit of Bill's solo push on April 8

Sump Four

Sump Five

Four Corners Lake (Sump Six)

Pyramid Rock

To Perseverance Hall

-1250

-1300

-1350

meters

drafted by Barbara Anne am Ende

They finished their snack, assembled their survey instruments—a compass, clinometer, and a thirty-meter measuring tape—and returned to Sump Two. From there, they began measuring their way into the cave.

Barbara's helmet began bothering her almost immediately. It was a lightweight model designed for kayaking, but popularly adapted by cave divers. It worked well underwater. But now the headband kept sliding down in front of her eyes, as a result of the weight of the solid brass carbide cap lamp clipped above her forehead. When she took it off the helmet to adjust the suspension, the baseball-sized cap lamp slipped loose from its mount. Unfortunately, she was standing atop the giant breakdown pile near Camp Six when this happened. The lamp tumbled into a deep crevasse, bouncing like a pinball on its way down.

"I, uh . . . I think we have a problem here," she said, haltingly.

Bill completed sketching the passage they'd just measured, methodically stowed the pencils and book in a carrying case strung over his shoulder, then bounded over to her. He joined her in gazing down the hole.

"You're pulling my leg!" he said. "Down there? Can you see it?"

Her head turned slowly left, then slowly right. "Your arms are longer than mine. Maybe you can reach it."

He handed his helmet to her and squeezed his head into the narrow slit of darkness. He flattened his nose against one of the smooth limestone slabs, while grinding his head of wispy brown hair against the other. He kicked his legs awkwardly outside the hole, and squeezed his shoulders deeper into the pile of tombstone-sized boulders. His right hand aimed a flashlight through another narrow opening. When he strained his arm, twisted his neck, and compressed his nose in unison, he could see the small brass cylinder teetering precariously on a small ledge three meters below. No matter how he contorted himself, the lamp remained well beyond his grasp. He writhed in reckless frustration, like an animal with its head caught in a trap.

After a moment of flailing, his six-foot, four-inch frame went limp. He gently clicked off the flashlight, and lay still in the darkness. "I can see it, but I can't reach it," he said.

"Damn! Not again!" she cried out.

He yanked his head from the fissure. "What's wrong?" he asked. Barbara clicked on her flashlight and began frantically searching the breakdown below her feet. "What on earth are you doing?" he asked again.

"I was . . . I was drying out the felt in your lamp," she stammered in disbelief. His lamp had been sputtering, probably a result of a felt pad that got wet during the dive. She had disassembled it in the dark, not wanting to waste the batteries in her electric lamp when she knew the parts of a cap lamp by feel. "And when I screwed the bottom on, the spring flew off the striker. It must have been loose. It just flew off."

Bill scrambled over to where she was sitting and looked at the floor. The tiny striker had launched the cap, flint, and spring out like little cannonballs into the void. Finding those tiny parts amid the breakdown would be impossible. He glared at Barbara, but said nothing. He didn't need to. She was overwhelmed by guilt so powerful he could feel it.

She switched off her light. The darkness suited her.

"I'm sorry," she stammered. "I screwed up."

Bill drew a deep breath. He was mad at Barbara for being careless. But mostly he was mad at himself for packing the little cap lamps instead of the carbide guzzling—but harder to lose—ceiling burners. He let out a long sigh. The fading of his breath echoed through the inky silence. He sat down next to her in the darkness.

He worked through the predicament in his head. In addition to the electric dive lights—which were good for about three hours each, or just a little more time than it would take to strike Camp Six, retrieve the rigs, kit each other up for the dive, and swim back through the sumps to Camp Five—they'd brought three of the small carbide lamps. They needed two for day-to-day caving. The third had been a backup. One was now down the hole. And a second was rendered inoperative unless lit by the third lamp. If anything should happen to that third striker—if its cap spun off, or if its flint wore out, or whatever—they were on a short fuse to reach Camp Five before their electrics ran out. As he sat next to Barb in silence, he was stunned by the irony: The most expensive and technologically ambitious probe of a deep cave ever mounted was now held hostage to a single, antique flint striker.

Barb had run out of light in a cave once before. Back when she was in high school she and her first caving buddy, Greg McCarty, decided to reexplore a tight Iowa cave that was considered a dead end. Hoping they might find a narrow continuation that previous cavers might have been unwilling to squeeze through, the two youngsters stripped off their caving packs and pressed into a narrow crawlway. At the end of a long belly crawl, they discovered a chimney-like hole. Excited at the prospect of scooping booty, they slithered down the tall and narrow fissure for about three meters, then down a second chimney for another four meters or so. The crevice was tight enough that they could jam their bodies against the sides and create enough friction to keep from falling. The problem came when it was time to get out. The walls were too smooth to get a grip on, and the crevice was too narrow for Barbara to shimmy up. She finally worked out a way to pull herself up, but it was slow going. Well before they made it back to the crawlway, their carbide had burned out. Their spare carbide was still in the packs they'd left at the cave entrance, along with the flash-lights they'd brought along as backups. They groped their way out of the cave in total darkness. In the two decades since, she'd never again stepped into a cave without plenty of carbide and a couple of spare flashlights. Yet here she sat.

Last time she was merely a few hundred meters from the cave entrance. This time she was a mile beneath the Mexican sky.

"It happens," Bill finally said. It was less an absolution than a reminder that there was simply no time to dwell on what could not be undone. Their predicament had now come down to this: Either they retrieved the lamp teetering deep in the breakdown hole, or they had to turn around while they still had battery power to light the way to Camp Five. If they retreated now, Bill knew well, they'd be sentenced to live out their days haunted by the knowledge that they had literally been to the edge of the unknown—and turned back. He concluded that they simply didn't have time to engineer their way out of this. The only thing to do was to muscle their way through, the way Doc Savage and crew so often overcame obstacles. He switched a flashlight back on. Bound together by its tiny beam, they became a team again.

He fashioned a sling out of nylon webbing, and looped it around one of the garbage-can-sized boulders. He pulled from one side while Barbara, crouched in the breakdown, used her long legs to push from the other. The boulders were smooth and glassy, as if shaken out of a giant rock tumbler. This was because for most of the year, the breakdown pile lay beneath a massive underground river. The force of the water, and small bits of sand it carried along, had been polishing these boulders every summer and fall for thousands of years. Bill's orange sling slipped off the rock a few times. And each time he rewrapped it, the glassy surface reminded him that they only had a few weeks before the river would reclaim the cave.

Bill pulled as hard as he could. The narrow nylon sling pressed through his Capilene pile sweater, and bruised his shoulder. Barbara wedged herself deeper into the breakdown to get more leverage. Over the next hour they managed to move several of the 200-pound stones.

Once they'd moved as many as they could, Bill began fashioning a fishing line from the parachute cord they'd used to lash their rigging ropes to the outside of the big orange duffel bag during the trip through the sump. It was made up of tied-together pieces and had a solitary overhand knot at one end. That, he hoped, was the hook that was going to catch the lamp. He could see the lamp better now. He lay face down with his ear in the crevasse. In his left hand was the flashlight. In his right was the guideline turned fishing line. He reeled it out, working his fingers like a winch. Innumerable times the end of the line swung tantalizingly close, only to miss. He was desperately aware that if he missed, and succeeded in only disturbing the lamp as opposed to hooking it, it might easily tumble deeper and completely out of sight. Sweat rolled off his forehead as he tried to gauge whether he had caught the lamp or not.

As the two-hour mark approached, Bill managed to trap the knot in the cord into the wedge between the cap lamp's brass cylinder and its flint wheel striker post that was screwed into the saucer-sized chrome reflector. Ironically it was the striker cap that had allowed the catch. He gathered the line in ever so slowly, fearful that one sudden move could tumble the lantern deeper into the breakdown. A moment later, the lamp was in his hand.

He beamed and held the prize aloft as if it were a fly ball caught in the last inning. Barbara whooped with joy. She stepped forward to offer him a kiss, but he hadn't yet let go of being annoyed. "Don't do that," he said, holding up his hand to stop her.

"Tell you what," he offered a moment later, "let's tether these things to our helmets so that doesn't happen again."

They continued surveying for several more hours, exploring a quiet, railroad-tunnel-sized borehole that ultimately dead-ended. They dubbed it the Silent Borehole and returned to camp for the night. After a big dinner of freeze-dried Stroganoff, they spread their sleeping bags out on the makeshift wetsuit mattress and crawled in. Yearning to make up for having been so standoffish after the cap lamp incident, Bill smiled at Barbara and offered her a back rub.

"Sure" she said, rolling over in the sleeping bag. He started rubbing her shoulders.

"You know," she said. "I think this is the first time we've been together in private since we left the hotel in Tehuacán."

"Yeah, you're right," he replied, as his strong hands pressed down her spine. "I don't know what we're going to find tomorrow, but we might be able to set some sort of . . . um . . . depth record . . . right here."

She laughed and nuzzled closer, musing, "I wonder who holds *that* record?"

Noel's pleas for help persuaded Steve and Jim to haul gear for one more day before departing. So on May 2, while Noel and Don carried equipment up from Camp Five, they made two more runs up to the 620 Depot. And on the following morning, they headed for the surface.

They crossed paths with Bill Steele on their way out. Sliding off the bottom of the One-Ten, Steele was struck by their appearance: Steve had grown a thick beard since he'd rolled through San Antonio three months earlier, and both men strode through the cave with an ease of motion unique to cavers entrenched in a long expedition. While his nervous recruits awkwardly inched their way down the awesome shaft above, Steele sat and chatted.

"It's been tough to keep this going," Steve said. "Stone's push has been almost more than we could bear."

Jim agreed. "He's off the deep end this time."

Steele was surprised by how spooked Steve and Jim were, how eager they were to leave the cave. He'd heard about Ian's death, but knew nothing of the dissension festering among the remaining team. He asked how the de-rig was proceeding.

"Stone wore out twenty people getting gear into the cave," Steve said. "You won't believe the pile of gear in Tommy's Borehole. And there's an equal pile at the sump. It's crazy."

"Is it all coming out?" Steele asked.

Jim and Steve looked at each other, then laughed.

"This is it for me," Steve said. "I'm not coming back in. I don't care about the gear. Leave it. It'll be here next year, or whenever. Too much was brought in. You'll see. It's crazy. Beyond reason."

Steele was startled by Steve's attitude. Was this the same eager young man he'd met only three months prior? Steele had seen this kind of thing before—a young caver feels pushed beyond the limits of what he feels is safe, then expresses that fear in the form of rebellion against the expedition leader—but rarely to this degree.

"We had no business staying after Ian died," Steve continued. "I've had a real bad feeling ever since. I don't want to die here."

Steele nodded. Though not a diver himself, Steele was a veteran expedition leader. The consequences of Steve's and Jim's imminent defection stunned him. Only three months before, the expedition was teeming with gung ho divers, each jockeying to be first into the sump. Was Noel really the only one willing to support Bill and Barbara? He turned to Jim Brown.

"If we need you," he asked Jim, "and we come back out to get you," he continued, eye-to-eye with Brown, "you'll come back down here, right?"

Jim shuffled his feet, looked at the limestone floor, and mumbled, "Yaaah."

It wasn't much of a commitment. But before Steele could say anything else, the first of the recruits dropped in, wide-eyed and panting. Another was having trouble negotiating a rebelay fifty meters overhead. Steele turned his attention to guiding his group. By the time they were all safely off rope, Steve and Jim were swiftly frogging their way out. Feeling a bit like Marlow on his way up the river to find Kurtz, Steele cautiously led his green scouts down the Upper Gorge.

At Camp Three, Steele found Noel and Don huddled around a solitary cap lamp. The recruits were exhausted and went straight to bed. Steele strode over to the cook circle, and took a seat at Stonehenge, where Noel and Don were conducting a morbid vigil: five more days.

Expecting to greet the lovably goofy doctor he'd known for years, Steele was shocked by the twisted apparition seated before him. Noel was silently suffering the onset of an ulcer, and had contorted his body into the awkward sitting position of a nervous madman. He'd lost weight, and shriveled skin hung loosely from his bones. His hair was a filthy mat with autonomous peninsulas jutting wildly in several directions at once. And dilated pupils wandered lazily across his large glassy eyeballs, which bulged eerily above a mud-caked beard.

"God, I hope they come out of there alive," Noel told Steele, after a rambling monologue outlining the status of the expedition. "I don't want to go back through there. Of course I will. I'm here. If they don't come out, I'm going in by myself. But I don't want to."

Steele looked to Don, hoping for some clue as to what had happened to Noel. Unflappable as always, Don offered only a subtle shrug. Then he poured Noel some more of the mildly spiked Crystal Light they'd both been drinking. When Noel leaned forward to pick up his mug, his twisted torso slid between the carbide lantern on the floor and the high rock wall behind. His shadow crept up the wall behind Stonehenge like some rising cave creature.

He rambled on. "Why has Stone done this?" he asked. "We could have pulled out while we were all still okay. But we had to carry on. And now they're over there. And we're here. Except Porter and Brown aren't here. They're up on the surface, not to be counted on."

Steele joined Broussard in trying to nurse Noel through his spell. "Oh, I suppose that's understandable," he mused. "What with the first death in Huautla in thirty-six years of caving here and all."

"Does that surprise you?" Don asked. "That Ian died?"

"It surprises me no one's been killed before," Steele replied. "We've had many close calls. We'd gotten by for many years. And now on top of it all we're diving, and extreme diving to boot, with experimental equipment. No, I'm not surprised."

Noel was closer to his old self in the morning. But Steele's volunteers, a group of middle-aged mountaineers, were exhaused. The one-day trip directly to Camp Three had wiped them out. For their health, and Noel's mental condition, Steele suggested the camp take a rest day.

At noon, the group went up the short drop to Anthodite Hall, the stadium-sized chamber just above Camp Three that Stone and Tommy Shifflett had discovered in 1979. Steele was surprised to learn that Noel had never been there; he saw it as indicative of how hard Bill had kept the team's nose to the grindstone. Noel introduced them to a game of tag that Kenny had taught the group during the 1993 training trip. One player was designated the detective and another the murderer. When the lights are off, everyone shuffles around. If the murderer whispers "you're dead" in a player's ear, then that player has to scream and fall to the ground; the detective's job is to find the murderer before everyone dies. With its flat floor and infinite darkness, Anthodite Hall was a grand place to play.

Afterward, they returned to Camp Three and fixed a huge dinner. Knowing they'd have to pack out whatever wasn't consumed, they ate as much as possible. Noel even poured sugar on his pasta, sprinkling liberally from a large one-liter Nalgene. Steele laughed and reminded him he could dump anything biodegradable into the river.

Noel retold the tales of the expedition to his new camp-mates: pushing the sump with Steve and Ian, the Tarot card reading, hauling Ian's body to the surface, the flood, Steve's falls, his visit to the *curandero*. There were four days remaining on Noel's grim vigil, and the strain of waiting was clearly taking its toll on him. "What do you think is gonna happen?" he kept asking Steele. "Are they gonna come back? If they don't, do you know what I've got to do?"

Steele had no more of a clue what would happen next than anyone. But he tried to comfort Noel anyway. "Every-thing's going to be okay," he said. "There's always been a fairy godmother watching over Huautla. There were so many close calls; so many times someone should have died. But it's as if there's a helping hand that always pushes us back up the wall. I've had it happen. There were a whole bunch of times I should have been a dead man, I was falling, and then, boom, I'm caught."

Steele gently teased Noel back to humor. "You know, Noel, what makes me uncomfortable is being here with you," Steele chided. "Because every time I've caved with a doctor, we needed a doctor. It's like a jinx."

Bill rose early the morning of May 2, and clenched a small electric flashlight in his teeth as he tiptoed over jagged breakdown to the latrine he'd dug the afternoon before. He and Barbara shared a breakfast of hot oatmeal at Camp Six, then donned their black pile jump suits and climbing har-nesses. Before leaving, he carefully inspected the flints on the two remaining carbide lamps, and tightened the retainer caps with a pair of pliers.

They headed south, past the Silent Borehole, toward the passageway where Bill had turned back on April 8. That going tunnel would have been the obvious route forward, except that it was headed east and, more disturbingly, was rising too steeply. Bill thought it unlikely the April 8 route would lead down toward the resurgence in the Santo Domingo canyon. With barely a week to explore, they didn't have the luxury of probing every going passageway. Instead, they'd have to make strategic choices about which routes to push, and which to ignore. The river would be their only guide. Floodwaters had carved the labyrinth, and seasonal rains left behind scallops in the rock and other clues that pointed the way forward. Relying on such geological clues—and on more than a little instinct—they returned to the flooded tunnel just west of the April 8 route, which they'd dubbed Sump Four.

There at the edge of yet another eerie black lagoon, Bill and Barbara faced their conundrum. Since they'd resolved not to dive any further, they couldn't follow the river itself. So in addition to being their guide, the river was also their gatekeeper. It teased them onward even while barring their progress. But rivers are restless creatures, too, when regarded in geologic time. On the surface, they meander through low-lying fields and forests as they rise and fall with the seasons, ever seeking the swiftest route to the sea. Underground, where their banks are constricted by rock, they rise and fall more dramatically, as if engaged in some geologic game of three-dimensional chess. A tumbling boulder might open the slow series of moves. Should the boulder come to rest atop a softer spot of rock, and should the river choose to spin the boulder for several thousand years, a pothole might result, like the one Ian dove into to retrieve his hammer. And should such a pothole lead the river to a lower layer of rock just a bit softer than its existing bed, the river might seize upon the opening to move down a level. At first, such a move might take the shape of a dramatic horsetail falls, like the Grand Cascade or the Washing Machine. Later, the river might abandon the upper bed completely, leaving an overhead passage that remains dry when the water is low. It was such an overhead passage that Ian and Noel were searching for as they hugged the ceiling during their early exploration of Sump One. It was such a "fossil riverbed" that Bill had followed when he bypassed Sump Three a month earlier. And it was exactly such a Swiss cheese mezzanine that he was hoping to locate on May 2.

He unpacked one of their high-intensity krypton dive lights, and used its piercing beam to probe the layers of limestone that rose above the south end of Sump Four. There, some eight meters above the sump, was an oval-shaped void. Barbara uncoiled the nine-millimeter rope and fed an end to Bill. He scouted the wall above the pool. It had small, jagged projections sticking out here and there, but was otherwise dead vertical. He tied a figure-8 knot in the end of the rope and clipped it into his harness. The rope wouldn't stop him from falling, but at least Barbara would be able to haul him in from the lake if he slipped. He edged out onto the mud-covered wall until there was no dry land below him. The wall was slick, but the projections made for good holds. Before long he'd free climbed the eight-meter wall and crawled into the opening. He set a bolt, rigged the line, and Barb followed. While she worked her way up, he began exploring the mezzanine. It wasn't that large, perhaps two meters wide and five tall. The walls were whitish gray, with large scallops carved in the rock walls and floor when the passage was flooded. He found a shaft leading down into the darkness—perhaps the remnant of some ancient pothole—and tossed a large rock down. It landed with a loud "splush." He sighed. Somewhere below him lay Sump Five.

He uncoiled another length of rope, tied it off, then began rappelling down the shaft. The sump's greenish hue faded to black as he rappelled through the floor, and he was certain he was in for a swim. But before he was all the way to the water's surface, he spotted a thin, steeply ascending ledge along the east wall. He started swinging on the rope, and was able to pendulum over to the ledge. He tied off the end of the line, and Barbara rappelled down behind him. Together, they scaled up the ledge system to the continuation of the higher, roof-level tunnel.

The new tunnel led eighty meters to the head of yet another drop-off. A massive slab of bedrock appeared to jut up below the drop, like a jagged marble pyramid. Bill rigged another line, and they rappelled onto the pyramid. About the size and pitch of a steep house roof, the pyramid stood in the middle of a large lake stretching in all directions. It was as if the passage had deposited them on some rock island in the middle of a black sea at night. Barbara shone her light across the black lagoon.

"This looks like your department, G," she said. "I don't like cold swims."

He looked at his dry, dusty pile jump suit. It wasn't going to do him much good in the black sea below. He might as well be wearing a Speedo in an icy mountain lake. He waded off in a southeast direction. The cold water hit like a knife. Barbara watched his light fade away, then listened as his echoing splashes did the same.

Bill's breath rolled over the black water like steam as he waded neck-deep through the ice-cold water. He held his stomach tight in a futile attempt to stave off the penetrating cold. After forty meters of swimming to the southeast, he turned back when the ceiling met the water. He tried again to the northeast; same result. The northwest branch led back where they had come from, likely connecting to the downstream end of Sump Five. He pulled himself out of the pond and onto the pyramid slab, shivering and breathing hard. "Well, we aren't going any of those ways," he said.

That left the longest-, deepest-looking southwest branch. When he was on rappel, he'd seen a gravel bar in that direction. Since he'd seen gravel bars adjacent to terminal sumps so many times before, he'd chosen to investigate the other routes first. Now there was nothing left but to swim over there and verify with his own two eyes what he feared would be the end of the San Agustín expedition: yet another sump.

He took a deep breath and swam furiously toward the distant sandbar. Not two strokes into the swim, a cold realization swept over him: He wasn't going to make it. Unlike the previous three attempts, he was no longer able to touch bottom. Despite the powerful strokes of his long arms, he was sinking. His metal vertical gear—ascenders, rack, carabiners—and his heavy rubber Bata boots were weighing him down like cement overshoes. It was too late to turn back, too late for Barbara to throw him a line. He paddled as hard as he could, but could just barely keep his head above water. After thirty meters, he was starting to wear out. He could feel the water splashing higher and higher up his head. *Swim, man, swim!* he scolded himself. Just as his head slipped under, however, his toes touched the sand bottom. He gasped for breath and took another large step. After that, he was able to wade again. He walked up on the gravel bar, shivering violently. Bent over, hands on his knees, he swallowed giant gulps of air. *You nearly bought it that time,* he scolded himself.

When he'd finally caught his breath, he stood up. Only then did he realize that the four-cornered lagoon wasn't, as he'd feared, a sump. The high sandbar and low ceiling had conspired to create a mirage: From the pyramid, they looked connected; but now that he was here, he could see that the ceiling rose abruptly just beyond the beach. He shook off the cold, dripping water like a soaked dog, then quietly walked across the sandbar. A hundred meters of gravel flats later, he found himself staring out into a gaping tunnel. It was fifteen meters wide at the start, then expanded into a void too massive to see in its entirety. He gazed into the utter blackness for a few seconds. Then he shot his right arm into the air and let out a yell.

"Aaahooooooooooo!" he shouted. "Ah-ah-ah-oooooo-oooie!"

As his voice echoed back in twisted refrain, he savored the moment. It was a sublime triumph. After so many years of struggle, he'd found the route, the secret doorway to the gaping, unexplored beyond. It was the unknown nature of what lay ahead that spellbound him. For the first time in years, the road ahead was wide open. All he and Barbara had to do was pick up their gear and stride victoriously through vast corridors leading into the heart of Huautla. Booty unbound.

CHAPTER ELEVEN

After stripping off his vertical gear and boots, Bill swam back to get Barbara. "You wanted booty?" he asked as he pulled himself up onto the pyramid slab. "We just busted this sucker wide open."

She stuffed her climbing gear into a large Nalgene bottle, tied her boots around her neck, and followed Bill back through the ice-cold Four Corners Lake. Once atop the sandbar, they suited back up and set out into the massive chamber beyond, secure in the satisfaction that each and every step forward was a step no one had ever taken before.

They climbed down through a massive breakdown field filled with polished boulders the size of pickup trucks. The rock had strange orange and red streaks that neither of them had seen before in Huautla. They were descending rapidly, but without rope. Gripped by exploration fever, Bill free climbed down each drop, then climbed back up just to be sure that they'd be able to get out. Then the both of them climbed down and moved on to the next drop.

"Wow! Would you look at that!" Barbara said, standing atop one of the truck-boulders. A towering stalagmite thrust up into the blackness, like a citadel guarding the gates of beyond. Its height made it a useful landmark in the massive chamber, which was 140 meters wide and more than thirty meters high. Their puny cap lamps were far too weak to light up much beyond whatever immediate area they happened to be climbing over, so the journey was like descending a boulder field at night on a mountain.

"What do you think we should call this place?" he asked.

"How about The Hall of Perseverance," she suggested.

Bill laughed. "Sounds like something a cough drop manufacturer would think up," he said. "What about Perseverance Hall?"

"I can live with that," she replied. "It certainly was hard-won."

He took off the orange backpack and fished out one of the high-intensity dive lights. He looked at the light carefully, moving his thumb back and forth over the on switch without touching it. Every second that lamp was turned on was one fewer that it would function where it would be needed most—getting back to Camp Five. But without better light, they were flying blind down here in inner space. He flipped the switch and played the laserlike beam out ahead of them. Only then did they see the chamber focusing far below into a funnel. "Man, I sure hope that's not a breakdown choke we're looking at," he said, playing the beam about the lowest point in the rubble field, fifty meters below. "We're just starting to pick up some depth here."

"Let's go find out," she said. "But as long as you've got that pack open, let's take a few pictures." Bill produced the waterproof camera, and Barbara a large strobe. She led the way, aiming the strobe down the tunnel while Bill composed photos of her in silhouette. In addition to making pictures, each burst of light lit up the chamber like sheet lightning and gave them a fleeting glimpse of what lay ahead. By the time he put the camera away, she was easily a football field ahead of him.

He hurried to catch up. Big mistake. He stepped on a

table-sized boulder and it started sliding. It moved rapidly down the V-shaped chute it had been resting in for who knows how many thousands of years, teetering patiently, just waiting for something to set it in motion. Like a bowling ball rolling down an inclined alley, the five-ton chunk of limestone began spinning downward. Bill was scrambling to stay atop it.

Barb heard the thunderous motion behind her and stopped cold. There was no mistaking the crashing sound of heavy, brittle limestone. She whirled around, fearing she'd have to dodge whatever was lumbering her way. But she saw nothing but darkness.

"G!" she shouted. "G!"

He lay inverted in the trough. His feet were in the air and his butt was jammed against the face of the boulder. He'd fallen into the path of the rolling block of rock, but the boulder had fortuitously jammed into another chunk of breakdown before crushing him. He pulled himself upright, then reached up to stroke the flint wheel on his cap lap. A reassuring "boom" echoed out into the chamber as the flame ignited.

"G! Are you all right?" Barbara asked as she scurried back to where he lay.

"Ah, well . . ." He wiggled about. Nothing felt broken. "Whew!" He caught his breath. "Two demerit points on that move."

"What happened?"

"The damn boulder just rolled right out from under me," he said. "Could have crushed my leg."

The seriousness of their situation struck hard: If Bill had broken his leg, he'd almost certainly have spent the next six weeks more or less right where he lay. Barbara could never have carried him back to Camp Six by herself. And even if she had, he never could have swum back through the sumps with a broken leg. She would have had to go back to Camp Six by herself, pack up their camping gear, carry it all to where Bill lay, and establish a new camp in which he would recuperate. Then she'd have had to go back to Camp Six again, kit up a rig, and swim back through the sumps alone to fetch Noel. Bill was still grappling with the enormity of the potential chain of events when Barbara reached him.

"Jeez," she said, reaching down to help him up. "Let's not do that again, okay?"

They continued together—and much more slowly—down to the lower end of the enormous room, where giant boulders had piled up against a high wall like marbles in a jar. Bill took out what was left of the rope and rappelled into a space between two of the largest. Twelve meters below, he landed on the bedrock floor. He'd returned to the river passage. The river had carved this cave, and knew its secrets better than anyone. Their job was to follow the river.

What had been an intimidating amount of water in the Lower Gorge seemed tame here in this massive chamber. The tunnel was scoured, scalloped, and polished—yet another testimony to the enormous volume of water that ran through here once the rains began. They came to a series of three long, narrow lakes that spanned the passage from wall to wall. The first two were only waist deep. Bill waded into the cold, clear water, and Barbara followed. They clung to the edge of the ten-meter-wide passage, where the water wasn't as deep. With no far shore visible, the third lake looked like a sump. The only way to find out was to go for another swim. But they were both cold and tired.

"I don't know about you, but this looks like a good place to start surveying our way back," Bill suggested. "Unless, of course, you feel up for a swim."

"No thanks," she said. "I reckon we're at least a mile beyond camp already. I'm cold."

He opened up the pack and produced the optical compass, clinometer, survey tape, and a waterproof notebook. Barbara took the instruments and tape, Bill the notepad.

Together they began surveying their way back to Camp Six. It was a slow, wet, cold retreat. Wisps of steam rose from their black jump suits as their body heat drove out the moisture.

When they reached Camp Six, Bill pulled off his Bata boots and inspected his feet. After a long day in wet rubber boots, they looked and felt like prunes. Barbara put some water on the stove. As a joke, she asked what he wanted to eat.

"How about a one-gallon Nalgene filled with Dairy Queen vanilla malt?"

She laughed. They'd been working hard for months, and sustaining themselves primarily on freeze-dried food. Bill had slipped from a wiry 205 pounds when he left Maryland to an almost emaciated 189 pounds when he last left the surface. Both were starving for some real food.

"Sure," she quipped back. "And I'll have Chinese. Something with lots of vegetables, maybe some chicken, all in a spicy brown sauce."

"Either that or a big old cup of, well . . ." Bill smiled. "What I could really go for would be some pulverized Stroganoff!"

She handed him a cupful. "Take all you want," she said. "It's on sale."

It was also the only dinner they had. Bill dug out two small Zip-loc bags filled with salt and cayenne pepper tucked into the freeze-dried food bottle. Barbara had thoughtfully placed them in there more than a week before. "Good thinking," he said.

Noel woke up sometime after midnight. He heard something stir at Camp Three. He lay still in the darkness—hoping it was Bill and Barbara—but he heard nothing more.

While lying there, he realized he also needed to use the latrine. That meant finding a light, finding shoes, walking across the camp, ugh. He tried to roll over and go back to sleep. But then he figured he'd just wake up again in another fifteen minutes, so he might was well get it over with. Before he was able to make up his mind, Bill Steele switched on a flashlight.

"Did you hear that?" Noel asked.

"Yeah," Steele replied. "I was hoping it was Bill and Barbara."

"Me, too, but I haven't heard anything else."

"Yeah. Now I gotta pee."

"Me, too," Noel replied.

The two of them padded over to the latrine and were standing there like guys at a urinal when they heard a low groan. "Who was that?" Steele asked. Once they'd finished relieving themselves, they started walking around and checking people. First the newcomers, then Broussard. They found Don a foot from his sleeping bag, face down in the dirt.

"Oh my God," Noel said.

Steele knelt down and turned him over. He was pale and drooling. His hands were raised at chest level, palms out, like he was being held up at gunpoint. And he stayed that way after Steele rolled him over. He was stiff as a rock, as if suffering from rigor mortis.

"Insulin overdose," Noel said, answering the question that had only begun to form in Steele's mind. "We gotta get sugar in him."

Relieved that Noel knew what to do, Steele woke the others.

"We gotta act fast, 'cause he's close to going unconscious," Noel said, snapping out of his deep funk and into doctor mode as instantly as he had when Steve slipped under the waterfall. "If he goes, it's a whole different ball game."

Noel ordered Cicheski to fetch the bottle of sugar they'd been joking about the night before, and some water. He and Steele then propped Don up into a sitting position, leaning against Steele's back. When Cicheski returned, Noel mixed the sugar and water into a thick syrup. Then he pried open Don's mouth, and began dribbling the syrup under his tongue.

"Can he swallow?" Steele asked.

"Doesn't have to," Noel replied calmly. "Sugar goes straight in, through the mouth and tongue."

Noel talked gently as he continued spooning the sticky paste into Don's mouth. He explained to Don everything that he was doing. Within half an hour, Don had loosened up and regained consciousness. Within an hour, he sat upright and said, "I'm gonna be okay."

After eating a candy bar and catching his breath, Don explained that he'd miscalculated his insulin. He'd adjusted his daily dose to compensate for the hard work of hauling gear. But when the group decided to take the day off and go up to Anthodite Hall instead, he'd wound up working less, and eating less, and needing less insulin. As a result, the amount he'd given himself was too much. Once he'd recovered, he traded his sleeping bag for another—the sugar water had splattered all over the one he'd been using—and went back to sleep.

Steele was still too wired to sleep. He and Noel sat down at Stonehenge.

"Is he gonna be all right?" Now Steele was pressing Sloan for answers.

"Oh yeah," Noel said nonchalantly. "It's just like your car running out of gas. You put gas in it and everything's normal again. He'll be fine."

"That was close, you know," Steele said, still rattled. "We could have lost a second person."

Noel nodded absentmindedly. He gazed down the flowstone slope toward the Lower Gorge, and added, "or two more."

Barbara whispered in the darkness. "Hey, G, what time is it?"

Bill rolled over and pulled his Rolex up to his face. It had become scratched and terminally mud-encrusted, but he could still read it.

"Six A.M. May 4. Time to scoop booty."

Barbara got up, fired up the stove, and mixed some instant oatmeal. Before entering the cave, she'd packed the bottle with fruit flavors. She threw in a bag of maple flavor, too, because it was Noel's favorite, and at that time she thought he'd be diving. She loathed the maple, so Bill volunteered to eat it.

"You're right, B," he said, after shoveling two spoonfuls into his mouth. "This stuff tastes like glue." Staring into his purple cup with disgust, he realized what the meal was missing.

"Noel should have been here," he said.

"Ian should have been here," she replied.

Bill nodded. They both should have.

After breakfast, they donned their wetsuits. They planned to wear them all day, on top of their fleece underwear. In addition to providing buoyancy and insulation for the cold sump swims, the thick neoprene wetsuits offered superior protection against bumps and bruises along the way. They packed two liters of carbide, a half-liter of gorp, the rest of their bolts, and every remaining bit of rope they had into the orange pack. They strapped on their harnesses, racks, and ascenders; helmets and gloves; and off they went.

It took almost three hours of fast hiking to work their way through Perseverance Hall and down to the lake where they'd turned around on their last push. They'd spent most of the preceding day surveying this territory, so the route felt familiar. Barbara climbed out on a ledge along the left-hand wall to get a better look. It looked like a sump. But there was a small horizontal slat where the ceiling came to the water. Maybe it was only a reflection. Or maybe it was a narrow airspace. They'd seen "near sumps" before, some so low that they'd had to roll over onto their back and run their noses along the roof for air.

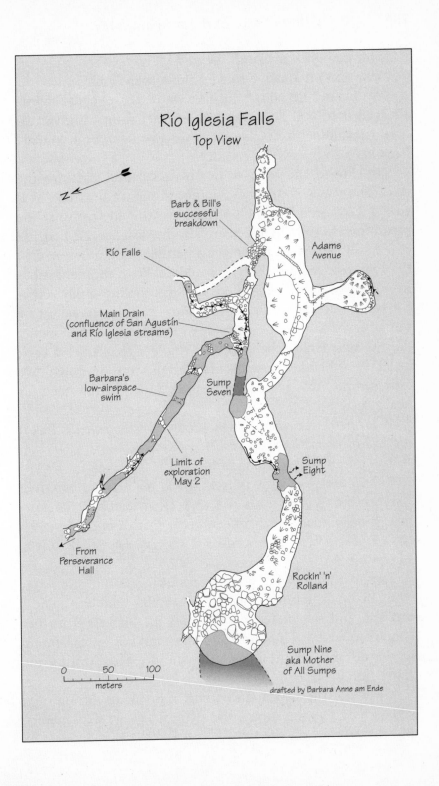

Río Iglesia Falls
Top View

N

Barb & Bill's
successful
breakdown

Río Falls

Adams
Avenue

Main Drain
(confluence of San Agustín
and Río Iglesia streams)

Barbara's
low-airspace
swim

Sump
Seven

Limit of
exploration
May 2

Sump
Eight

From
Perseverance
Hall

Rockin' 'n'
Rolland

Sump Nine
aka Mother
of All Sumps

0   50   100

meters

drafted by Barbara Anne am Ende

"You going for a swim?" he said.

"You mind if I take a look? I think there's air."

"Go for it," he said. "But first we better give you a line. I'll feed it to you from here. If you get sumped, give two hard tugs, and I'll hold it for you so you can pull yourself back in."

She clipped the rope to her harness, then slid into the lake. The water was bone-chilling, though not as bad as it would have been had she not been wearing her wetsuit. She swam toward the tiny black arch in the distance. At first Bill could still hear the cap lamp on her helmet grating against the low rock ceiling, then he couldn't. For a moment more he could see the reflection of her light rippling dimly across the black water, then he didn't. She was gone. As he sat by the edge of the dark water, slowly paying out the orange line, he wondered if he'd feel her tug. He recalled that back in 1979—when he made his first nervous, upside-down dive into Sump One—neither Zeman nor Lloyd had noticed his heavy tugs.

What if I can't tell? he wondered. *How long should I wait before I start hauling her back?*

Ten minutes passed. Then fifteen.

Fifteen years later, he mused. *We've got laptop computers. Lightweight Acurex tanks. The Mk-IV rebreathers. Specialty gear from a dozen corporate sponsors. Everything money can buy. And it still all comes down to waiting for your buddy to tug on a rope!*

Twenty minutes. He was just about to get into the water when he finally felt her tugs. He braced his long legs against the wall and she pulled herself back in. Flickers from her lamp reappeared. Then he heard the sound of water lapping in the distance. A moment later, she popped through the restriction.

"It goes," she said, the excitement breaking through her voice. "Used all the rope. That swim is at least sixty meters. Big river tunnel on the far side."

"All right!" Bill said. He looked again at the small gap she'd come through. "It wouldn't take much rain to trap us over there. Look, I'm going to bolt-rig this rope on both ends so that it goes right through. That way, if it floods while we're over there, we'll be able to free dive it by pulling ourselves back along the line."

Barbara swam back through while Bill set the bolt. He then followed her through the low-air arch. On the far side he pulled out the hammer and drill, and set a bolt in a boulder at the far end of the lake. He'd seen cavers trapped beyond obstacles like this before. Even a light rain could easily seal them in for good. Barbara returned about the time he finished securing the line.

"Do you want the good news or the bad?" she asked.

"Uh-oh. Give me the bad first."

"I followed the water downstream past another lake. It turns into a sump. I swam the whole perimeter. There's no way on."

"So what's the good news?"

She struggled to disguise the disappointment in her voice and focus on the positive. "About a hundred meters beyond a pile of boulders is a huge river coming in from the left. It must have four times the flow of this one!"

"Four times?" he asked. "That's incredible."

"Yeah, but it leads upstream. That's not the direction we want to go. I think we're at the end of the road."

He wasn't ready to believe it: "We'll see about that."

They waded down the tunnel together. Within 100 meters they could hear the rush of the new river. It flowed in from the left, forming a T confluence. Downstream, to the right, was Sump Seven. A cursory inspection suggested Barb was right: no way on without dive gear. Upstream, to the left, was a different story. The new river she'd discovered flowed down a dramatic canyon, twelve meters across and twenty meters high. They hiked up the passage. It jogged abruptly to the left, then scrambled over a large breakdown pile. Mist covered their faces as they climbed, and they soon found themselves standing before a massive waterfall. Twelve meters overhead, an enormous river plunged out of a six-by-six-meter tunnel and arched out into space. The deafening cascade was without question the largest waterfall either of them had ever seen underground.

"The Río Iglesia!" Bill shouted.

"You think?" Barb yelled back.

"No doubt about it!"

The largest among the many surface rivers that twisted across the top of the Huautla Plateau, the Río Iglesia had been a source of speleological fascination—and frustration—ever since that drizzly summer day in 1965 when Bill Russell and his buddies from Austin arrived in San Agustín. In 1967, a Canadian expedition followed the river down through the Sótano del Río Iglesia to the minus-300-meter level, only to see it disappear into a breakdown pile. Since then, no fewer than twenty-six international expeditions had come hunting for the master river, the subterranean Holy Grail that they believed would tie together the crazy quilt of surface streams that made the Huautla Plateau such a hydrologic riddle.

"The Main Drain!" Bill shouted, recalling how John Fish had referred to the master river. "We're standing in it!"

He broke out the survey instruments, and handed them to Barbara. He flipped open his waterproof notebook, and asked, "How about Río Falls?"

"Sounds good to me," she yelled.

He then thought for a second, set the book and pencil down, and fished out the bolting kit from the bag.

"What are you doing?" she shouted.

"Going to set a permanent survey marker," he said. "Someday, some way, someone is going to come down that shaft. And when they do, I want to make it easy for them to tie the two surveys together. You never know, it might be us! We'll appreciate the favor," he said, laughing.

While he set the symbolic bolt, Barbara fished the camera out of the pack. "I think this deserves a picture, don't you think?"

Bill nodded. They took several photos, then began to survey downstream. Río Falls was no place to hang around. The wind-driven spray was whipping past and they were cooling off rapidly. "Well, I guess this is it," Barbara said, referring to the dead-end sump back at the T. Her disappointment was obvious. "I guess we finish this survey and we're done."

"Maybe," Bill said. "Why don't you take a break here. I need to play out a hunch."

"What do you mean?" she asked.

"You see how this big tunnel makes a ninety-degree bend here," he explained. "I bet you there's something over here." He dug out the dive light, switched it on, and played the beam across the southeast wall. "See . . . there," he exclaimed. "There's a small fissure. Give me five minutes."

She followed him to the entrance of the small passage and sat down. No sense in both of them going up into some body-sized crack that probably didn't go anywhere. But her curiosity got the better of her. And within ten minutes, she, too, was in the crack. It was awkward, but going.

"Hey G, you up ahead there?" she yelled, her voice dampened by the muddy walls.

A muffled "In here" filtered back. She found him sitting in a small chamber. "I think there is something headed out behind me," he said. "Give me a few more minutes."

Barbara got bored waiting, and started looking for an alternate route. She couldn't see an end to the fissure above her, so she climbed up to investigate.

"Where are you?" Bill yelled, after his passageway looped back to a balcony overlooking Río Falls.

"Up here. It keeps going," she shouted back down. She continued wending her way into the darkness above. When

Bill could barely hear her boots scraping the rock, he decided to follow.

Fifteen meters above, she broke into a gigantic room. It was fifty meters wide, 363 meters long, fifteen meters high, and descended steeply. High mounds of dirt covered the floor. Hundreds of years of farming had eroded the steep slopes of the Río Iglesia valley, and over countless rainy seasons the river had deposited much of that fertile soil here in this room. It looked like a landscaped golf course—in monochrome brown—beneath a broad arched ceiling of tan limestone.

Barbara sifted the soil through her glove. "Never seen these in a cave before." She pulled a tiny bug from the soil. When touched, it curled into a tight, protective ball.

They combed the edges of the room, and Bill found a small tunnel that descended. Very low at first, almost like something playing tricks on his ears, he heard a rumbling. The passage continued descending. The rumble grew louder. And within another 100 meters he broke out into a twenty-meter-wide stream way with a clean cobble floor.

He reviewed the passages they'd been through since Barbara's low-air swim: east through the Río Iglesia tunnel, south through the breakdown fissure, then west through the big dirt chamber. They'd been working their way around a giant bypass. He'd doubled back on the active river. He was sure of it now. The sound grew louder with each step. Soon he could see the turbulent river. It boiled out of a deep pool, and thrashed down through boulder-strewn rapids. Looking up at the pool, he realized he'd found the way around Sump Seven, the one they'd thought had stopped them back at the T that led to Río Falls.

The current was much stronger down here, below where the Río Iglesia had joined the Main Drain. The river rushed down into a lake measuring twenty-five meters in diameter: Sump Eight. Waves churned on its surface, and radiated toward the south wall where the river suddenly disappeared into a sump. Barbara took the lead end of the tape and began swimming across the turbulent lake. She pulled herself out onto the polished boulders at the far shore. Bill took the survey measurements, then followed her across.

The tunnel rose gradually on the other side of the lake in a forty-meter-wide boulder pile. The river, strangely, had disappeared. Barbara raced ahead while Bill sketched the room. She returned a moment later, breathless.

"It gets . . . really big . . . over this next rise," she panted.

"You don't call this big?" Bill asked, waving his arm across the boulder-filled passage.

"You don't understand," she said. "I mean, it gets HU-MON-GOUS!"

They crested the boulder field and were soon gazing down an immense funnel. It was easily 100 meters across. And the ceiling rose out of sight. It was breathtaking. They stood together on the precipice in a moment of silent triumph.

"Right," Bill said, finally breaking the trance. "Let's shoot a survey line down there."

Barbara hiked down the slope with the tape. Within 100 meters they came to the edge of what, from above, appeared to be the blackness of a lower tunnel. But as they grew closer the tunnel didn't brighten. It was as if the beams from their lamps had struck a black sponge. That's when they realized it was a lake. A big lake. Only when Bill reached Barbara's final survey station did he realize how big. It was at least twenty-five meters across, and twice that long. Steep sand banks sloped down from two sides; the other two were guarded over by sheer stone buttresses rising into the gloom.

He knelt down at the water's edge and shone a dive light under the surface. Its beam went far enough to show that the sand slope continued underwater, maintaining the same descent rate. And he could see that this immense cobble borehole—and the river he'd lost track of on the other side

of this giant funnel—continued down right there, underwater. This was no lake. He switched off the light and sat
down for the first time in hours. The disappointment was
evident in his face as he looked up at Barbara.

"Welcome," he said slowly, "to the Mother of All
Sumps."

Bill was mesmerized by giant ripples in the sand. They
were like small dunes. "Can you imagine the flow that must
come through here to do that?" he said.

Barbara stepped over a dune and picked something out of
the sand. It was a Popsicle stick. Then she found a plastic
toothbrush. "Where do you suppose these came from?"

"San Miguel?" he guessed, referring to a small village to
the southeast of San Agustín. Like the dunes, the debris was
evidence that the coming rains would transform the towering funnel into a torrential 100-meter-wide whirlpool,
with the power to suck anything in its maw deep into the
earth.

"G, what's the date?" Barbara asked.

"Uh, May 4."

The Popsicle stick had reminded her: The rainy season
was nearly upon them. "I'm starting to think this won't be
such a good place to be standing in, say, another week or
three," she said.

"Yeah," he replied. "Me, too."

They probed the cliffs above the Mother Sump with the
dive light, searching for some upper gallery that would
bypass the deep water, but found no route onward. The
sense of impending opportunity that had driven Bill to
search for high routes around Sump Four and Sump Seven
was gone. Standing there in Sump Nine, he felt like a bug
caught in a toilet bowl. It was only a matter of time before
someone yanked the chain.

"It's checkmate," he said. "No time for a dive. No other
way on. Time to go home."

His legs felt heavy as he started walking back up the hill. Every sinew of his soul wanted to keep going, to find some other way down. But his head knew the game was over—for this year, at least.

Barbara fiddled with the beat-up toothbrush as she hiked alongside. Bill hadn't let her pack one. Space in the big orange duffel was just too precious. So it had been days since she'd brushed her teeth. There wasn't much left of this one, but if she scraped off the mud and then sterilized the bristles in boiling water . . . Then the sad realization set in. She'd be back at Camp Three within a few days. Her time beyond the sump was nearly through.

They continued up the funnel together in silence. At the top, they turned to gaze at the spectacular view one more time.

"I've got a name for this," Barbara finally offered.

"Yeah?"

"Rockin' 'n' Rolland," she suggested. "It describes the boulders and hillocks. And Ian always enjoyed a good pun."

Bill laughed, and penciled the name in his little yellow book.

"That's a great name," he said. "And how about Adams Avenue for the big dirt-floored room? Rolf would have loved this place."

They surveyed their way back, finally reaching Camp Six some twenty-two hours after they'd departed. After recuperating for most of May 5, they suited up for the return dive. Everything went fine until Bill got in the water. He fired up the rig, and his main computer crashed.

He examined the rig. The entire unit had absorbed substantial abuse on the long haul down to Sump One and the cable leading to the main computer display had come loose a fraction of a millimeter, hardly enough to be noticed, but enough for a few drops of water to work their way inside. And that's all it took to short out the computer.

"Dammit!" he cursed. "I'm screwed."

Barb looked over. "What's wrong?"

"Computer's crapped. Gonna have to run this dive on manual—"

He stopped in mid-sentence. The rig snapped to life. The second and third computers—fully redundant backups built in for just such an emergency—had assumed command. The head-up display flickered, and the green LED lit up. "I'll be damned . . . Good job, Nigel!" Bill exclaimed, referring to Nigel Jones, Cis-Lunar's electronics designer. The backup computers ran the rig perfectly for the rest of the trip.

Bill's last swim through the sump that had held his imagination hostage for so many years was stunning. After such a long stretch of dry weather, the visibility was the best he'd ever seen it. With Barbara in the lead, Bill turned his lights off and let hers light up the deep for him. For the first time since he'd gazed into the great blue void in 1979, he could appreciate the awesome complexity of the underwater canyon. The rebreathers were working flawlessly. No bubbles. The whole voyage home was totally silent.

As he floated along, he wondered if just maybe this wasn't even better than a space walk. Not merely orbiting the earth, but floating within her exploring her secrets firsthand. And he realized that after so many years, his own life had finally come full circle: Here in the boundless depths of inner space, he'd finally fulfilled his boyhood aspiration to be like John Glenn.

Bill burst into the cacophonous Camp Five canyon a few moments later. As soon as he reached the shallows beneath the dive platform, he stood up and gave Barb a long, wet hug. "We did it!" he said. "By God, we did it."

The couple staggered into Camp Three late that night. It had taken five hours to break down the rigs, and two more to claw their way up the Lower Gorge with a forty-three-pound rebreather in tow. Noel heard them coming, and jogged down the flowstone slope to meet them.

"Hoooooie," Bill howled when he saw Noel's light bobbing down the hill. Noel returned the welcome.

"Bill! Barbara! Oh man! I can't begin to tell you two how relieved I am to see you!"

Bill thrust out his open hand in greetings. Noel batted it away and seized his old friend in a long bear hug. After he'd squeezed Barbara just as hard, he stood back and asked, "Well?"

"Dr. Sloan," Bill began in mock officiousness, "welcome to the deepest cave in the Americas."

They hiked up to Stonehenge. Steele and his group of volunteers had left for the surface, but Noel and Don were on the edge of their stone seats as Bill and Barbara related the highlights of their week beyond the deep. Bill ceremoniously opened the Nalgene in which he'd secured his survey notebook and the four rolls of film they'd shot; four months of bruising work distilled into one small plastic bottle. He read from his notes as he and Barbara described the three kilometers of virgin passage and seven new sumps they'd discovered, all heading south toward the Santo Domingo Canyon.

It was an emotional reunion. Noel could feel his body relax; his ulcer faded away, and with it, his Mr. Hyde posture. And whereas Camp Three had once felt like a remote place—Wes and the Moles felt like they were trapped on the far side of the moon during the flood—it now felt warm and homey to Bill and Barbara, as comfortable as the living room in Gaithersburg. After Bill went to bed, Barb stayed up for another hour and did some needlework.

The four of them—Bill, Barbara, Noel, and Don—spent the next five days hauling gear up the cave. They dismantled Camp Five, and stowed the platform components in a high alcove for future use. They scoured Camp Three, and began moving the mountain of gear up the cave to successively higher temporary camps. Much to everyone's welcome surprise, Jim Brown reappeared, cajoled into rejoining the de-rig by Bev Shade, the teenager Don had recruited in Austin. They established an interim bivouac called Camp 2B in Tommy's Borehole, near the 620 Depot. And Camp 1B was pitched at the top of the sixty-meter drop that nearly claimed Angel Soto. "I feel better with each gorge we leave behind," Noel told the six of them one night. "We've got the data. And everyone is safely above flood stage."

Hauling more than a ton of gear up the long drops of the Bowl Hole Series was painful, thankless work, even more physically challenging than hauling Ian out had been. A seemingly endless line of duffels awaited to be hauled up each pitch. Both Bill and Noel developed staph infections on their fingers, due to the constant grinding against the grit-covered inside of wet rubber gloves. Everyone suffered from sore muscles and severe harness chafe, due to working on rope for eighteen-hour days. Upon reaching the top of the One-Ten, the group decided to head to the surface for a few days of rest before ferrying everything up the Stairway to Hell.

After eighteen days below ground, Bill could smell the dense vegetation of the surface from the Cracked Slab. It was nighttime when they reached the Slip-n-Slide, and a torrential thunderstorm was assaulting the surface. Bill dragged himself up the Jungle Drop. His arms and legs burned with every motion, chafing old wounds each time he stood in his harness. The long, thin line swayed in the howling wind, and sheets of rain soaked his muddy clothes.

As Barbara started up the last drop, Bill crawled out the entrance tunnel, and into the cornfield below. The tiny seedlings he'd studiously avoided stepping on during the early days of the expedition had ripened into high stalks. He staggered down into the clearing, and threw back his head. The wind blew out his carbide lamp, and the hard rain peppered his unshaven face.

"Let it rain," he shouted to He Who Knows the Sky, or whatever other spirits might be listening. "We're done. You let it come."

EPILOGUE

Barbara rose early the next morning, and washed her hair at sunrise. Bill slept a bit later, and after an extended breakfast of—well, everything in sight—he started entering their survey data into a portable computer. Barbara read aloud the figures they'd scribbled in their survey notebooks, while Bill keyed them into the computer program. When they were done, they discovered they'd lengthened Sistema Huautla to fifty-six kilometers.

And at 1,475 meters deep, Huautla recaptured its status as the deepest cave in the Americas, and moved from twelfth to fifth place in the world rankings.

"Damn," Bill said, frustrated that they were still 127 meters shy of the longtime record holder, the 1,602-meter Reseau Jean Bernard.

By the summer of 2001, the French cave had been bumped down the list three times itself. First by another French cave, the Gouffre Mirolda (−1,616 meters) in January of 1998. Then by Austria's Lamprechtsofen (−1,632 meters) in the summer of 1999. And in a stunning surprise, a cave called Voronja, on the Arabika massif in the former Soviet republic of Georgia, was pushed in January of 2001 to a reported depth of 1,710 meters. Thus Sistema Huautla had slipped to eighth place on the list.

A gap of only 235 meters remains, however, and the rapidly shuffling list illustrates the rising intensity of deep cave exploration. Sistema Huautla remains a strong contender because it harbors another 400 meters of "depth potential," while many of the other caves on the top ten list have essentially bottomed out. Surveyed depth is the depth confirmed by the physical passage of humans, and the subsequent mapping of those passages; only these figures count in the record books. Depth potential is generally measured by calculating the distance between the uppermost passable entrance, and the lowest spring from which water entering above emerges. (Potential is measured by releasing non-toxic dyes into high streams or sumps, then testing for the appearance of those dyes in resurgence springs below.) There are at least three locations in Mexico—including both Sistema Huautla and its sister, Sistema Cheve—that have potential depth in excess of 1,710 meters. The game has just begun; and each major expedition represents another bold move in this international game of subterranean chess.

These numbers understate the relative difficulty of reaching the bottom of Sistema Huautla. The Rockin' 'n' Rolland chamber remains the most remote place yet reached by humans inside the earth. As with any claim to a superlative, one must qualify what is meant by "remote." One might be tempted to equate remoteness with distance from the nearest entrance. Under this simple definition Tennessee's Blue Spring Cave would vie with Canada's Castleguard Cave and mexico's Sistema Cheve for the record. All three terminate roughly ten kilometers from the nearest entrance. However, as with any frontier, one must consider physical efforts, the level of enabling technology required, and the degree of psychological commitment necessary. It is the presence of 655 meters of flooded tunnels—not to mention the more than three kilometers of nylon highway one must traverse in order to reach those sumps—that place a journey to Sump Nine and the Rockin' 'n' Rolland chamber in a class by itself. By comparison, the most remote points in Voronja and Lamprechtsofen can each be reached on a three-week expedition without diving.

"I don't know what you're whining about," Barbara ribbed Bill as the noonday sun heated up the cookshed. "We scooped three lakes, four sumps, and Perseverance Hall. We found the Río Iglesia, and extended the underground system to—what?—thirty-five miles long. As far as I'm concerned, this was a great expedition."

Bill laughed. Even he had to agree.

Several more trips were made to de-rig the cave over the next week. All were day trips. After a combined total of forty-four days underground, Bill and Barbara felt no need to sleep again in the stygian gloom.

On May 17, some twenty-three packs were hoisted up the One-Ten, and then transported up to within 280 vertical meters of the entrance. Noel reorganized the way the thin remaining team worked in an effort to make it more fun for everyone. Instead of having individuals traveling back and forth like ants in a maze, Noel persuaded the group to line up in a little chain—each caver a few feet from the next—and pass the duffels along like a bucket brigade. This provided more personal contact, and the few team members remaining actually wound up joking and laughing their way through the last few painful days of what they'd begun to call the Endless De-Rig.

Two days later, all of the remaining equipment was transported to the base of the Jungle Drop. On May 21, a system of ropes and pulleys was rigged, and the rest of the gear was pulled out from above. The endless bucket brigade gave the few remaining team members a chance to mourn Ian as a group.

Though an autopsy had been performed in Oaxaca eight

days after Ian was found, it indicated only that Ian had died by asphyxiation due to immersion in water. There was no chance of examining blood sugar levels after so much time.

The notion that the rebreather had somehow killed Ian lost momentum after Barbara traveled to Camp Six and back on the same rig, without incident. And the theory was disproved after the memory chip that Bill removed from Ian's rig was studied. Like the black boxes that record flight conditions aboard commercial aircraft, the chip revealed that Ian had been swimming along the surface for some time before mysteriously plummeting to a depth of three meters. The data showed that throughout the dive, his oxygen level had been at or above that for normal air. So at no point had the breathing mix gone hypoxic.

An exhaustive investigation considered and ultimately rejected each of four possible causes of death: hardware or software malfunction of the rebreather; "pilot error"; or being knocked unconscious due to tripping while walking with the rig. Only one viable scenario remained: Ian hiked out onto the sandbars wearing a rig that weighed as much as he did, and—in the excitement of discovery—failed to compensate for the heavy toll this excess exertion had taken on his blood sugar levels. Shortly thereafter, he blacked out from diabetic hypoglycemia, apparently while swimming back to the beach. Eaten in time, a candy bar would have saved his life.

Ian Rolland's ashes were scattered at the summit of Ben Nevis in Scotland, where he'd often climbed, usually in the gloom of winter when the ice was good. Rob Parker led the eulogy for his longtime friend. Members of the RAF Mountain Rescue Team and the distinguished British Cave Diving Group attended the service. Ian's wife, Erica, remarried another member of the RAF rescue team in the spring of 1995.

In the fall of 1997, Bill Stone returned to England's Wookey Hole district to deliver yet another eulogy—for

Rob Parker. After years away from cave diving—and with a prospering climbing wall business—Parker had returned to the blue holes of the Bahamas to assist in filming a BBC documentary about Rob Palmer, a British cave diver who perished in a freak accident in the Red Sea. After the filming was done, Parker and partner Duffer Mallone went on an open-circuit exploration of Four Sharks Blue Hole. But they stayed down too long—scooping booty at 100 meters—and Parker ran low on his deep mix. He was forced to transfer to a bottle of compressed air at a depth of eighty meters, and the instant blast of nitrogen narcosis left him unconscious. Had he been diving a rebreather, Parker would still be alive.

Farmers from San Agustín Zaragoza were hired to haul the equipment from the cave entrance up into the village. And on the afternoon of May 21, mules began arriving at the gear shed, with rebreathers on their backs.

The technology that made the 1994 San Agustín expedition possible—the Cis-Lunar Mk-IV rebreather—was an experimental device. So much so that it had frightened even steadfast professional divers. Myth, superstition, and suspicion persisted for years afterward. Some members of the expedition continued to believe—in spite of digitally logged data to the contrary—that the rebreather had somehow killed Ian. But the Mk-IV's performance during the expedition was undeniable: Eighteen dives were conducted at the San Agustín sump, most below a depth of twenty-five meters. Yet the gas consumed during the entire project— barely eighty cubic feet of heliox and fifty cubic feet of oxygen—was less than an average scuba diver would suck through in a leisurely afternoon of recreational diving.

Tentatively at first, then with increasing enthusiasm, the Cis-Lunar rebreather was embraced: first by the scientific diving community—notably the Bishop Museum in Hawaii, which used it to discover more than sixty new species of fish at depths in excess of 120 meters—and then by the under-water film community, where silent running meant the ability to mingle with aquatic fauna previously frightened away by noisy exhaust bubbles. In 1999, a National Geographic Society expedition to Wakulla Springs provided convincing evidence that rebreathers had become mainstream technology.

Bill Stone, Nigel Jones, and Mike Stevens went on to develop a commercial version, which reached the market in 1997. Forty were produced before the much improved Mk-V-Mod1 was introduced in 1998. Fifty of those were sold over the following year. But by 2001, Cis-Lunar had become a victim of its own success. No fewer than ten diving manufacturing firms were producing commercial rebreathers. Due to lack of investment funding, and an unwillingness to compromise on safety features, the fledgling Cis-Lunar was unable to compete with those long-established firms. The plant in South Lancaster, Massachusetts, was closed in a cost-cutting measure while the company reorganized and sought capital to reenter the market.

The Cis-Lunar remains the tool of choice for those at the frontiers of underwater exploration, however. When the National Geographic Society fielded an expedition to the massive ice island floating off the coast of Antarctica in the spring of 2001, they took the Mk-VP with them.

On May 22, the remaining team members held a sparsely attended press conference in Huautla de Jiménez. A television crew from Telemundo was there, as were a few journalists from Oaxaca, and two of Huautla's three *presidentes*. As Renato García and Sergio Zambrano gave eloquent speeches of introduction, Bill glanced around the clean white-tile dining room of the Bellas Rosas—which the owner's son, Leonardo Casimiro Altamirano, had hastily rearranged for the event—and reflected on how many team members were missing.

Kenny Broad had left Huautla a month earlier. The following summer, working for the National Science Foundation's Ocean Drilling Program, he was dropped off on a desert isle in the South Pacific with a gas-powered drill, an inflatable boat, and a supply of food and water. Logistical snafus prevented the support helicopter from retrieving him on schedule, and his ten-day trip stretched into a six-week odyssey. In the spring of 2000, Kenny earned his Ph.D. in anthropology from Columbia University in New York. He accepted a teaching position in his native South Florida, where he continues to dive regularly.

After wrestling for weeks with his decision to leave, Steve Porter caught a ride back to Texas with Bill Steele in his van of volunteers. On May 4, Steve left a note for Noel that read: "Noel— My buddy, my buddy, my pal. I hope this all ends on a happy note for you. And soon. Looks like I'll be leaving with Steele and company . . . I plan to be at my parents' house when you drive through Texas. How about stopping in for an evening out on Dallas . . . Get my cap lamp for me from Bill, okay?" Steve returned to his life as a transportation analyst in Minneapolis, and subsequently married. Though no longer an active expeditionary caver, he continues to be an ardent wreck diver in the Great Lakes and regularly leads rescue and recovery efforts.

Lined up at the press conference were Noel, Barbara, Bill, and Angel, who, though he never set foot below the One-Ten again, graciously served the expedition in a supporting role until the bitter end.

Jim Brown skipped the event. Back in San Agustín Zaragoza, he helped Don Broussard, Bev Shade, and Chris Sobin pack the trucks. He moved to Florida after the expedition, and became a part of the Mole fraternity. To free himself up to dive as much as possible, Jim lived cheaply: sleeping in a camp trailer owned by Tom Morris and subsisting for more than a year on freeze-dried food and MREs left over from the '94 expedition. He moved to the Pacific

Northwest in 1999, where he works as a Web computer programmer. He's continued to dive on caving expeditions, including at Wakulla Springs, in Belize, and on a 2001 push of the Infiernillo sump at Mexico's Sistema Purificación.

Noel Sloan lived to regret his decision not to join the final push. "I was completely demoralized about having missed that segment of the cave. I was beating myself up over it. Trying to reconcile it all out," he said in the spring of 2000. "It's weird how things play on you." He returned to his position in the anesthesiology department at Indianapolis General Hospital, and subsequently divorced. He participated in a 1995 expedition to Huautla, making important contributions to the exploration of the Huautla resurgence springs. "I had to return," he said, "after what happened in 1994." Over the last several years he's grown more interested in motorcycles—Harleys, specifically—and joined a motorcycle club. He remarried in October of 1999. His new wife, Becky, gave birth to their first daughter in March of 2000.

Barbara am Ende completed her Ph.D. in geology in December of 1995, and lectured at the University of Maryland through the spring of 1998. Drawing on her experience mapping caves, she became a computer graphics programmer. She served as the visualization programmer for the 1999 National Geographic Society expedition to map Wakulla Springs, and is creating the first three-dimensional cave map. This virtual fly-through of the Florida system will allow nondivers to visualize the underground environment. Barbara currently works at the National Institute of Standards and Technology, where she is collaborating with chemists and physicists on projects ranging from semiconductors to superconductors.

Though Bill and Barbara's expedition succeeded, their relationship did not. Working with an entirely different tribe of expeditionary cavers, Barbara has been busy caving overseas in locations she and her new teammates are keeping secret, at least for now.

Bill stepped up to the microphone in Huautla wearing clean washed jeans and a denim shirt—both of which villager Olivia Pereda had kindly scrubbed for him after she heard he'd be speaking. His appearance contrasted starkly with his last public appearance in Huautla. Gone was the intensely nervous man with the scruffy beard and disheveled hair who, on April 10, spoke so passionately about the need to return to the sump quickly. In his place was a freshly shaved scientist, on his way back to the States. He returned to his job at the National Institute of Standards and Technology, where he subsequently conducted groundbreaking work using electromagnetic impulses to track firefighters inside burning buildings. He later became leader of the Construction Metrology and Automation Group, a team researching the use of robotics and information technology at construction sites.

He's also maintained a hectic expedition schedule since the San Agustín project, most notably leading the three-month National Geographic Society project at Wakulla Springs, Florida. With financial support and encouragement from Jim King—the Tennessee businessman who loaned the big white Step Van to the '94 team—Bill designed a scooter-mounted mapper that uses sonar arrays and ballistics missile guidance technology to precisely plot the walls of an underwater cave. During January and February of 1999 the Digital Wall Mapper collected 10 million data points inside Wakulla Springs—data that would have taken lifetimes to be recorded by individual divers. In recognition of his advancements in life support, propulsion, and underwater imaging, the Explorers Club awarded Bill Stone the Willard Bascomb Quadrennial Prize in 2001.

Once all the rope was stashed and the goodbyes said to the villagers, what was left of the ragtag caravan—Jim Brown in the Step Van that had become his exoskeleton, Don Broussard and volunteers Chris Sobin and Bev Shade in Big Dog, Noel behind the wheel of his pickup, and Bill and Barb together in the battered blue Toyota—streamed north and crossed the border at Laredo on May 24, and began the awkward ascent back into their daily lives.

There's a joke that cavers sometimes tell when noncavers ask why it is that seemingly normal people spend all their free time so far from the sun. In a twist on the old why-do-men-climb-mountains cliché, the caver deadpans: "Because it's not there." At this point, the caver laughs nervously while the questioner quietly reconsiders the "seemingly normal" premise of the question.

"Because it's not there" does a good job of explaining why expeditionary cavers like Bill, Barbara, and so many others keep searching for the bottom of the earth. For while every climber knows which mountain is the world's tallest, *no one will know which cave is the deepest until cavers bottom them all.* And for the past several decades, that's what expeditionary cavers have been doing—in Mexico, Austria, France, Spain, Croatia, the former Soviet republics of Georgia and Uzbekistan, and elsewhere. Through a heartbreaking process of elimination, they've explored one promising entrance after another, only to discover time and again that wherever the depth might be, it was "not there."

Bill hasn't given up on the Mother of All Sumps. He's been back to the area on several expeditions, probing the Sótano del Río Iglesia and Cueva San Agustín, hoping to find the shortcut by which that Popsicle stick made its way to Sump Nine. And in March of 2001, he and Bev Shade co-led an expedition puckishly dubbed the InnerSpace Odyssey, on which divers were able to crack the Huautla resurgence spring. Using Cis-Lunar Mk-VPs and heliox, the team laid line through a sixty-five-meter-deep tunnel, then surfaced in an air-filled corridor 1,059 meters inside the plateau, thereby opening the possibility of a back door to the Mother Sump.

On the day after he and Barbara climbed out of the

Sótano de San Agustín in 1994, Bill completed calculating their survey data, then made the following entry in his personal journal:

... the sun was shining in the window and it was just kind of a magic moment. I realized that after ten years, everything we'd tried to do had actually come to pass. Granted, we'd suffered some serious losses along the way with Ian and Rolf Adams. But nonetheless we'd done what we set out to do. And the fact that there's still some unexplored cave between the Mother Sump and the Santo Domingo Canyon, hell, that just leaves the lure of the cave calling. It goes.

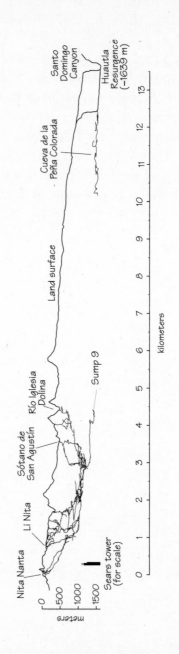

Huautla Cave System and Resurgence
Side View

Nita Nanta

Li Nita

Sótano de
San Agustín

Río Iglesia
Dolina

Land surface

Santo
Domingo
Canyon

Cueva de la
Peña Colorada

Huautla
Resurgence
(-1639 m)

Sump 9

Sears tower
(for scale)

meters

0
500
1000
1500

kilometers

0 1 2 3 4 5 6 7 8 9 10 11 12 13

drafted by Barbara Anne am Ende

GLOSSARY

Airbell – a small, air-filled chamber with flooded passages both upstream and down.

Ascender – a hand-sized mechanical device used for climbing ropes. A metal frame, usually made of aluminum, surrounds the rope and provides a handlelike grip. A spring-loaded locking cam mounted inside the frame allows the ascender to slide up the rope but holds it tightly in place on the rope when weight is applied.

Bailout bottle – a scuba tank and regulator taken on a dive in case an emergency supply of breathing gas is needed.

Bolt – a steel rock anchor used to form a fixed attachment point on an otherwise flat wall. A rigging plate, known as a *hanger*, must be attached to the bolt in order for it to be used. Climbing *carabiners* and *rapide* links may then be clipped to the hanger for attachment of ropes and slings. Bolts are used both for permanent rigging of a vertical shaft as well as for scaling smooth walls to reach high-level passages.

Booty – cavers' slang for unexplored passageway. The act of exploring such virgin territory is often referred to a "scooping booty."

Borehole – a subterranean tunnel that is large enough for easy walking.

Breakdown – rock that has fallen from the ceiling and lies on the cave floor. Breakdown piles vary in size from a few small boulders to stadium-sized mountains of rubble. These rocks generally fall down from the ceiling when water that filled the cave drains away and the water no longer supports the weight of the roof.

Buddy light – a pair of red and green LED lights affixed on Cis-Lunar *rebreathers* to show a diving partner the relative *partial pressure* of oxygen in his or her system.

Buoyancy compensator (BC) – a vestlike piece of diving equipment containing a waterproof bladder and a mechanism for letting in and releasing gas, supplied from a diver's tanks. The BC is used to make up for loss of buoyancy due to compression of the diver's wetsuit as one descends into the water. When coming up, a diver must vent the expanding gas from the flexible bladder.

Cap lamp – a small, one-piece-style *carbide lamp*, usually mounted on the front of a helmet. These lamps were used by nineteenth-century miners and are still used by many *cavers*. It typically provides light for two to three hours. Cap lamps are ignited by striking a flint wheel mounted on a small reflector attached to the body of the lamp.

Carabiner – a coffee-mug-handle-sized metal loop used to temporarily connect pieces of climbing equipment together. Carabiners are generally oval or D-shaped and have a hinged gate on one side for attaching and detaching items. Locking carabiners have an additional safety mechanism that, when locked, prevents the gate from opening.

Carbide – (aka calcium carbide) comes in gray, gravel-sized to nut-sized chunks that are used to fuel *carbide lamps*.

Carbide lamp – are built with two chambers; an upper one contains water and the lower one *carbide*. An adjustable dripper allows the water to trickle into the carbide chamber. Acetylene gas is produced from the chemical reaction between the water and *carbide*. The gas flows to a tip where it is burned forming a bright white glow.

Caver – the term to describe someone who explores caves by those who participate in caving. The lay term spelunker is purposely not used by the vast majority of active cavers.

Ceiling burner – a style of *carbide lamp* in which the water and *carbide* chambers form a belt-mounted generator that is connected to a lightweight headpiece by a hose. Because the burner is generally mounted on the front of a helmet and directed upward, its flame can touch the roof of a constricted tunnel, hence its nickname. Ceiling burners commonly have a built-in piezoelectric ignition system for lighting the flame.

Chi Con Gui-Jao – the Lord of the Cave, according to traditional Mazatec belief. A capricious and vengeful deity. Because the literal translation reads, "He Who Knows What Lies Beneath the Stone," the Mazatec sometimes use the same phrase to describe cavers.

Cow's Tail – a short safety line, made of stiff rope or nylon webbing, no more than eighteen inches long, that attaches to the harness, and has a *carabiner* on the other end. The carabiner is gripped tightly so that it stands out for ready attachment to a safety line or to a bolt hanger.

Crack – to succeed at overcoming an obstacle, as in "to crack" through a difficult passage and discover the route onward.

Crawlway – a cave passage so small that a *caver* must crawl through on his or her knees or belly.

Cretaceous – a period of geologic time ranging from about 145 to 65 million years ago. During the Cretaceous, more of the earth was underwater than today and the climate was warmer. Much cave-forming rock was deposited during this time.

Decompression computer – a computer that monitors a diver's time, depth, and breathing gas mix to calculate whether a diver must stop periodically on the way back to the surface in order to prevent *decompression sickness.*

Decompression sickness – a condition where pressure on a body is released faster than the gas dissolved in the blood can escape through the lungs. Gas bubbles then form in the blood, oftentimes lodging in a diver's joints causing pain and potentially permanent damage or death. Also known as the bends. An analogy is when a shaken soda bottle is uncapped. The pressure is suddenly released and bubbles foam out of the liquid.

De-rig – the process of removing ropes and equipment from a cave at the end of an expedition.

Diluent – a breathing gas used to dilute the concentration of potentially dangerous pure oxygen in a *rebreather*. For safety, the diluent—commonly air, nitrox, or heliox—contains a small amount of oxygen so that in an emergency the diluent can be safely breathed by itself.

Dolina – a closed depression, or sinkhole, where all surface water flows into the ground, and no stream or valley leads out (except underground).

Drop – a *pit* or other sharp drop-off in a cave. Usually drops require ropes to negotiate.

Drysuit – a waterproof suit used for diving in cold water. Tight rubber seals around the neck and wrists keep water out. Insulation for the diver comes from thermal underwear, fleece, etc., worn underneath.

Flowstone – a type of *travertine* formation that forms as water flows down the walls or across floors of caves.

Free flow – an unwanted loss of air from a scuba regulator.

Frog – both a noun that describes a way of arranging one's ascenders, and a verb that describes the act of ascending via that setup. The frog uses two ascenders: one at the waist, attached to the seat harness, and a second at head level, attached to a foot loop (and safety line). To frog, a caver alternately sits in the harness, and then stands in the foot loop. Most members of the 1994 expedition used the frog system.

Hanger – a metal plate, usually made of three-millimeter-thick stainless steel, with two holes; one to attach to a *bolt* and the other for the attachment of a *carabiner* or *rapide* link.

Huautla – (pronounced WOW–tla) a county-sized area in the state of Oaxaca, Mexico. The name comes from the town of Huautla de Jiménez, the seat of Mazatec authority in the region. It is also used to refer to the spectacular limestone plateau to the east of the town as well as to the cave system below. The name is derived from the Nahuatl meaning "place of eagles."

Hyperbaric chamber – a small chamber that can be pressurized with air to simulate the pressure a diver would encounter at various depths underwater. These chambers are generally scattered at individual hospitals and at a few tropical diving sites far from normal medical facilities. Divers suffering *decompres-*

sion sickness are repressurized in a hyperbaric chamber to redissolve the bubbles in their blood. The chamber is then slowly depressurized at a rate that does not allow bubbles to re-form. Additionally, hyperbaric chambers can be used to simulate diving conditions to test equipment or diver physiology.

Hypoxia – a condition where a body does not receive enough oxygen for proper functioning. Under extremely low oxygen concentrations, worsened by heavy exercise, a diver may black out or die.

Jughole – a rock protrusion on a cave wall or floor that has an opening through it that may be used as an anchor for a rope.

Jumar – a Swiss brand of *ascender*. Because Jumars were one of the first commercial *ascenders*, their name is used by some *cavers* synonymously with *ascender*, even for other brands.

Karst – a terrain formed on soluble bedrock characterized by few or no surface streams. Karst features include caves, *dolinas*, sinking streams, and pinnacles.

Kitting up – a British term for assembling and donning equipment in preparation for a cave dive.

Limestone – a common type of rock composed of calcium carbonate. Limestone is soluble in groundwater, thereby forming caves and other *karst* features.

Lithium hydroxide – a highly reactive chemical substance that absorbs carbon dioxide from the gas in the breathing loop of a *rebreather* and gives off water in exchange. The material is similar in appearance to whitish kitty litter.

Meter – a unit of distance approximately equal to one yard. There are 3.28 feet per meter.

Nalgene – a commercial brand of durable plastic bottles that have caps that form a waterproof seal when screwed on properly.

Neutral buoyancy – the condition where an object neither rises nor sinks in the water. To achieve neutral buoyancy, either lead is added or a type of *buoyancy compensator* is inflated with gas.

Onboard computer – any of three computers built into the Cis-Lunar Mk-IV rebreather to control and monitor oxygen concentration, depth and tank pressure, and decompression requirements.

Partial pressure – the amount of pressure exerted by one component of a mixture of gases. For example, at sea level, the oxygen in air exerts a partial pressure of 0.21 atmospheres because air exerts 1.0 atmosphere of pressure at sea level, and it contains 21 percent oxygen. Air from a tank breathed at thirty meters of water depth would have a partial pressure of oxygen of about 0.84 atmospheres, since the total pressure there is approximately four atmospheres. This concept is crucial to understanding and operating a *rebreather*, since the hallmark of such a device is the active control of the partial pressure of oxygen.

Pit – a vertical shaft or drop-off in a cave. Generally pits are encountered first from the top. If a vertical shaft is discovered from the bottom it is usually referred to as a dome. Pits usually require ropes to negotiate them safely. Also known as a *shaft* or *drop*.

Pitch – a vertical or near-vertical section of cave that must be rigged with rope to negotiate safely. Nearly synonymous with *drop*, and both terms may refer to the path a caver takes down a *pit* or *shaft*.

Pony bottle – a very small scuba tank, oftentimes a quarter the size of a normal, full-sized tank. A pony bottle may be used for a variety of purposes, such as providing the small amount of gas required by a *rebreather*, diving very short sumps, or inflating *drysuits*.

Rapide – a metal link, similar to a small *carabiner*, with a screw gate instead of a hinged one. Generally, rapides are used for anchors where they will not be opened and closed very often and where the more secure gate is needed.

Rappel rack – a U-shaped bar, typically of stainless steel, that attaches to a *caver*'s harness and controls the rate of descent down a rope. The rope is threaded over and under metal bars that cross the U. Adding or removing bars (five or six bars are commonly used) controls the amount of friction and thus speed of the descent, as does the spacing of the bars.

Rebelay – a secondary rope anchor point used to pull a rope away from a chafing rock, thereby avoiding a dangerous fray. Rebelays may also be used to break a deep drop into a number of smaller segments that allow more than one climber to ascend or descend the rope at the same time without adding additional weight to the rope segments.

Rebreather – an efficient life-support device that contains small scuba tanks. Exhaled breath is kept in a counterlung for reuse. Built-in computers (with manual override) monitor and add a small amount of oxygen to make up for what the diver metabolizes. Exhaled carbon dioxide is removed by scrubbing with a chemical such as *lithium hydroxide*. The most important feature of a rebreather is that gas is not wasted when a diver exhales and no bubbles are produced.

Reel – a spool used to lay a guideline through an underwater cave. A typical dive reel may contain about 100 meters of two-millimeter nylon line knotted at regular intervals and used for surveying. A safety reel, also frequently known as a gap reel, is barely bigger than a fist and is used for emergencies such as finding a lost guideline in low or no visibility.

Regulator – a valve that reduces the pressure of gas flowing from a pressurized tank to that of the surrounding water, and delivers such "regulated" gas on demand.

Rig/rigging – catchall terms used to describe the rope and climbing hardware used to prepare a cave for descent. These terms are also used as verbs to describe the work of installing such equipment.

Scoop – to be the first to explore a cave passage, as in "scooping *booty*."

Shaft – a vertical passage in a cave, essentially synonymous with *pit*.

Silt-out – occurs when a diver disturbs the sediment in an underwater cave, reducing the visibility of the water to zero. In such a situation it is generally impossible to read gauges, displays, or to see a hand in front of a diver's mask.

Sótano – the Spanish word for basement. However, in Latin America it is also used in mountainous regions to describe a *karst* pit—a deep vertical shaft leading into the earth.

Spelunking – a term used by the general public to describe cave exploring. This term is not used by *cavers* and its use indicates a lack of knowledge on the subject.

Stalactite – a type of *travertine* formation that forms on the roof of a tunnel or chamber when water drips from the cave ceiling. Small stalactites may look like icicles or soda straws, whereas large stalactites may be meters across.

Stalagmite – a type of *travertine* formation that forms when water drips onto the cave floor and leaves behind a mound of calcite.

Sump – an underground tunnel flooded entirely with water. Sumps commonly begin as lakes where the ceiling of the passage eventually dips under the surface of the water. A sump is sometimes called a siphon.

Survey – to gather data used to create a map. In dry caves, such data is obtained with a compass, clinometer, and tape measure. Underwater, a compass, depth gauge, and knotted line are used. A line is surveyed through the cave between stations where measurements are recorded along the way. The walls are sketched around the survey line. The survey data is later drafted into a final map.

Tether – a length of nylon webbing used to suspend a duffel bag from a caver's seat harness. Usually about as long as the caver is tall, the tether moves the pack's center off gravity to where it is less likely to pull the caver backward while rappelling a freefall drop or working against a sloping wall.

Tie-off – a place where an underwater guideline is tied to a rock to securely fix it in place.

Travertine – a deposit found in caves made of crystalline calcite. Travertine forms as water saturated with calcium carbonate leaves behind calcite when the water can no longer hold the dissolved mineral matter. This is the basis for most common cave formations—e.g., *stalactites, stalagmites.*

Vertical gear – the equipment a *caver* uses to climb up and down ropes. Typically this equipment includes ascenders, a *rappel rack*, a harness, slings, and *carabiners.*

Wellingtons – a British brand of knee-high rubber boots.

Wetsuit – a tight-fitting neoprene rubber suit that allows a thin layer of water to be trapped between the suit and a diver's skin. The water is warmed by body heat, which then insulates a diver, though not as well as a *drysuit.*

1994 SAN AGUSTÍN
EXPEDITION PERSONNEL

Expedition Leader:
Dr. Bill Stone (U.S.)

Dive Team:
Dr. Barbara am Ende (U.S.)
Dr. Kenny Broad (U.S.)
Jim Brown (U.S.)
Steve Porter (U.S.)
Ian Rolland (U.K.)
Dr. Noel Sloan (U.S.)

Support Team:
Leonardo Altamirano (Mexico)
Dick Ballantine (U.K.)
Don Broussard (U.S.)
Harry Burgess (U.S.)
Mike Cicheski (U.S.)
Don Coons (U.S.)
Jaime Escudero (Mexico)
Bill Farr (U.S.)
Tony Finnegan (U.K.)
Renato García Dorantes (Mexico)

Pete Hall (U.K.)
Joe Ivy (U.S.)
Patty Kambesis (U.S.)
Ted Lee (U.S.)
Mark Madden (U.K.)
Karlin Meyers (U.S.)
Don Morley (U.S.)
Matt Oliphant (U.S.)
John Palmer (U.K.)
Rob Parker (U.K.)
Nancy Pistole (U.S.)
Bev Shade (U.S.)
Chris Sobin (U.S.)
Angel Soto (Mexico)
Shirly Sotona (U.S.)
Carleton Spears (U.S.)
Rick Stanton (U.K.)
Bill Steele (U.S.)
John Thorpe (U.K.)
Carol Vesely (U.S.)
Alex Wade (U.K.)
Pete Ward (U.K.)
Paul Whybro (U.K.)
Yvo Wiedman (Germany)
Sergio Zambrano (Mexico)

Photo Team:
Neeld Messler (U.S.)
Tom Morris (U.S.)
Wes Skiles (U.S.)
Paul Smith (U.S.)
James York (U.S.)

1994 SAN AGUSTÍN
EXPEDITION SPONSORS

Air Products and Chemicals, Inc.
Air UK
AT&T
Autodesk, Inc.
Bill Mixon
British Sports Council
Canyon Industries, Inc.
Cascade Designs, Inc.
Charles Pease Jr.
Combined Services Caving Association
Cumberland Tool & Die Co.
Deep Breathing Systems, Inc.
Delaware Underwater Swim Club
Dive Rite Manufacturing, Inc.
Dogwood City Grotto
Dudas Diving Duds
Duracell Incorporated
Explorers Club
Florida Public Utilities Co.
Forestry Suppliers, Incorporated
Forty Fathom Grotto
Ginnie Springs, Inc.

Haley, Bader, & Potts, Inc.
Haskel, Inc.
Johnson Camping Incorporated
Keela
Keson Industries
KLM
Liberty Mountain Sports, Inc.
Luxfer, USA
Machining Services, Inc.
Medisense Britain Limited
Mike Emmerman
Miss Leslie Smart Memorial Fund
National Geographic Society
NiteRider
NOKIA/Amron International
Novo Nordisk Pharmaceuticals Limited
NSS Cave Diving Section
Oceanic USA
Oregon Freeze Dry, Inc.
Panasonic
Patagonia, Incorporated
Pigeon Mountain Industries, Inc.
Professional Scuba Association
Professional Sports, Inc.
Rasna Corp.
R.D. Werner Co., Inc.
Richmond Area Speleological Society
Rolex Watch U.S.A.
Royal Air Force
Royal Geographical Society
ScubaPro
Sea Quest, Incorporated
Sheriff's Office, Jackson County, Florida
Sherwood/Harsco Corp.
Sierra Precision, Inc.
Skedco, Inc.

Star Foods
Teledyne Analytical Instruments
Tilos, Inc.
Underwater Kinetics
Visionics Corp.
Warm Wind
Welsh Sports Council

SUMMARY OF MAJOR EXPEDITIONS TO SISTEMA HUAUTLA, 1965–2001

July 1965. After viewing recently released military topographic maps, Texas caver William Russell predicted the presence of deep caves in the Huautla Plateau. His team made it to Huautla but only explored relatively small caves near Puente Fierro to the northwest.

June 1966. A team led by William Russell returned to Huautla and traveled on foot to the village of San Agustín Zaragoza, where in the course of a single afternoon they discovered the entrances to the Sótano de San Agustín, the Sótano del Río Iglesia, the Cueva San Agustín, and the Cueva de Agua Carlota.

December 1966. William Russell and Terry Raines led early exploration of Cueva San Agustín and Sótano de San Agustín, where the team ran out of rope at a depth of 280 meters.

January–February 1967. A team led by John Fish ran out of rope at a depth of 449 meters, making San Agustín the second deepest cave in North America.

April 1967. A push on the Sótano de San Agustín led by John Fish, Terry Raines, and Orion Knox, was cut short by an early rainy season and dangerously high water levels in the cave.

December 1967. An all-Canadian team led by Peter Thompson pushed the Sótano del Río Iglesia to an apparent bottom at –535 meters. The river disappeared at the –285-meter level, giving rise to a controversy that took nearly thirty years to resolve.

December 1968–January 1969. A joint team from McMaster University and the University of Texas at Austin established the first underground camp (Camp One) in San Agustín at a depth of 250 meters. They reached a sump at a depth of 612 meters, establishing San Agustín as the deepest cave in the Americas. A large horizontal passsage at the –540 meter level carrying a substantial wind was left uninvestigated; memories of this tunnel haunted team member Richard Schreiber for eight years.

December 1969. A small team led by John Fish and Terry Raines bottomed Cueva San Agustín at a depth of 474 meters.

December 1970. In the final caving expedition fielded to Huautla before Mexican military roadblocks closed off the region, a team led by Mike Boon bottomed Cueva de Santa Cruz, the river cave west of San Andrés at –320 meters. Cueva de Agua Carlota was pushed to a sump at –163 meters.

December 1976. Upon learning that the military road-blocks had loosened, Richard Schreiber quietly organized a return to San Agustín and reached a depth of 625 meters by following the windy tunnel he discovered in 1968.

December 1976–January 1977. A group of Texans led by Bill Stone established Camp Two at a depth of –536 meters in the Sótano de San Agustín and discovered the Metro beyond the Upper Gorge. Their five-day assault netted a new depth of 800 meters.

March 1977. From a base at Camp Two, a team led by Richard Schreiber and Bill Steele discovered the Sala Grande de la Sierra Mazateca. A team member exiting the cave early accidentally pulled the rope up a 100-meter shaft, trapping the team below for five days. Jim Smith and Jean Jancewicz became the first to reach the San Austín sump.

May 1977. With San Agustín sumped, the Texas-based team established a camp at the –260 meter level of La Grieta and, during a ten-day underground push, reached a depth of 665 meters.

December 1977–January 1978. Bill Stone and Bill Steele led a large team from Texas, Georgia, and Australia that pushed La Grieta to an apparent end at –760 meters; however, maps suggested the underground passage was headed toward the Sótano de San Agustín. After La Grieta was de-rigged, the combined team reached a depth of 780 meters in Sótano de Agua de Carrizo.

May 1978. A team led by Bill Stone and Bill Steele pushed two separate routes deeper than –800 meters in Agua de Carrizo. The deepest reached –848 meters and ended in a breakdown chamber very near the end of La Grieta. Summer storms hit early and four members of the camping crew were trapped underground for eighteen hours.

February–May 1979. A small team consisting of Steve Zeman, Dino Lowrey, Hal Lloyd, Tommy Shifflett, and Bill Stone established Camp Three in San Agustín. During the next three months they discovered seven kilometers of new galleries below the –500-meter level. Bill Stone dived the San Agustín sump for the first time.

December 1979. A scouting team led by Bill Steele discovered the diminutive entrance of Li Nita and explored it down to a depth of 130 meters.

January–February 1980. A Polish team led by Maciej Kuczynski suffered two serious accidents below the –600-meter level in San Agustín. An international rescue involving Belgians, Mexicans, Brits, and the American team led by Bill Stone and Bill Steele was successful, but Polish team member Josef Cuber was paralyzed due to a fractured spinal column.

February–May 1980. A team led by Bill Stone and Bill Steele established a camp at –630 meters in Li Nita and pushed the cave down to a depth of 1,030 meters, making it the first kilometer-deep cave outside of Europe. At the end of the expedition Bill Stone made a dive through the –1,030-meter sump in Li Nita and emerged in the Sótano de San Agustín near Camp Three. The combined system— Sistema Huautla—reached a depth of 1,220 meters and became the world's third deepest cave. Also, Mark Minton discovered Nita Nanta, a small cave located 120 meters vertically above Li Nita.

February–May 1981. A team led by Bill Stone and Mark Minton established Camp One in Nita Nanta at the –400-meter level, and pushed the grimly narrow cave to depth of 927 meters. Though only 100 meters distant from a connection with Li Nita, the fissure became too tight to follow. Stone also pushed the San Agustín sump using new high-pressure fiberglass scuba gear, and increased the depth of Sistema Huautla to 1,248 meters. Bill Stone and Pat Weideman discovered the Cueva de la Peña Colorada.

March–May 1982. A team led by Mark Minton and Bill Steele established a second camp in the "Football Stadium" at the –640-meter level of Nita Nanta. A climb led by Doug Powell opened up a new route toward Li Nita, but it was plugged with flowstone. Meanwhile, a new discovery, Nita Nashi, was pushed to a depth of 641 meters, where it sumped.

April 1982. Bill Stone, John Zumrick, and Pat Wiedeman explored the Cueva de la Peña Colorada on the south end of the Huautla Plateau. They dived the 524-meter-long first sump and discovered 2.1 kilometers of borehole leading north toward San Agustín. The Huautla resurgence, as well as the resurgence spring from Cueva Cheve, were discovered.

March 1983. A team led by Mark Minton and Jim Smith squeezed past the flowstone choke and pushed Nita Nanta to a depth of 1,030 meters.

December 1983–January 1984. Nita Nanta pushed to a sump at a depth of 1,098 meters, but the survey was not completed at the time.

February–May 1984. An international team of eleven cave divers established a three-month camp at the bottom of the Peña Colorada canyon. Using seventy-two fiber-composite scuba tanks, the team led by Bill Stone and Bob Jefferys discovered 9.4 kilometers of tunnels leading north toward Huautla, of which 1.3 kilometers were flooded in seven sumps. Two underground camps were set beyond the sumps, marking the first time subterranean bases were established beyond underwater tunnels. During the de-rig, Zumrick proposed rebreathers as a way to surpass the logistical barrier posed by ferrying tanks forward.

March–May 1985. Work continued deep within both Nita Nanta and Sótano de San Agustín in search of a connection. Computer maps showed the Nita Nanta sump, the northern limits of San Agustín, and the bottoms of La Grieta and Agua De Carrizo all converging in one giant collapse chamber located 800 meters beneath the village of San Andrés Hidalgo. After weeks of meticulous route finding through the rubble pile, a team led by Mark Minton and Jim Smith emerged into the bottom of La Grieta and added nine kilometers of length (but no depth) to Sistema Huautla.

March–May 1987. A team led by Jim Smith and Mark Minton established Camp Four in the Sótano de San Agustín at the end of the northern tunnel known as Kinepak Kanyon, some 600 meters below the San Agustín entrance. They carried four scuba tanks to an upstream sump, which Smith penetrated on the first attempt, surfacing at the bottom of Nita Nanta. The connection brought the system depth to 1,353 meters and briefly made Sistema Huautla the world's second deepest cave. Bill Steele and Mark Minton discovered the Fools' Day Extension near the entrance of San Agustín, and quickly pushed it down to its connection with the Upper Gorge. The new route halved the transit time to Camp Three, and made possible the world's most spectacular through trip (in Nita Nanta, through San Agustín and out La Nita).

January–May 1988. Jim Smith, assisted by Ed Holladay, conducted dye trace experiments in Sistema Huautla as part of his Master's Thesis in geology. During the five-month field study he and Holladay made more than thirty-five descents below –500 meters to set activated charcoal traps and to release various dyes. Smith achieved the first positive dye trace to the Huautla resurgence. The Sótano del Río Iglesia was linked to the Huautla resurgence, providing indisputable evidence of the existence of a subterranean confluence of the two rivers. Nita Ka was discovered and was pushed to –758 meters.

December 1988–January 1989. Nita Ka bottomed disappointingly at –760 meters without connecting to Sistema Huautla.

February 1990. Jim Smith continued his hydrology studies of Sistema Huautla by revisiting the Cueva de Agua Carlota, bypassing the 1970 sump, and pushing the cave another three kilometers to a depth of 504 meters at a collapse.

January–May 1994. An international team of forty-four cavers and divers established Camp Five at the San Agustín sump. Using computer-controlled rebreathers, the team was able to pass two long sumps and establish Camp Six in the void beyond. During a six-day assault, Barbara am Ende and Bill Stone mapped three kilometers of new tunnels leading south toward the Huautla resurgence and discovered the presumed junction with the subterranean Río Iglesia before being stopped by Sump Nine at a depth of 1,475 meters.

February–March 1994. Jim Smith and Ron Simmons re-explored Cueva de Santa Cruz without finding any routes leading onward.

April–May 1995. Hoping to find a "back door" to Sump Nine, a team led by Bill Stone, Barbara am Ende, and Noel Sloan established a month-long base camp in the tiny village of Río Tuerto, halfway between San Agustín and the Huautla resurgence. All of the numerous sinks, pits, and river swallets were found to be plugged with dirt from nearby sugar cane fields. The Huautla resurgence was dived to 850 meters penetration by Paul and Jill Heinerth and Noel Sloan.

January 1997. A team led by Bill Stone and Barbara am Ende descended the Armadillo canyon and established a base camp at the Agua Frio spring in an effort to perform an "end run" around the Cueva de la Peña Colorada and reach Sump Nine in the Sótano de San Agustín. But dives by Rick Stanton, Jason Mallinson, and Bill Stone were all terminated due to zero visibility in the silt-covered tunnels. The team mapped 1.2 kilometers of dry and underwater tunnels.

January–May 2001. A team led by Bill Stone and Bev Shade returned to Cueva San Agustín, hoping to discover a connection to the lost Río Iglesia river. New leads were discovered in the Sótano del Río Iglesia, but there was no time to push them. Later, in the Santo Domingo canyon, divers Rick Stanton and Jason Mallinson used Mk-V rebreathers to crack the Huautla resurgence at a distance of 1,059 meters from the spring rising. An air-filled borehole led northward inside the east wall of Peña Colorada canyon.

DEEP CAVES OF THE WORLD: MAY 1994 (In meters)

RANK:	1
NAME:	Réseau Jean Bernard
COUNTRY:	France
PROVINCE:	Haute-Savoie
DEPTH:	1,602
LENGTH:	17,900

RANK:	2
NAME:	Gouffre Mirolda/Lucien Bouclier
COUNTRY:	France
PROVINCE:	Haute-Savoie
DEPTH:	1,520
LENGTH:	9,000

RANK:	3
NAME:	Shakta Vjacheslav Pantjukhina
COUNTRY:	Georgia
PROVINCE:	Abkhazia
DEPTH:	1,508
LENGTH:	5,530

RANK: 4 _____
NAME: Lamprechtsofen-Vogelschacht
COUNTRY: Austria
PROVINCE: Salzburg
DEPTH: 1,483
LENGTH: 14,657

RANK: 5 _____
NAME: Sistema Huautla
COUNTRY: Mexico
PROVINCE: Oaxaca
DEPTH: 1,475
LENGTH: 56,953

RANK: 6 _____
NAME: Sistema del Trave (La Laureola)
COUNTRY: Spain
PROVINCE: Asturias
DEPTH: 1,441
LENGTH: 7,300

RANK: 7 _____
NAME: Boj-Bulok
COUNTRY: Uzbekistan
PROVINCE: Uzbekistan
DEPTH: 1,415
LENGTH: 5,000

RANK: 8 _____
NAME: (Il)laminako Aterneko Leizea (BU56)
COUNTRY: Spain
PROVINCE: Nararra
DEPTH: 1,408
LENGTH: 11,893

RANK:	9
NAME:	Sistema Cheve
COUNTRY:	Mexico
PROVINCE:	Oaxaca
DEPTH:	1,386
LENGTH:	22,499

RANK:	10
NAME:	Sniezhnaja-Mezhonnogo
COUNTRY:	Georgia
PROVINCE:	Abkhazia
DEPTH:	1,370
LENGTH:	19,000

DEEP CAVES OF THE WORLD:
FALL 2001 (In meters)

RANK: 1 —————————————————
NAME: Voronja Cave (Krubera Cave)
COUNTRY: Georgia
PROVINCE: Abkhazia
DEPTH: 1,710
LENGTH: unreported

RANK: 2 —————————————————
NAME: Lamprechtsofen-Vogelschacht
COUNTRY: Austria
PROVINCE: Salzburg
DEPTH: 1,632
LENGTH: 44,000

RANK: 3 —————————————————
NAME: Gouffre Mirolda/Lucien Bouclier
COUNTRY: France
PROVINCE: Haute-Savoie
DEPTH: 1,616
LENGTH: 9,379

RANK: 4 _____

NAME: Réseau Jean Bernard

COUNTRY: France

PROVINCE: Haute-Savoie

DEPTH: 1,602

LENGTH: 20,000

RANK: 5 _____

NAME: Torca del Cerro (del Cuevon)

COUNTRY: Spain

PROVINCE: Asturias

DEPTH: 1,589

LENGTH: 2,685

RANK: 6 _____

NAME: Shakta Vjacheslav Pantjukhina

COUNTRY: Georgia

PROVINCE: Abkhazia

DEPTH: 1,508

LENGTH: 5,530

RANK: 7 _____

NAME: Ceki 2 (Cehi II) "La Vendetta"

COUNTRY: Slovenia

PROVINCE: Rombonski Podi

DEPTH: 1,480

LENGTH: 3,959

RANK: 8 _____

NAME: Sistema Huautla

COUNTRY: Mexico

PROVINCE: Oaxaca

DEPTH: 1,475

LENGTH: 56,953

RANK: 9 _____

NAME: Sistema del Trave (La Laureola)
COUNTRY: Spain
PROVINCE: Asturias
DEPTH: 1,441
LENGTH: 9,167

RANK: 10 _____

NAME: Boj-Bulok
COUNTRY: Uzbekistan
PROVINCE: Uzbekistan
DEPTH: 1,415
LENGTH: 14,270

RANK: 11 _____

NAME: (Il)laminako Aterneko Leizea (BU56)
COUNTRY: Spain
PROVINCE: Nararra
DEPTH: 1,408
LENGTH: 14,500

RANK: 12 _____

NAME: Sustav Lukina Jama—Trojama (Manual II)
COUNTRY: Croatia
PROVINCE: Velebit
DEPTH: 1,392
LENGTH: unreported

RANK: 13 _____

NAME: Sistema Cheve (Cuicateco)
COUNTRY: Mexico
PROVINCE: Oaxaca
DEPTH: 1,386
LENGTH: 24,300

INDEX

Huautla

San Agusti...

Top View

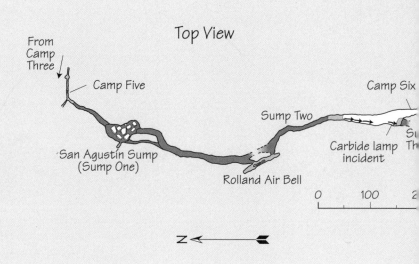

From Camp Three

Camp Five

Camp Six

Sump Two

San Agustin Sump (Sump One)

Carbide lamp incident

Su Th

Rolland Air Bell

0   100   2

N ← ◄

Side View

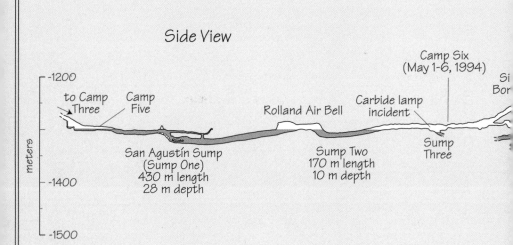

-1200

to Camp Three

Camp Five

Rolland Air Bell

Camp Six (May 1-6, 1994)

Si Bor

Carbide lamp incident

meters

San Agustín Sump (Sump One) 430 m length 28 m depth

Sump Two 170 m length 10 m depth

Sump Three

-1400

-1500